SAVE YOURSELF, MAMMAL!
A SATURDAY MORNING BREAKFAST CEREAL COLLECTION

By Zach Weiner

breadpig

BROOKLYN · SOMERVILLE · THE INTERNETS

Printed in the United States of America

For information about special discounts for bulk purchases,
please contact Breadpig, Inc. at IncredibleBulk@Breadpig.com

Manufacturing by RR Donnelley

Weiner, Zach.
Save Yourself, Mammal!
ISBN 978-0-9828537-0-2
Breadpig, Inc.
www.breadpig.com

Breadpig is not a traditional publisher. The majority of the profits of this book are going to the artist, Zach Weiner. And as with all of Breadpig's projects, the company's profits are being donated to a worthy charity. We selected the organization DonorsChoose.org, which makes it easy for anyone to help students in need. For as little as $1, anyone can help fund a project requested by a public school teacher anywhere in the United States of America. We'll be spotlighting many of the classrooms to which we donate our non-sustainable profits on our website, *breadpig.com*. Wait until they find out whence those microscopes came...

For support in this publishing venture, breadpig thanks
Marie Mundaca, LeeAnn Suen, and the friends and family
who've always unhesitatingly supported team breadpig.

Even our winged porcine hero couldn't have done it alone. Thank you.

Cover art designed by Zach Weiner, colored and made awesome by Jim Zubkavich.

0 1 1 2 3 5 8 13 21 34

To my mother and father, Phyllis and Martin Weiner,
for believing in me despite reason, prudence, and good taste.

Acknowledgments

Thank you to my wife Kelly for enduring the neverending horror that is life with me. Thank you to my managers, Mark Saffian and Josh Morris, for supporting me in hopeless times. Thank you to my longtime good friends, Angel, Chason, Katie, James, and Amanda for reading thousands of bad joke ideas, thereby saving me and the readers from some truly horrible ideas. Thank you to Marty for running all the tech stuff I ever had, going back to the days when SMBC was run off a computer upstairs in his house. That room also used to house our Team Fortress 1 server, but now houses children. I suspect he finds this rather bittersweet.

I have had a great deal of help from fellow cartoonists, but I wanted to give special thanks to the following people: R Stevens, for liking my jokes back when they were terrible. Chris Crosby, for being a neverending font of information. Chris Hallbeck, whose business sense helped more than I care to think. The explosm boys - Rob DenBleyker, Kris Wilson, Matt Melvin, and Dave McElfatrick for being surprisingly friendly despite being a gaggle of degenerate perverts. And, Randy Munroe, for being an intellectual fellow traveler.

OH HEY.

If you're reading this, you hold in your hands the first English language publication of *Saturday Morning Breakfast Cereal*.

You may not be aware, but there once was a short print run of SMBC books in Finnish. I mention this because it may be important to your understanding of the profundity of your personal character. You see, SMBC was published in the Helsinki Metro train line for all of one month before it was canceled due to complaints. Thus, this book (and by association, you) are THFF: Too Hot for Finland.*

Part of why you're THFF may be your reckless financial choices. For instance, you buy books whose content can be viewed online for free. It's part of your wild and brazen nature to read dirty comics and spend tens of dollars as if they were mere fives of dollars.

Nevertheless, you've made a good choice. The comics in this book are a special selection of favorite strips from the ten year history of SMBC. That is to say, you're about to enjoy some vintage Weiner.

And, unlike those who read online, you're privy to a bonus feature found only in this book. Weaved through the pages is a choose your own adventure. At the bottom of this foreword, you'll get your first "block." On the left and right of this block are choices, each of which indicates a page number and a position (top or bottom). Use this information to navigate to the next block, which gives you a picture indicating your previous choice and presents you with more choices.

If you solve for all 64 possible endings, the book will transmute into pure diamond. Unless you got a dud, in which case sorry.

So, sit back, curl up with a glass of wine, and enjoy your Too Hot for Finland comic strips and choose your own adventure book. If I can get wine to spurt out of your nose, I'll consider it a success. If I get wine to spurt out of anything else, this sentence limits my liability for any bodily harm that may result from the reading of anything contained herein.

Your fan,

ZACH WEINER

LIFE   DEATH

*If you are reading this in Finland, you are in fact THFH: Too Hot for Here.

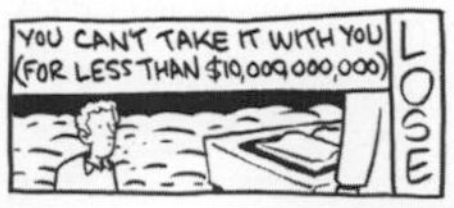
YOU CAN'T TAKE IT WITH YOU
(FOR LESS THAN $10,009,000,000)
LOSE

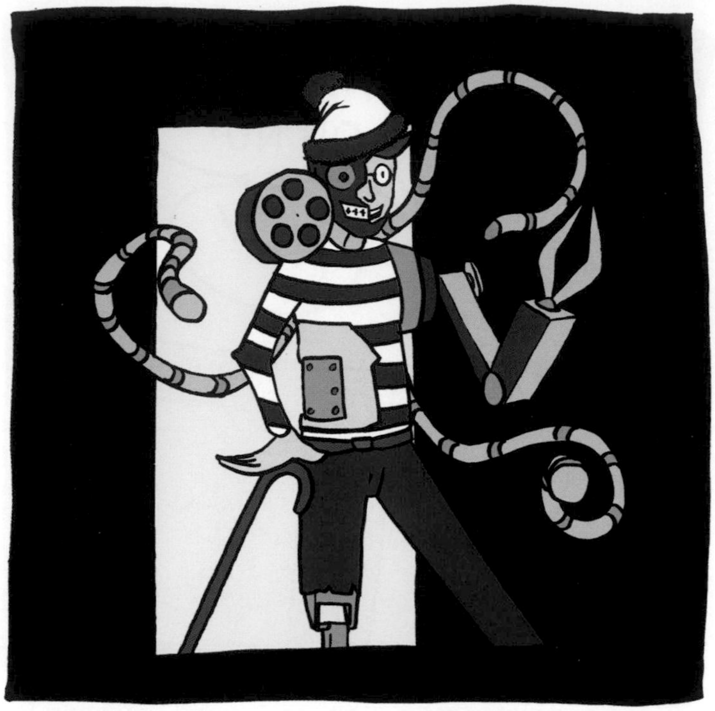

We found Waldo, but it was too late.
He was already one of them.

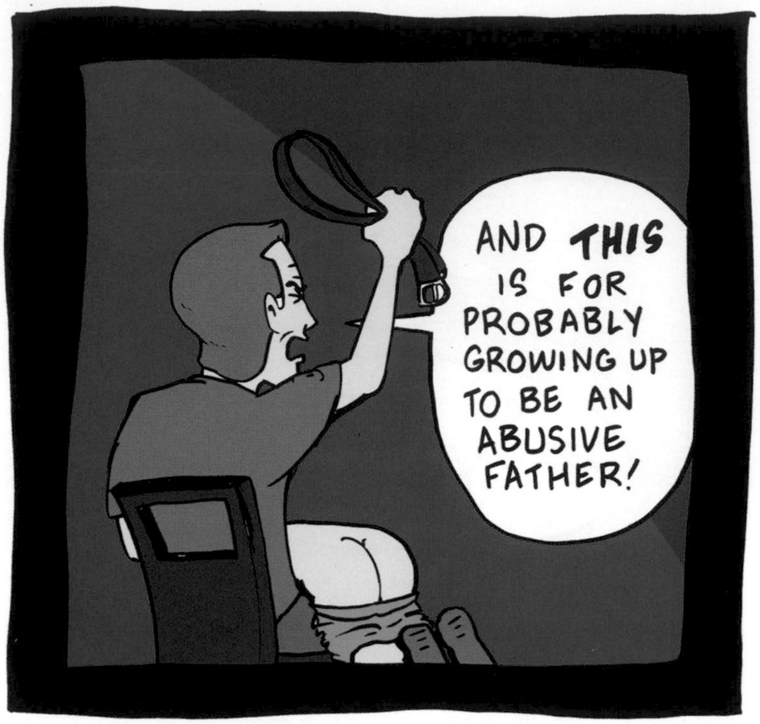
AND **THIS** IS FOR PROBABLY GROWING UP TO BE AN ABUSIVE FATHER!

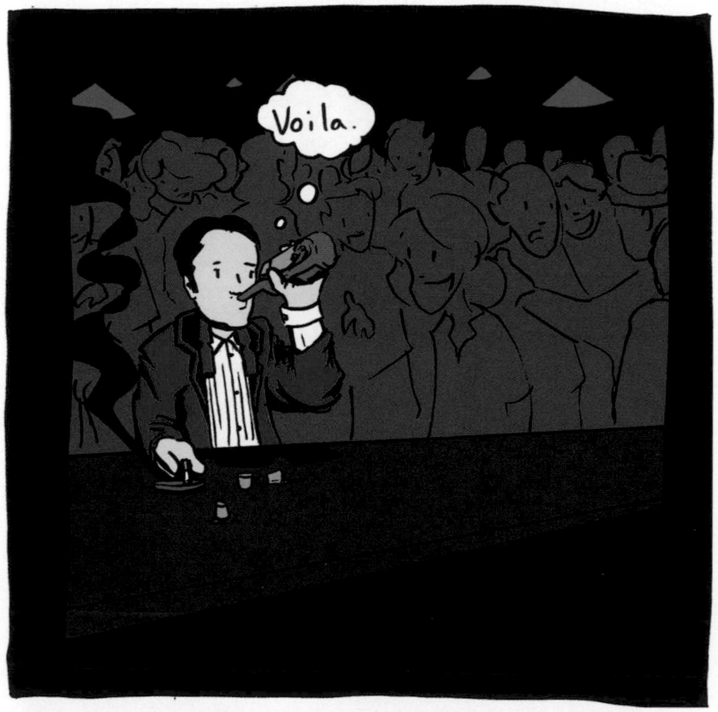
Voila.

Harry Houdini does his famous
"escape from reality" trick.

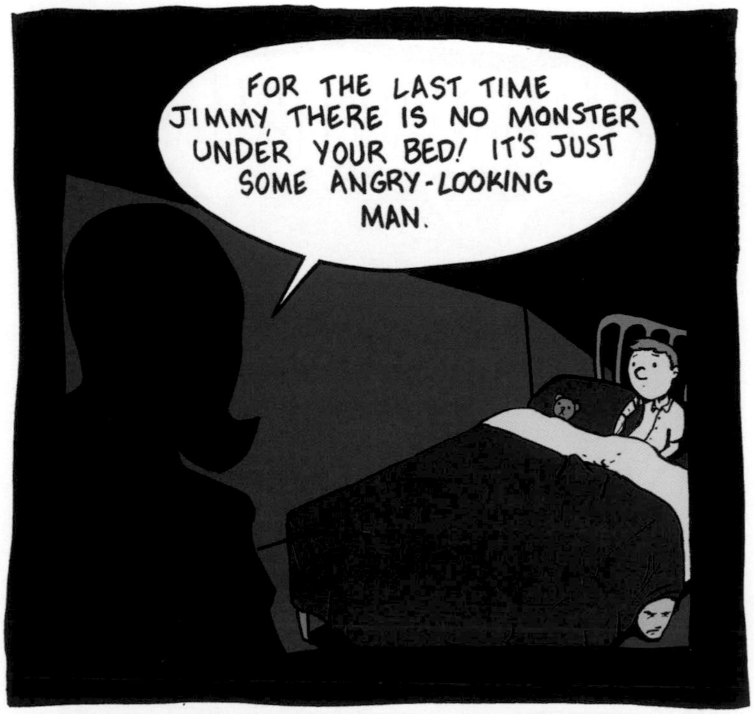
FOR THE LAST TIME JIMMY, THERE IS NO MONSTER UNDER YOUR BED! IT'S JUST SOME ANGRY-LOOKING MAN.

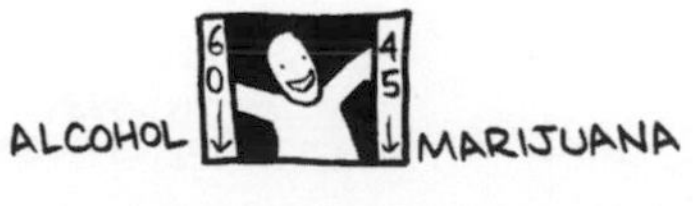
ALCOHOL
60↓
45↓
MARIJUANA

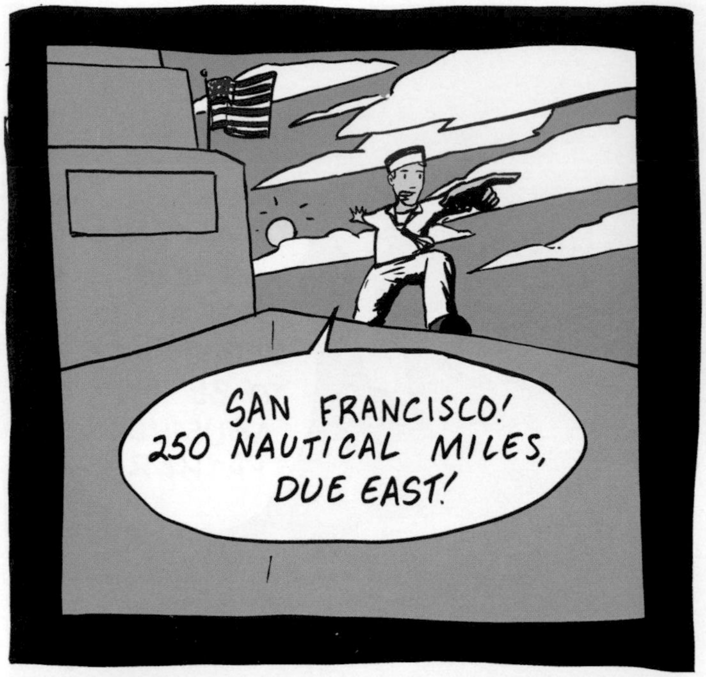
SAN FRANCISCO! 250 NAUTICAL MILES, DUE EAST!

Their GPS disconnected, their radio dead, the crew of the Arizona are forced to use the only tool they have left: Dave's gaydar.

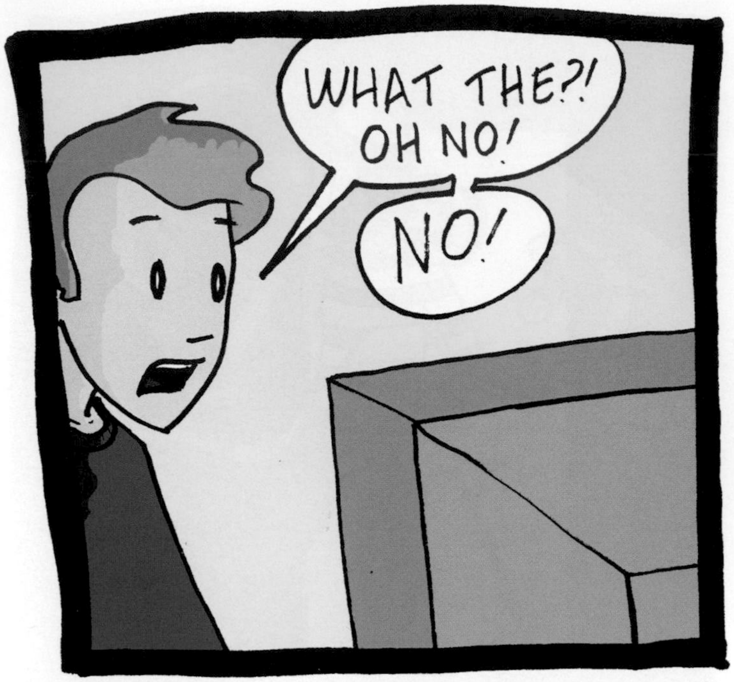
WHAT THE?! OH NO!
NO!

Steve had just received the rarely used emoticon for "Your mother was just crushed to death in a compactor and cursed your name with her dying breath."

For those wondering, it's][>:=~+.

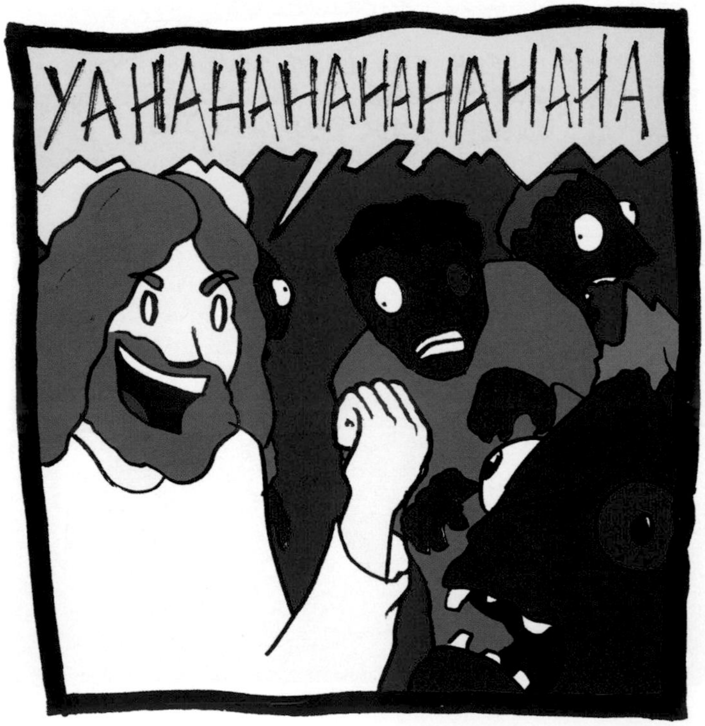
YAHAHAHAHAHAHAHAHA

The human body is ninety percent water.

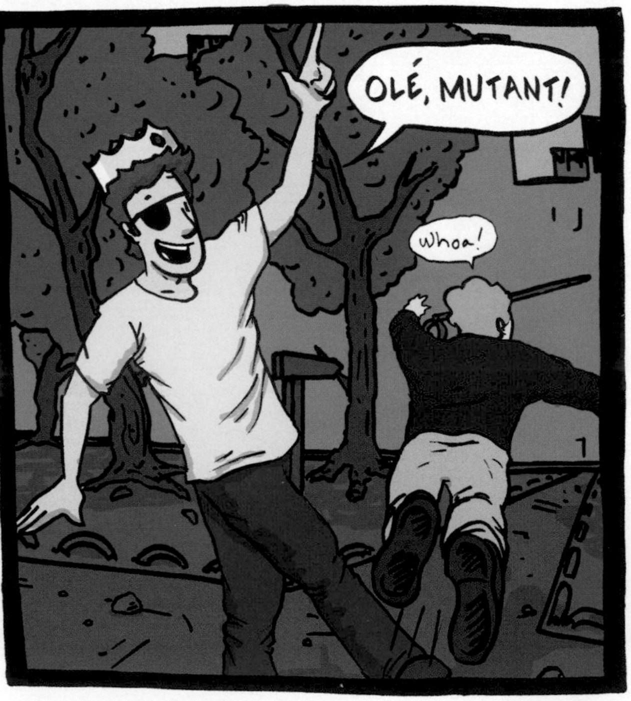
OLÉ, MUTANT!
Whoa!

In the land of the blind, the one-eyed man is an ass.

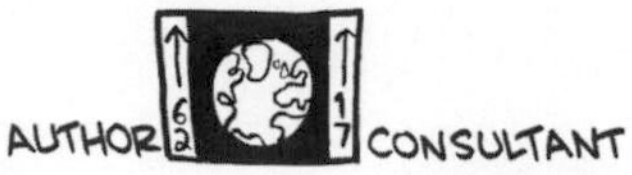
AUTHOR
62
117
CONSULTANT

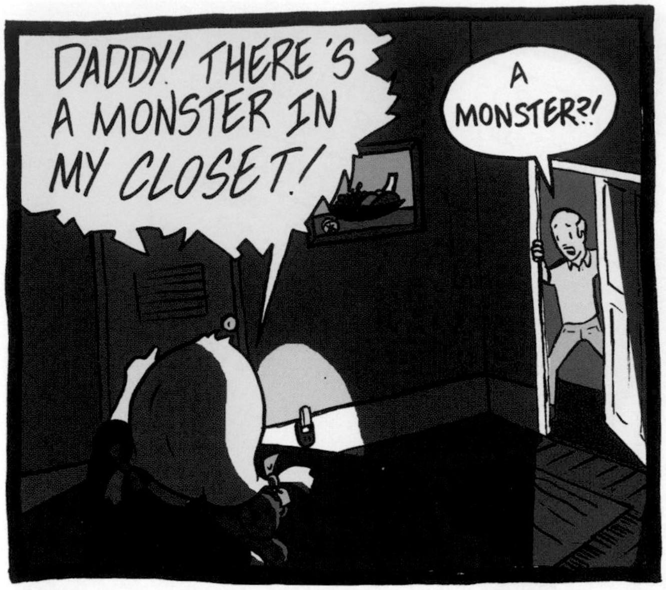
DADDY! THERE'S A MONSTER IN MY CLOSET!
A MONSTER?!

Fortunately, Susie's door locks from the outside.

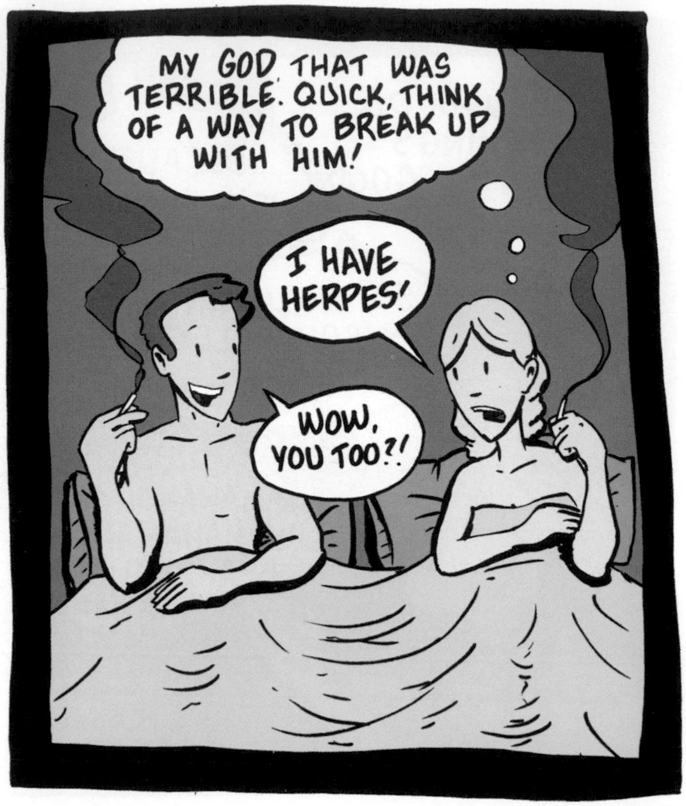
MY GOD THAT WAS TERRIBLE. QUICK, THINK OF A WAY TO BREAK UP WITH HIM!
I HAVE HERPES!
WOW, YOU TOO?!

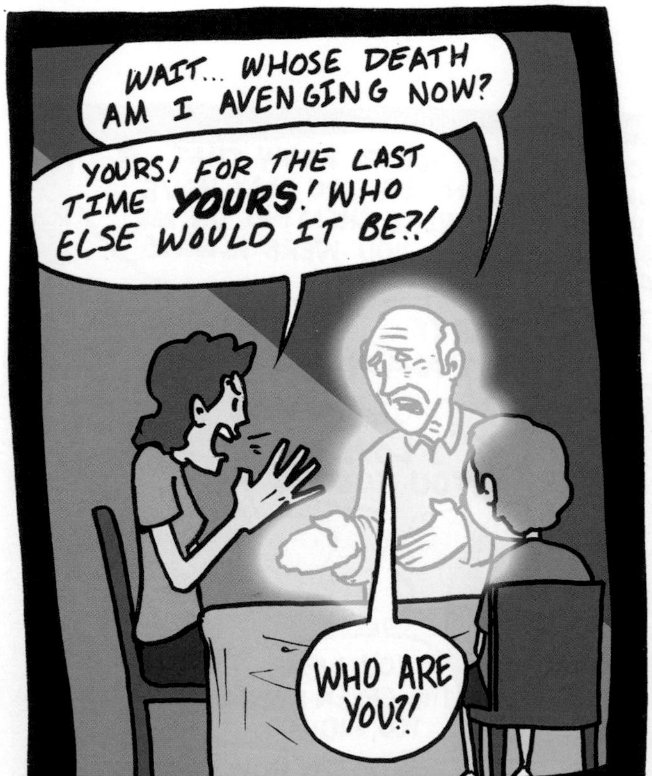
WAIT... WHOSE DEATH AM I AVENGING NOW?
YOURS! FOR THE LAST TIME YOURS! WHO ELSE WOULD IT BE?!
WHO ARE YOU?!

We all kinda wished grandpa had been brutally murdered *before* he went senile.

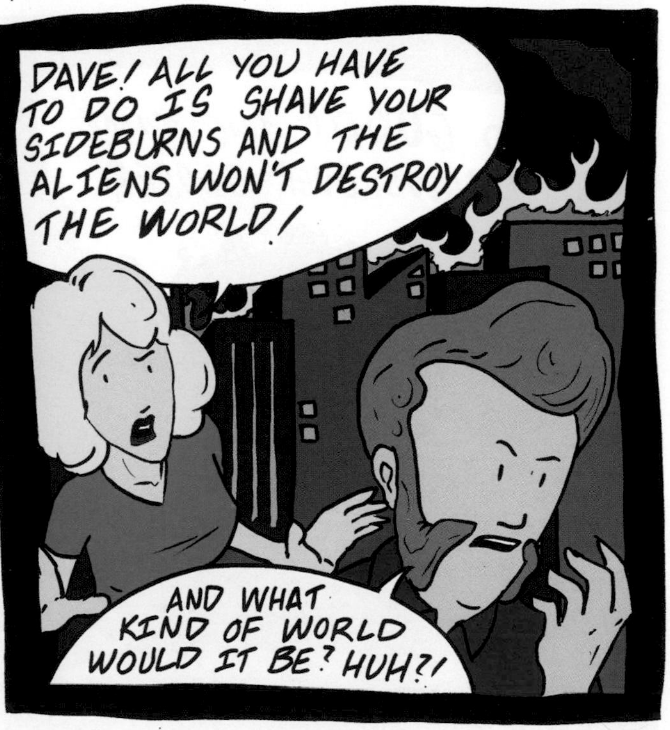
DAVE! ALL YOU HAVE TO DO IS SHAVE YOUR SIDEBURNS AND THE ALIENS WON'T DESTROY THE WORLD!
AND WHAT KIND OF WORLD WOULD IT BE? HUH?!

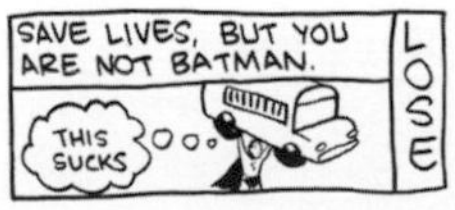
SAVE LIVES, BUT YOU ARE NOT BATMAN.
THIS SUCKS
LOSE

GOD, WHY DO BAD THINGS HAPPEN TO GOOD PEOPLE?
BECAUSE IT'S FUNNY!
SO, WHEN MY MY SON FELL OFF THAT BRIDGE-
HAHAHAHAHAHAHAHAHAHAHAHAHAHAHAHAHAHAHAHAHAHAHAHA

TODAY'S CROSSWORD
BY: CROSSWORDIN' SAM
TITLE: THE ANSWER IS YOU
ACROSS
① THE PROBLEM WITH OUR RELATIONSHIP
DOWN
④ THERE IS NO FOURTEEN DOWN BECAUSE YOU'RE A STUPID BITCH.

"Wow! I've never completed a crossword puzzle before! I should have cheated on Sam years ago!"

GOOD GOOD! THE TIME DRAWS EVER CLOSER!

Soon the fish sticks would be done.

LOIS, I WANT YOU TO KNOW THAT... I WAS SUPERMAN. SO, YOU MAY HAVE THOUGHT YOU WERE CHEATING ON ME, BUT, IN MY EYES, YOU WERE ALWAYS FAITHFUL.
OH CLARK! SOMEHOW I ALWAYS KNEW...
I LOVE YOU.
I LOVE YOU TOO.
...
...
YOU WERE THE GREEN LANTERN, TOO, RIGHT?
HUH?
NOTHING!

UNIVERSITY PRESS BESTSELLER (14.5 COPIES).
LOSE
BOETHIUS: PROMETHEUS?

HALT!
ALL WHO ENTER MUST PROVE THEY HAVE RENOUNCED ALL LOVE, DESIRE, AND PLEASURES OF THE FLESH. IT MAY TAKE YEARS, BUT-
DUNGEONS &DRAGONS PLAYER'S HANDBO
YOU MAY PASS.

BIGGER HAMSTER
5 4
1 9
BIGGER WHEEL

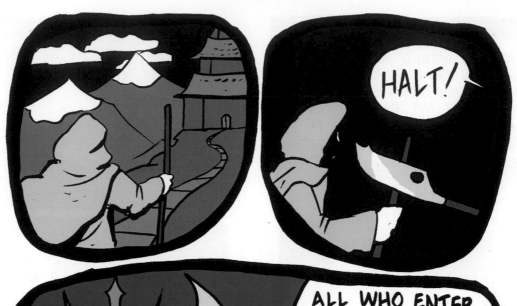

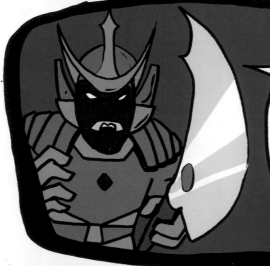

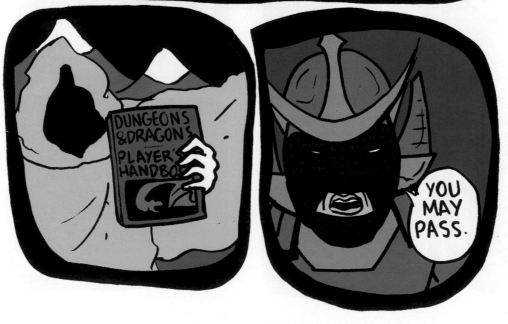

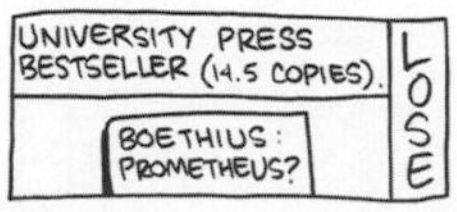

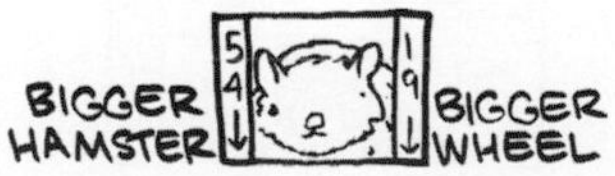

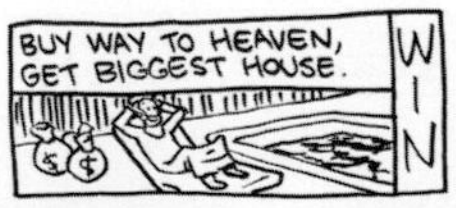
BUY WAY TO HEAVEN, GET BIGGEST HOUSE.
WIN

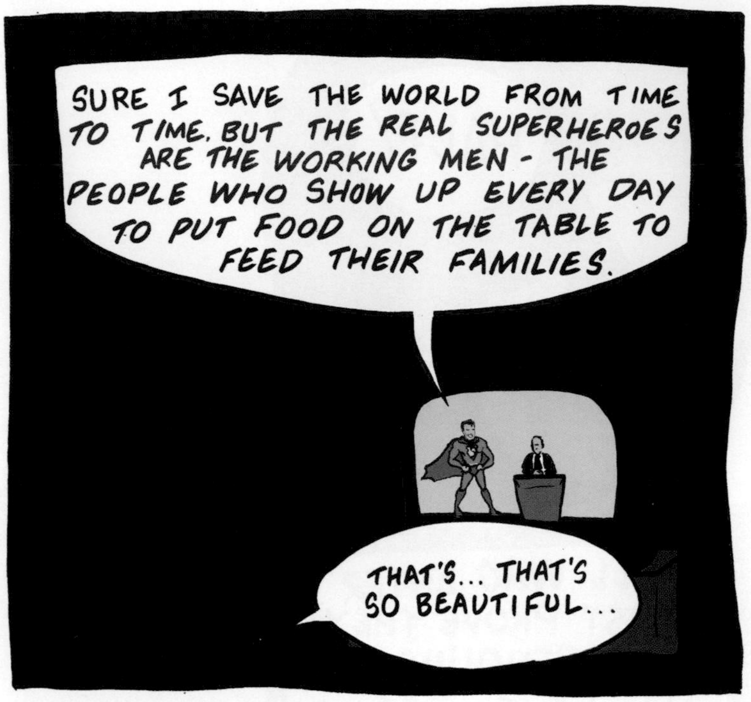
SURE I SAVE THE WORLD FROM TIME TO TIME. BUT THE REAL SUPERHEROES ARE THE WORKING MEN - THE PEOPLE WHO SHOW UP EVERY DAY TO PUT FOOD ON THE TABLE TO FEED THEIR FAMILIES.
THAT'S... THAT'S SO BEAUTIFUL...

Lex Luthor had a much easier time killing all the “real” superheroes.

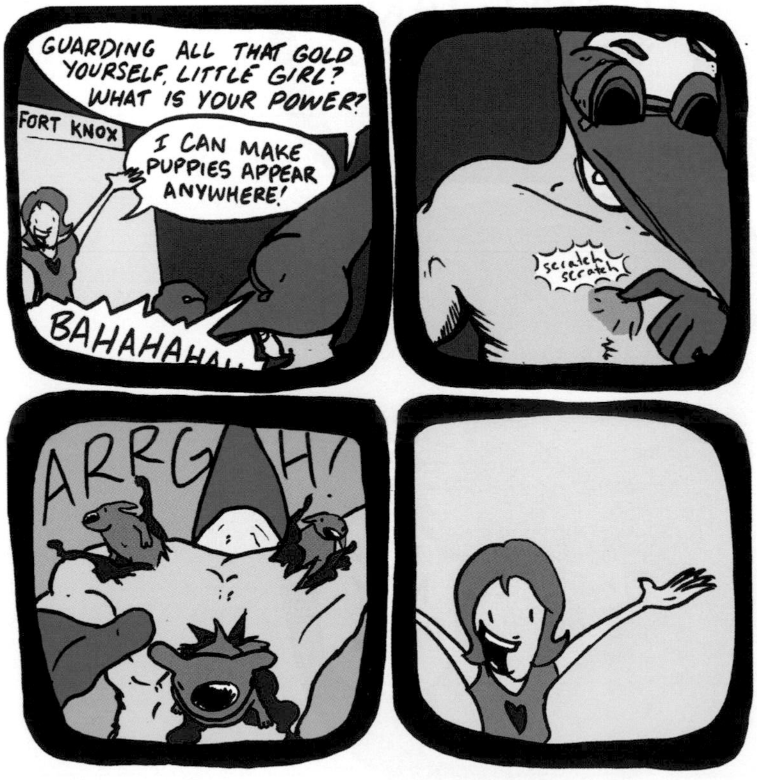
GUARDING ALL THAT GOLD YOURSELF, LITTLE GIRL? WHAT IS YOUR POWER?
FORT KNOX
I CAN MAKE PUPPIES APPEAR ANYWHERE!
BAHAHAHA
scratch scratch
ARRGH!

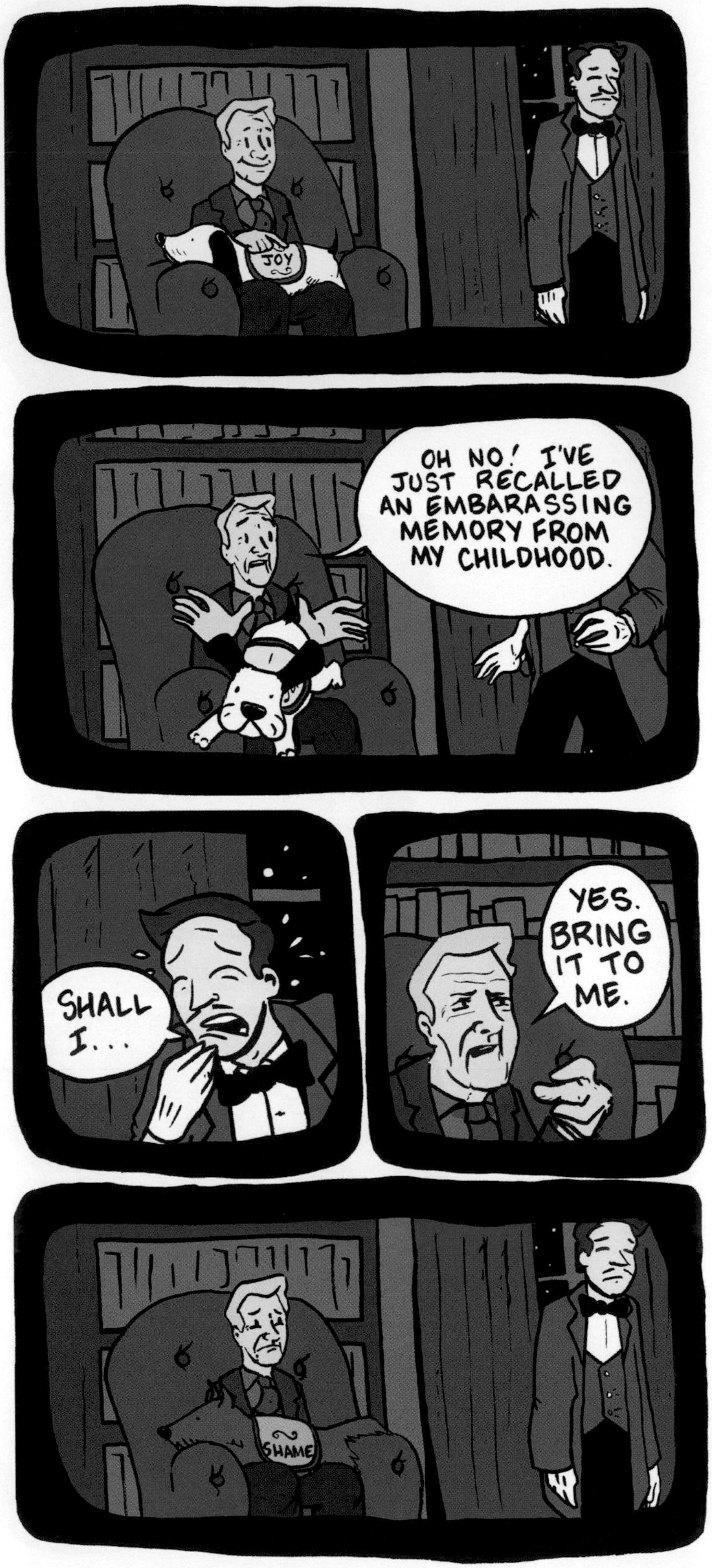
JOY
OH NO! I'VE JUST RECALLED AN EMBARASSING MEMORY FROM MY CHILDHOOD.
SHALL I...
YES. BRING IT TO ME.
SHAME

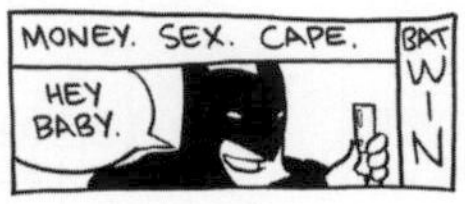
MONEY. SEX. CAPE.
HEY BABY.
BAT WIN

↑ 6 3
2 9 ↓

SMBC PRESENTS A TALE OF SUPERHERODOM "SO-DAMN-AWESOME-MAN"
GIMME YER PURSE! HAHAHA!
NOT SO FAST, CROOK!
BANG!
SDAM
OH MY GOD! YOU SHOT ME! BUT... BUT YOU DON'T EVEN HAVE A GUN!
THAT IS SO DAMN AWESOME.

PFFF...
LOSE

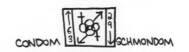

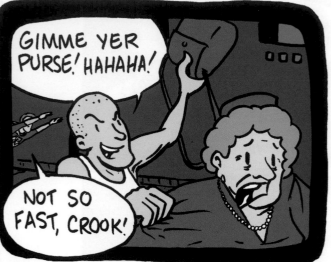

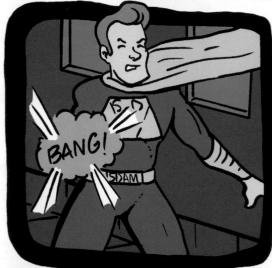

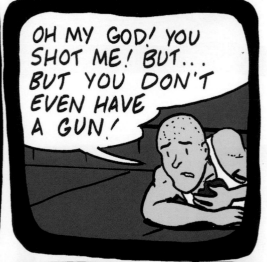

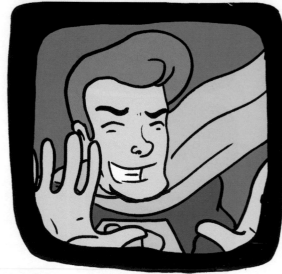

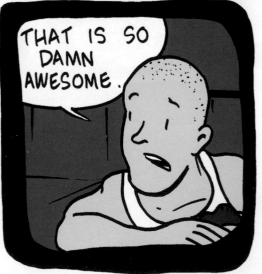

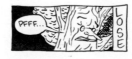

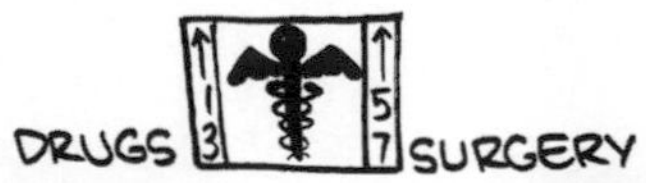
DRUGS
13
57
SURGERY

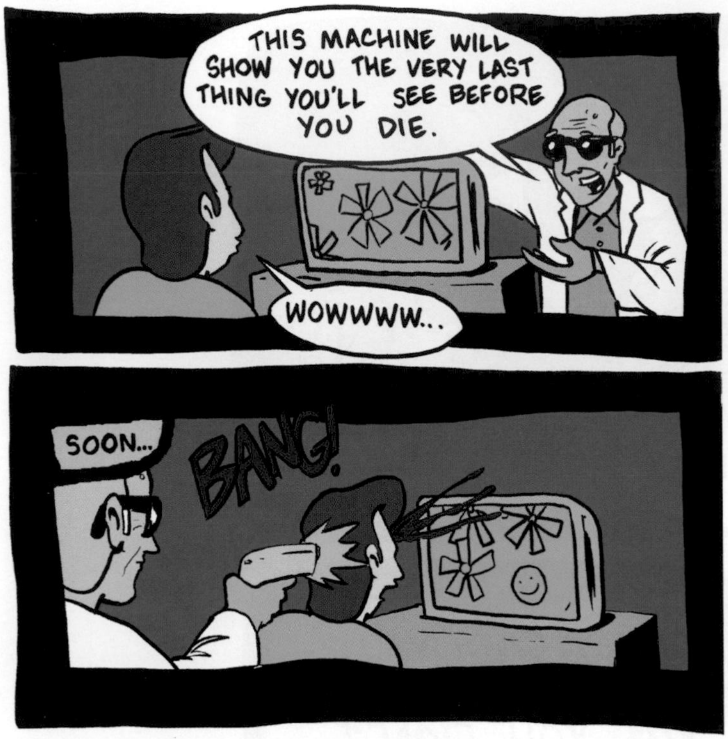
THIS MACHINE WILL SHOW YOU THE VERY LAST THING YOU'LL SEE BEFORE YOU DIE.
WOWWWW...
SOON...
BANG!

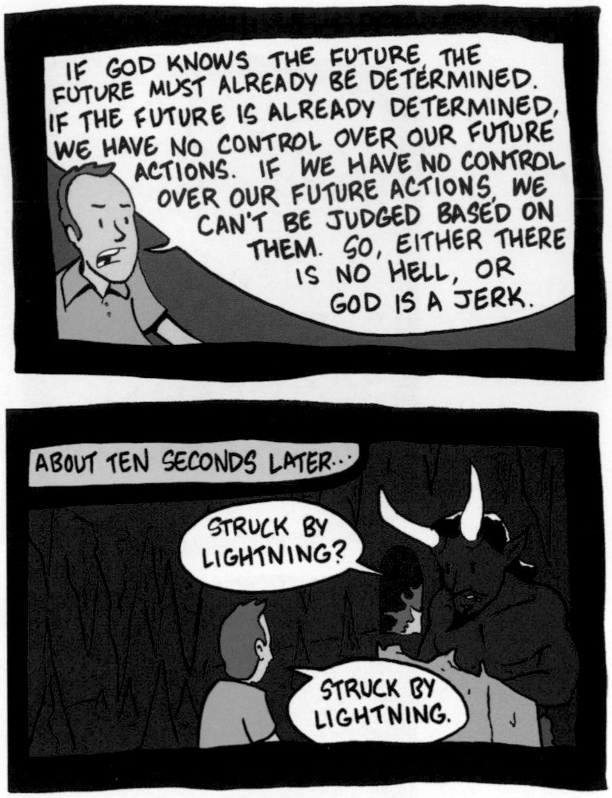
IF GOD KNOWS THE FUTURE, THE FUTURE MUST ALREADY BE DETERMINED. IF THE FUTURE IS ALREADY DETERMINED, WE HAVE NO CONTROL OVER OUR FUTURE ACTIONS. IF WE HAVE NO CONTROL OVER OUR FUTURE ACTIONS, WE CAN'T BE JUDGED BASED ON THEM. SO, EITHER THERE IS NO HELL, OR GOD IS A JERK.
ABOUT TEN SECONDS LATER...
STRUCK BY LIGHTNING?
STRUCK BY LIGHTNING.

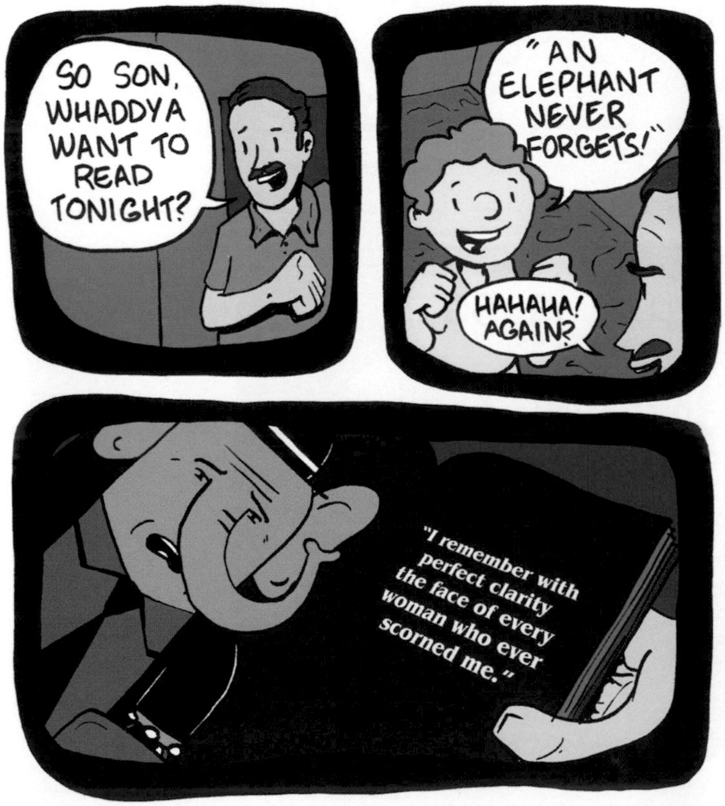
SO SON, WHADDYA WANT TO READ TONIGHT?
"AN ELEPHANT NEVER FORGETS!"
HAHAHA! AGAIN?
"I remember with perfect clarity the face of every woman who ever scorned me."

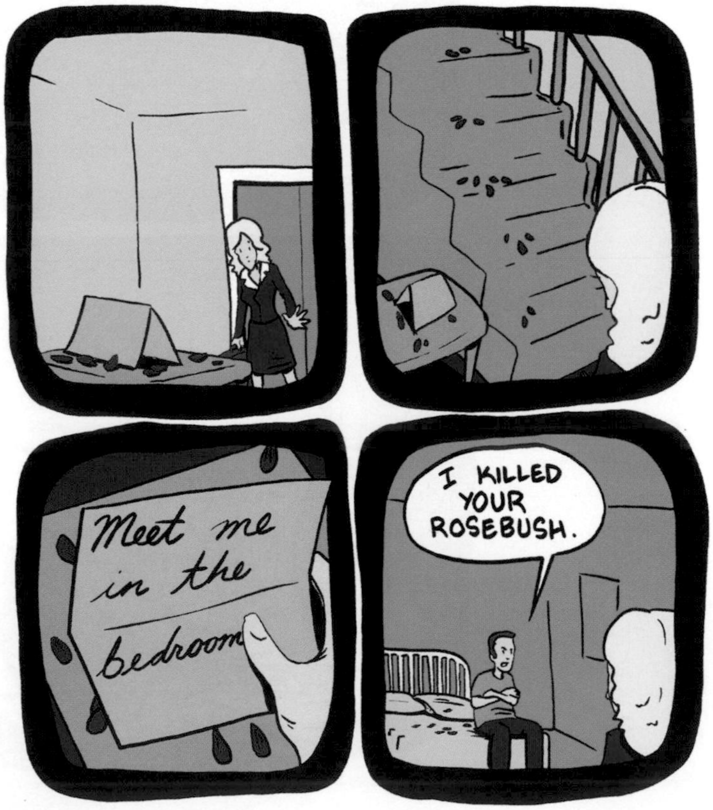
Meet me in the bedroom
I KILLED YOUR ROSEBUSH.

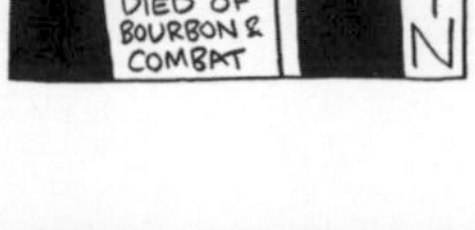
HERE LIES
— YOU —
DIED OF
BOURBON &
COMBAT
WIN

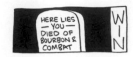

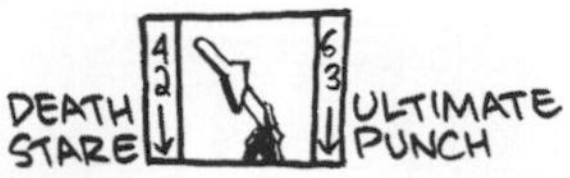
DEATH STARE
42↓
63↓
ULTIMATE PUNCH

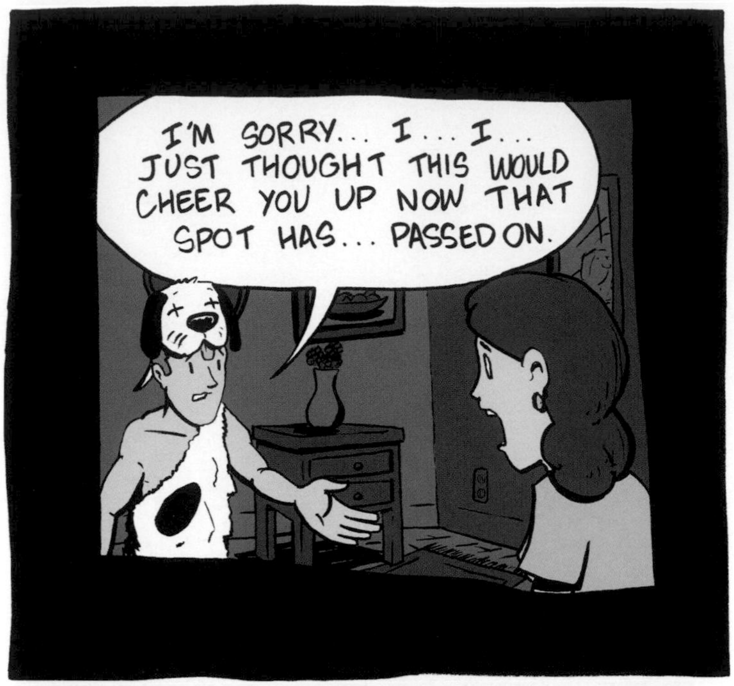
I'M SORRY... I... I... JUST THOUGHT THIS WOULD CHEER YOU UP NOW THAT SPOT HAS... PASSED ON.

Maybe she would have been happier if she hadn't just watched me kill Spot.

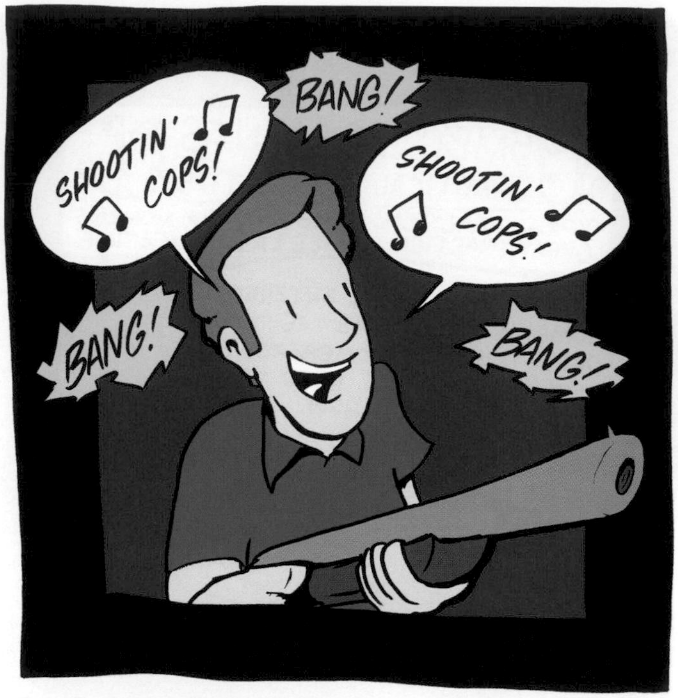
SHOOTIN' COPS!
BANG!
SHOOTIN' COPS!
BANG!
BANG!

Great Practical Joke #12:
Convincing your friend he has diplomatic immunity.

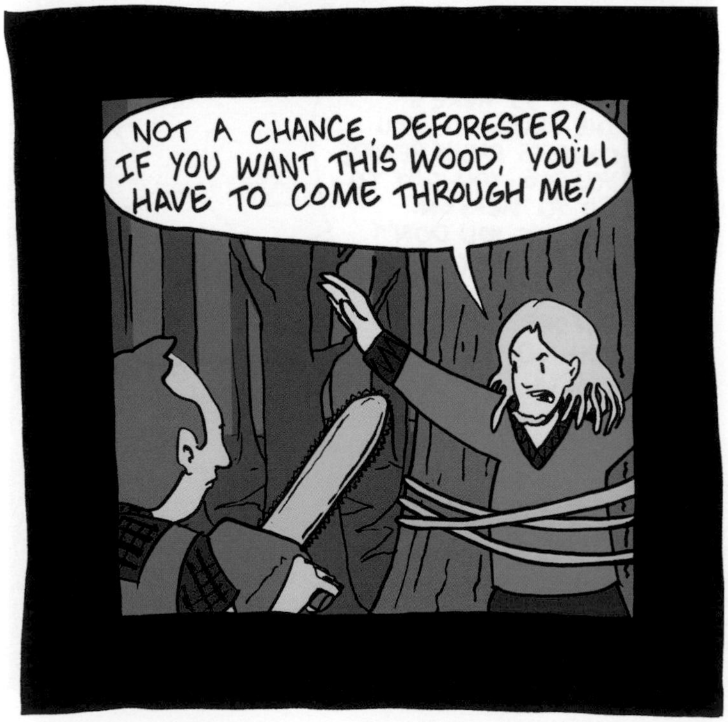
NOT A CHANCE, DEFORESTER! IF YOU WANT THIS WOOD, YOU'LL HAVE TO COME THROUGH ME!

The average toothpick is 0.01% hippie.

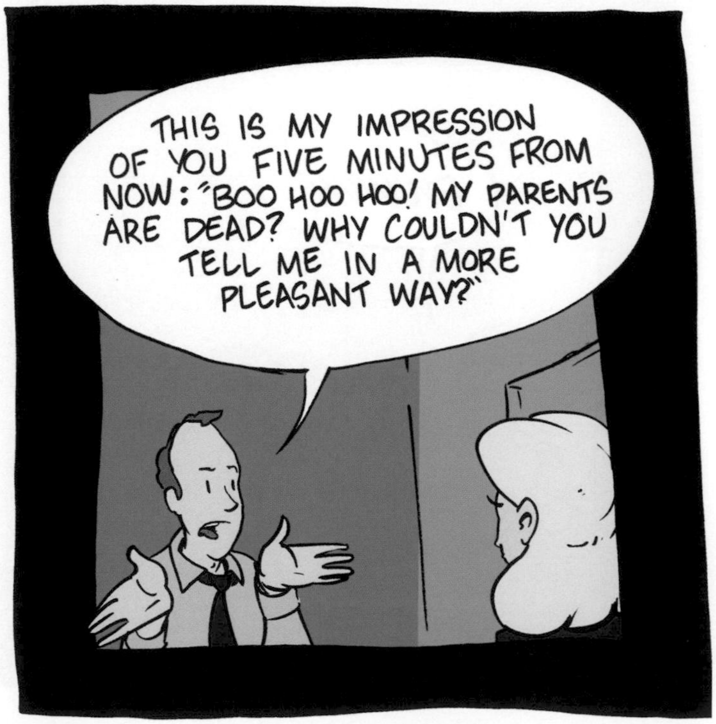
THIS IS MY IMPRESSION OF YOU FIVE MINUTES FROM NOW: "BOO HOO HOO! MY PARENTS ARE DEAD? WHY COULDN'T YOU TELL ME IN A MORE PLEASANT WAY?"

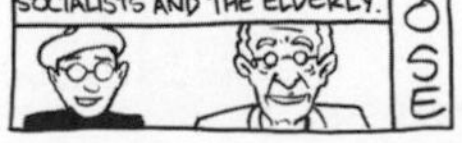
BELOVED BY COLLEGE SOCIALISTS AND THE ELDERLY.
LOSE

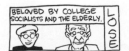

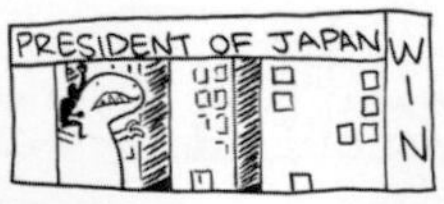
PRESIDENT OF JAPAN
WIN

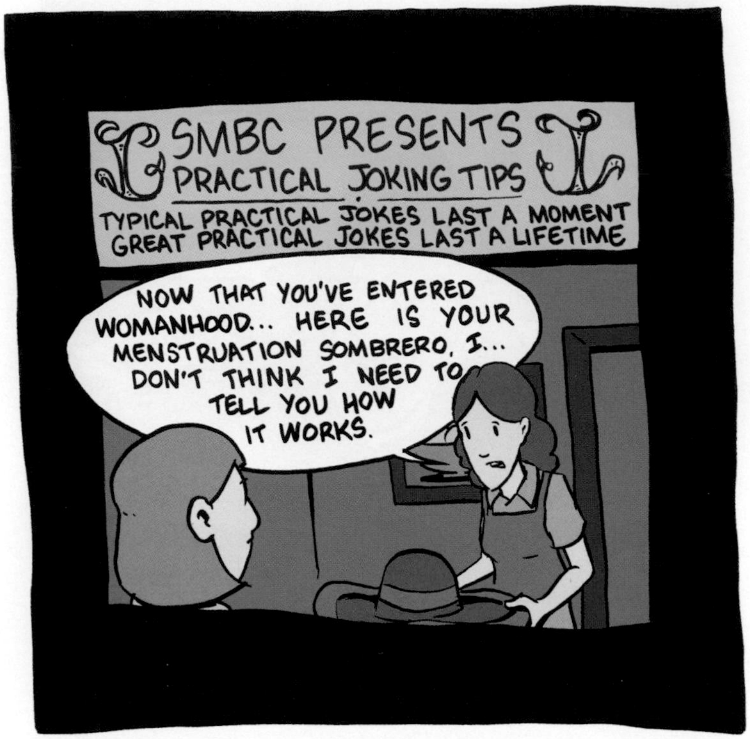
SMBC PRESENTS
PRACTICAL JOKING TIPS
TYPICAL PRACTICAL JOKES LAST A MOMENT
GREAT PRACTICAL JOKES LAST A LIFETIME
NOW THAT YOU'VE ENTERED WOMANHOOD... HERE IS YOUR MENSTRUATION SOMBRERO. I... DON'T THINK I NEED TO TELL YOU HOW IT WORKS.

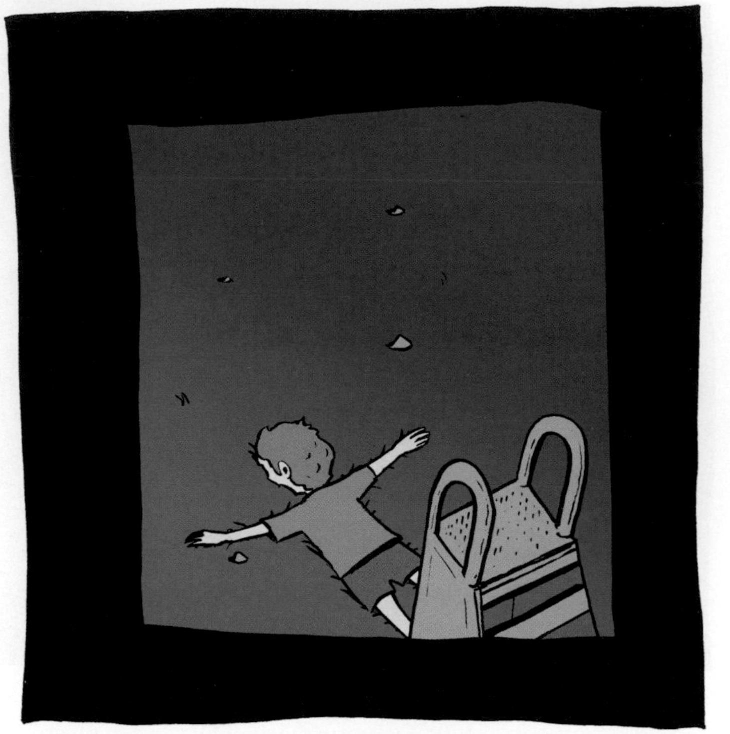

Before slides.

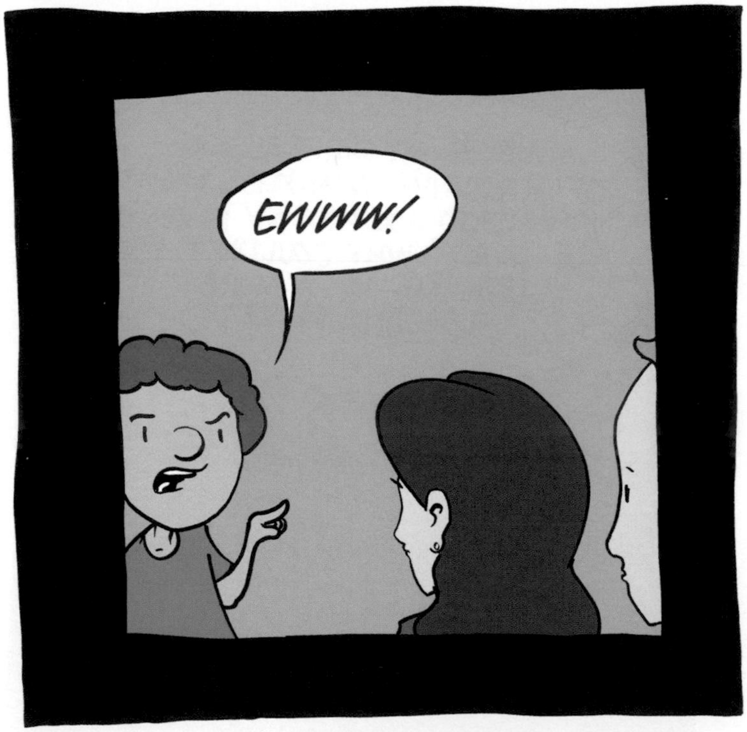
EWWW!

Never hire a sex therapist
under the age of 12.

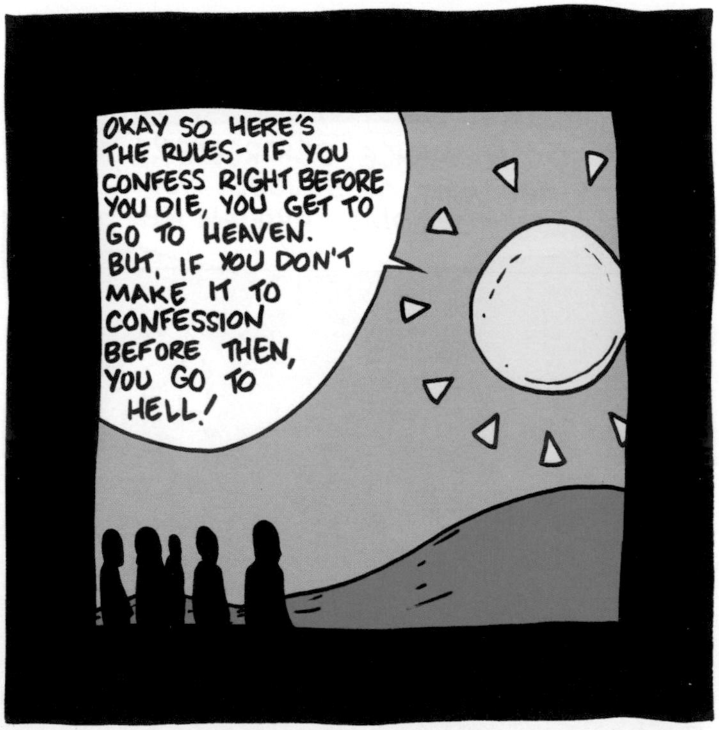
OKAY SO HERE'S THE RULES- IF YOU CONFESS RIGHT BEFORE YOU DIE, YOU GET TO GO TO HEAVEN. BUT, IF YOU DON'T MAKE IT TO CONFESSION BEFORE THEN, YOU GO TO HELL!

God also enjoys
Freeze Tag and Hopscotch.

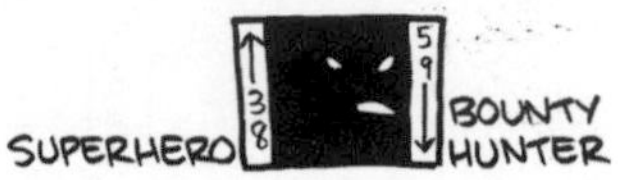
SUPERHERO
BOUNTY HUNTER

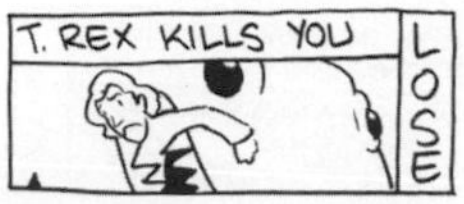
T. REX KILLS YOU
LOSE

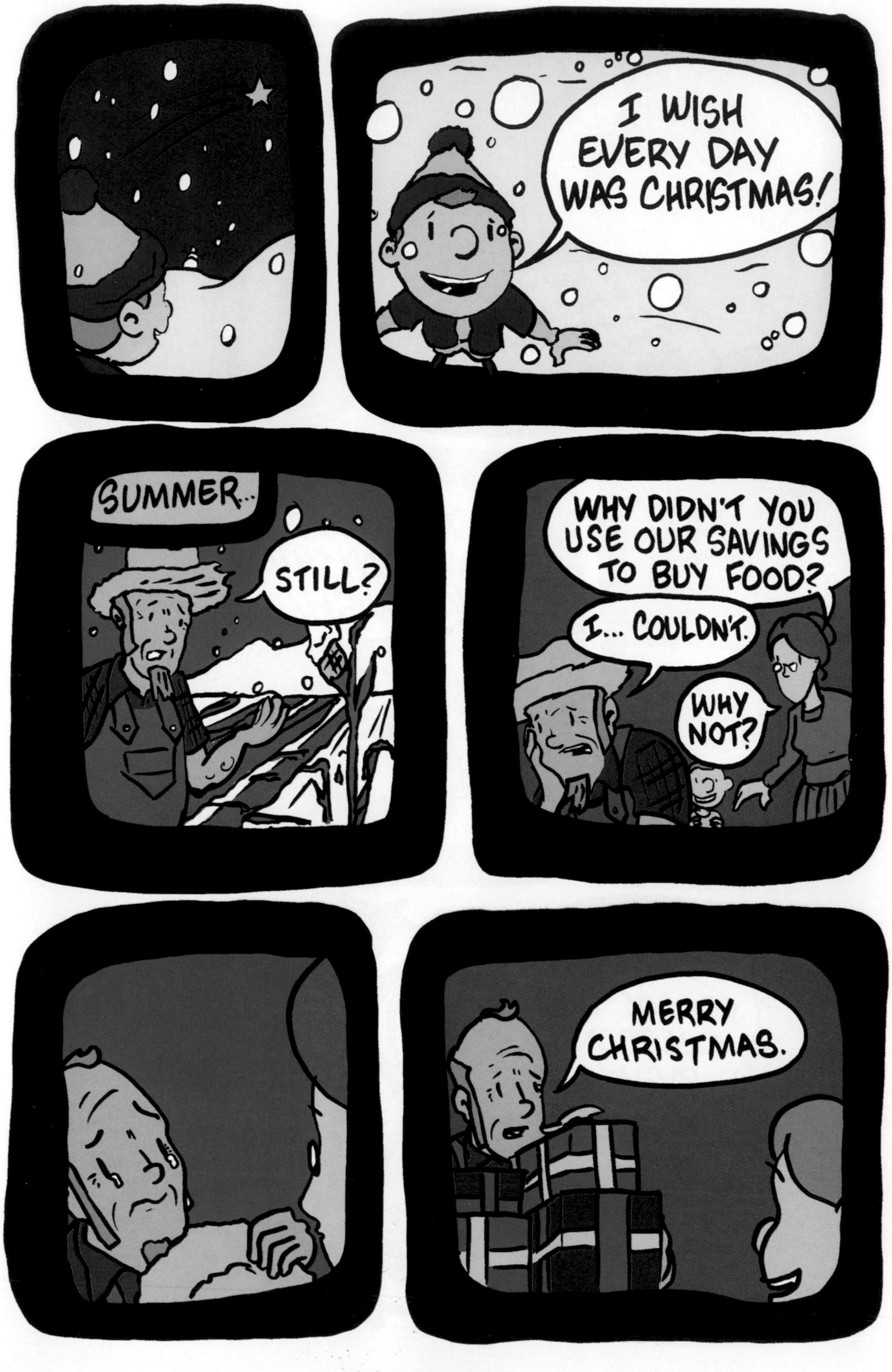
I WISH EVERY DAY WAS CHRISTMAS!
SUMMER...
STILL?
WHY DIDN'T YOU USE OUR SAVINGS TO BUY FOOD?
I... COULDN'T.
WHY NOT?
MERRY CHRISTMAS.

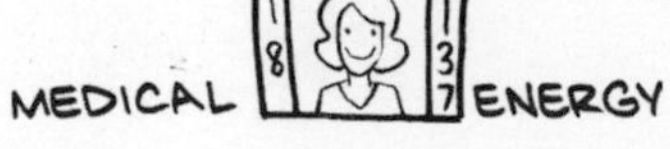
MEDICAL
8
37
ENERGY

DIE IN PUDDLE OF ENERGY DRINKS AND OWN FILTH.
??? LOSE ???

(12) HOW MANY VALENCE ELECTRONS IN A HYDROGEN ATOM? two. one
LATER...
YOU MAY HAVE ANYTHING YOU WISH!
I WISH I'D GOT THAT QUESTION RIGHT.
BOOM!!

LAWYER PROFESSOR
20↓
↑47

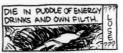

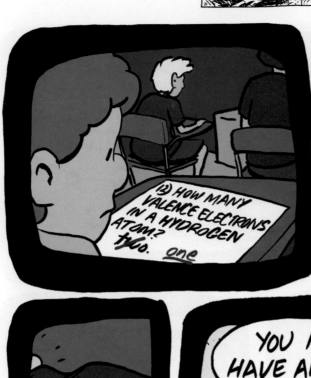

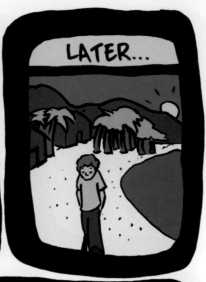

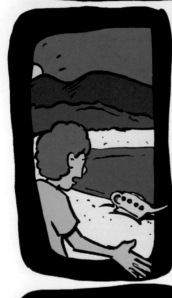

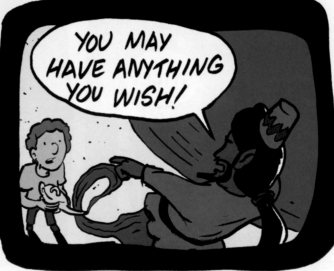

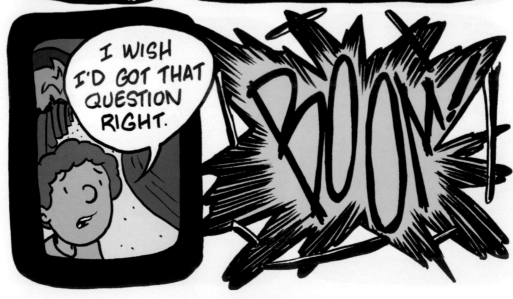

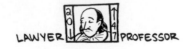

ACCORDING TO THIS STUDY, YOUNG CHILDREN ARE LESS ANXIOUS WHEN IN THE PRESENCE OF A CLOWN.
THAT COULD HELP BILLY'S PANIC ATTACKS.
BUT WE DON'T HAVE A CLOWN SUIT.
UNLESS...
LATER...
BILLY! SOMEWHERE IN HERE... IS A CLOWN!
GOODNIGHT!

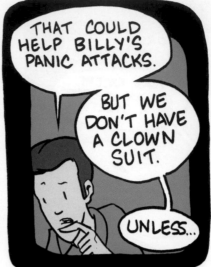

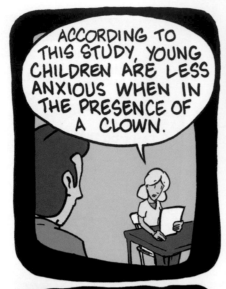

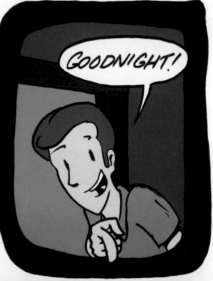

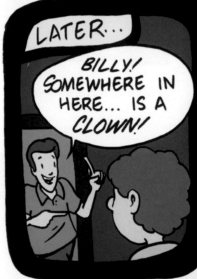

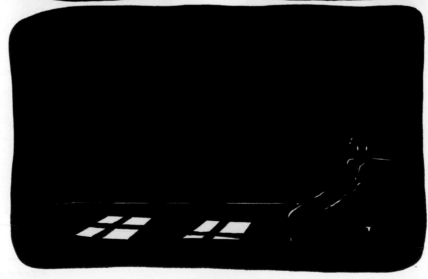

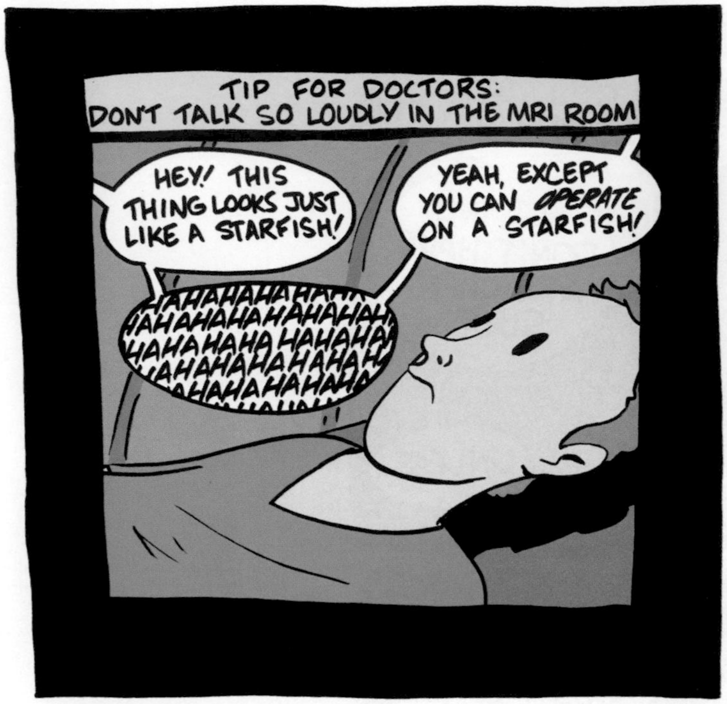
TIP FOR DOCTORS:
DON'T TALK SO LOUDLY IN THE MRI ROOM
HEY! THIS THING LOOKS JUST LIKE A STARFISH!
YEAH, EXCEPT YOU CAN *OPERATE* ON A STARFISH!

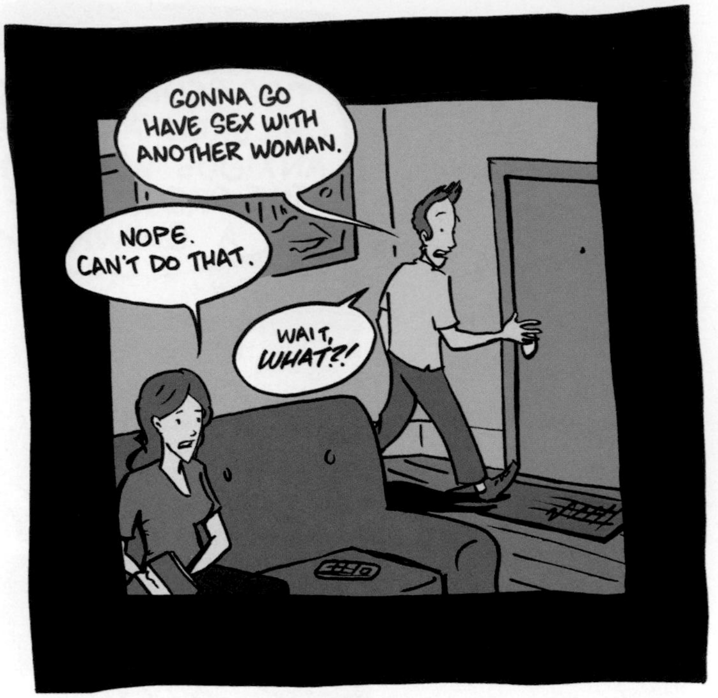
GONNA GO HAVE SEX WITH ANOTHER WOMAN.
NOPE. CAN'T DO THAT.
WAIT, WHAT?!

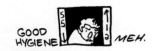

There are some *serious* downsides to marriage.

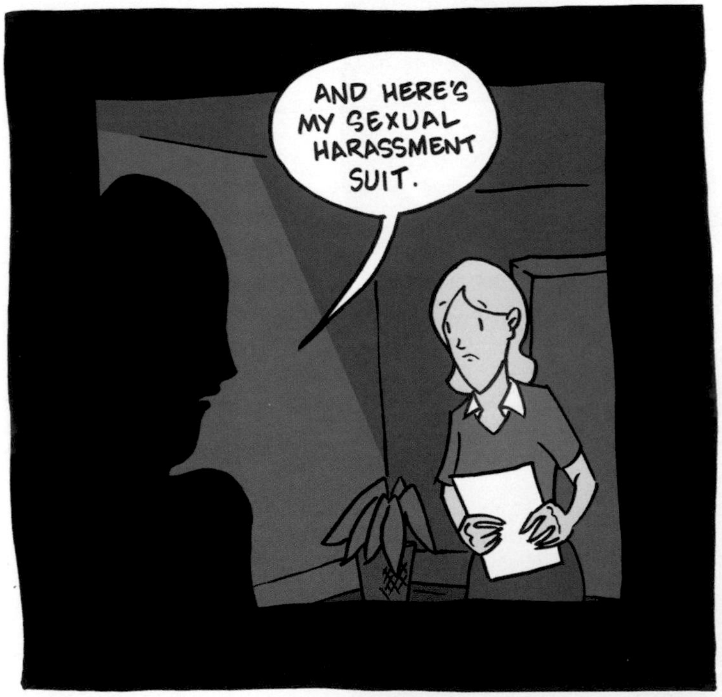
AND HERE'S MY SEXUAL HARASSMENT SUIT.

It was a poor euphemism for being naked.

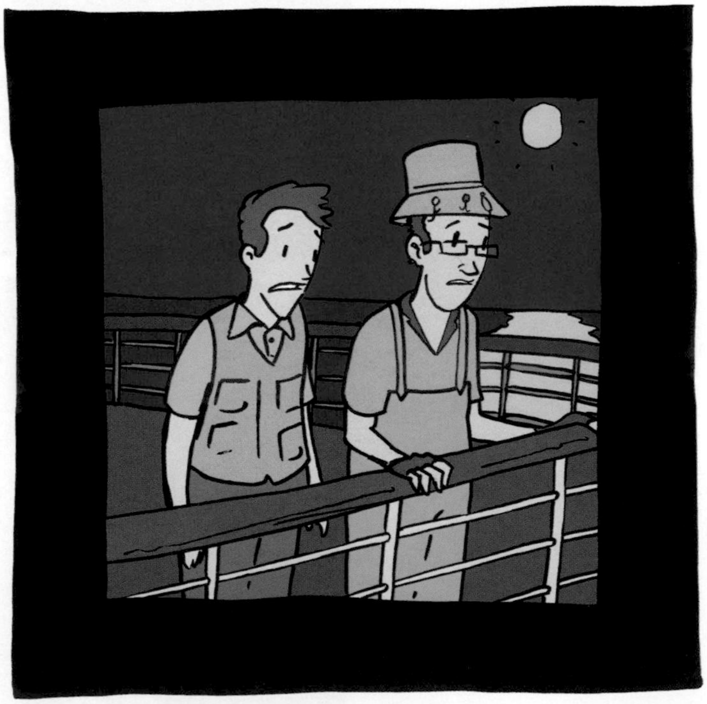

Feb 5,

Things I now believe in:
Mermaids
Things I no longer believe in:
Dynamite fishing.

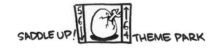

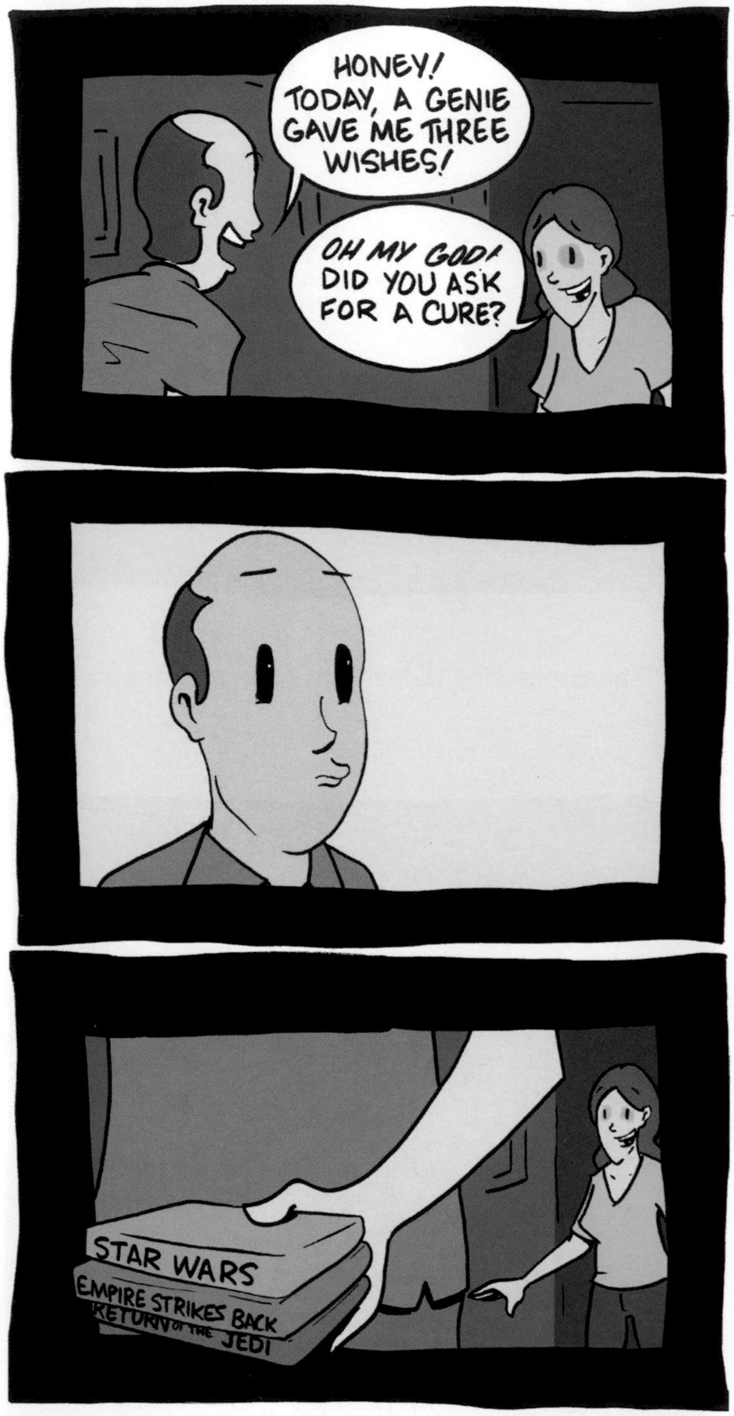
HONEY! TODAY, A GENIE GAVE ME THREE WISHES!
OH MY GOD! DID YOU ASK FOR A CURE?
STAR WARS
EMPIRE STRIKES BACK
RETURN OF THE JEDI

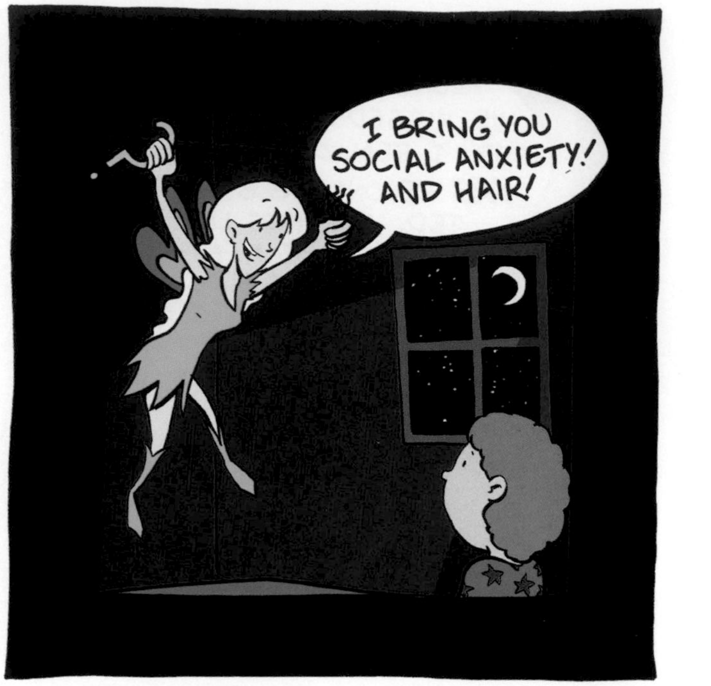
I BRING YOU SOCIAL ANXIETY! AND HAIR!

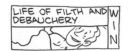

Nobody likes the Puberty Fairy.

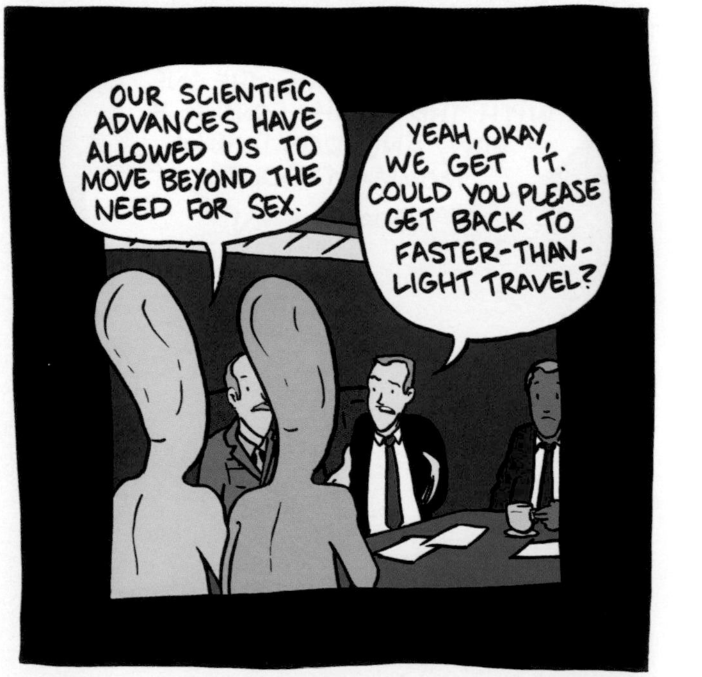
OUR SCIENTIFIC ADVANCES HAVE ALLOWED US TO MOVE BEYOND THE NEED FOR SEX.
YEAH, OKAY, WE GET IT. COULD YOU PLEASE GET BACK TO FASTER-THAN-LIGHT TRAVEL?

I don't know about you, but I'm starting to get tired of those constantly masturbating aliens.

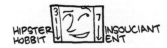

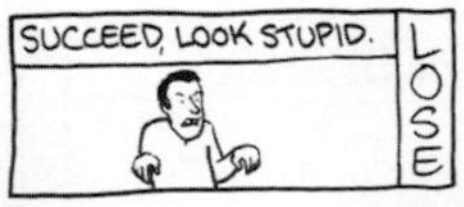
SUCCEED, LOOK STUPID.
LOSE

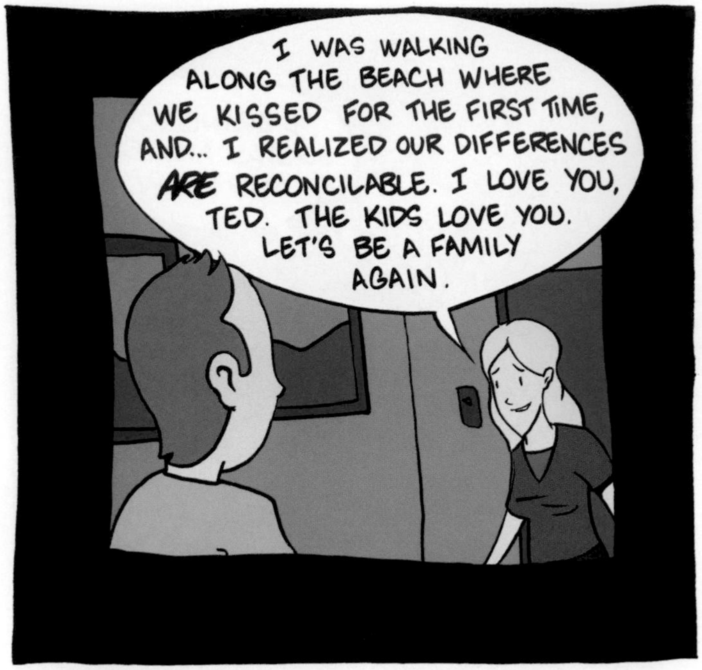
I WAS WALKING ALONG THE BEACH WHERE WE KISSED FOR THE FIRST TIME, AND... I REALIZED OUR DIFFERENCES *ARE* RECONCILABLE. I LOVE YOU, TED. THE KIDS LOVE YOU. LET'S BE A FAMILY AGAIN.

It didn't occur to me what day it was until she got me to sit on the whoopie cushion.

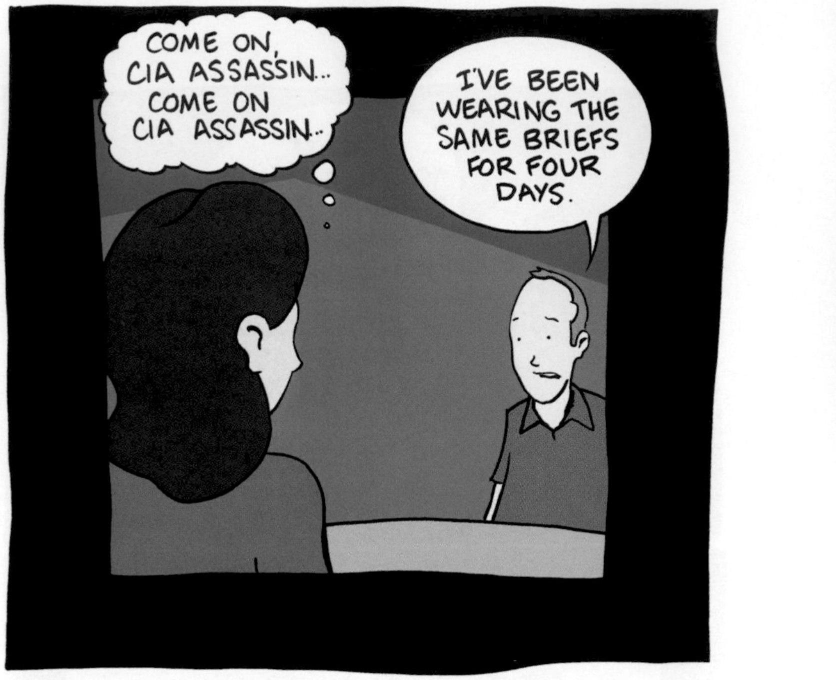
COME ON, CIA ASSASSIN... COME ON CIA ASSASSIN...
I'VE BEEN WEARING THE SAME BRIEFS FOR FOUR DAYS.

The confession didn't go as she had hoped.

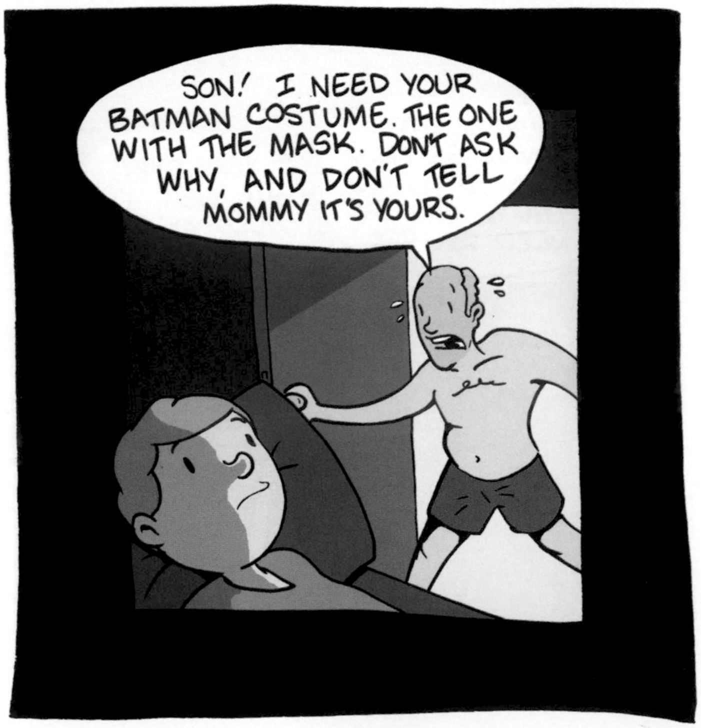
SON! I NEED YOUR BATMAN COSTUME. THE ONE WITH THE MASK. DON'T ASK WHY, AND DON'T TELL MOMMY IT'S YOURS.

I consider this the last moment of my childhood.

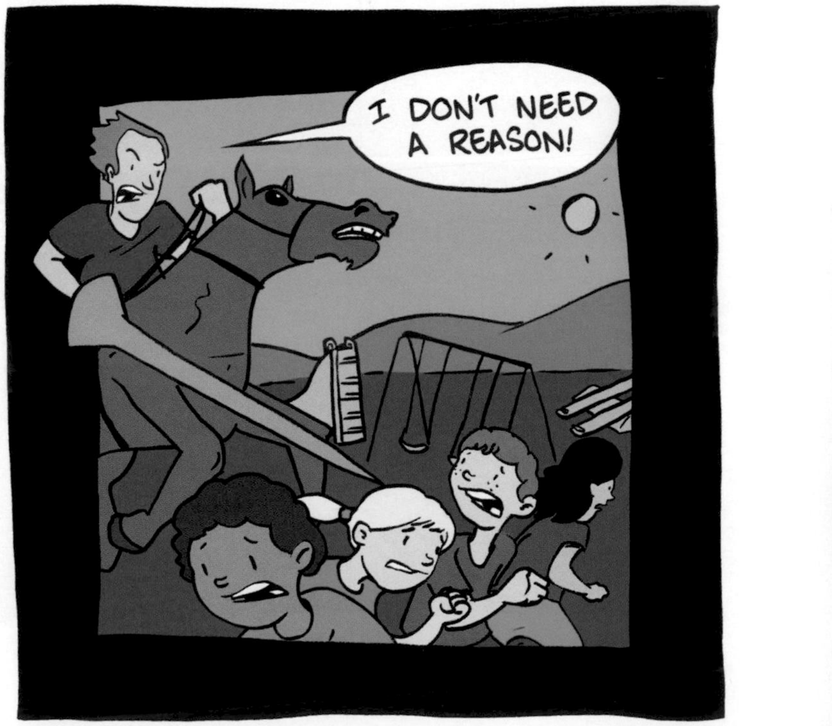
I DON'T NEED A REASON!

I consider myself something of a moral activist.

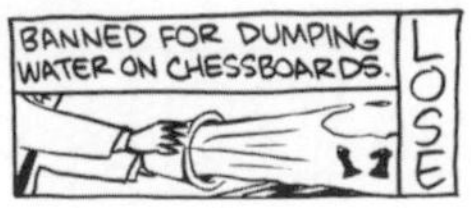
BANNED FOR DUMPING WATER ON CHESSBOARDS.
LOSE

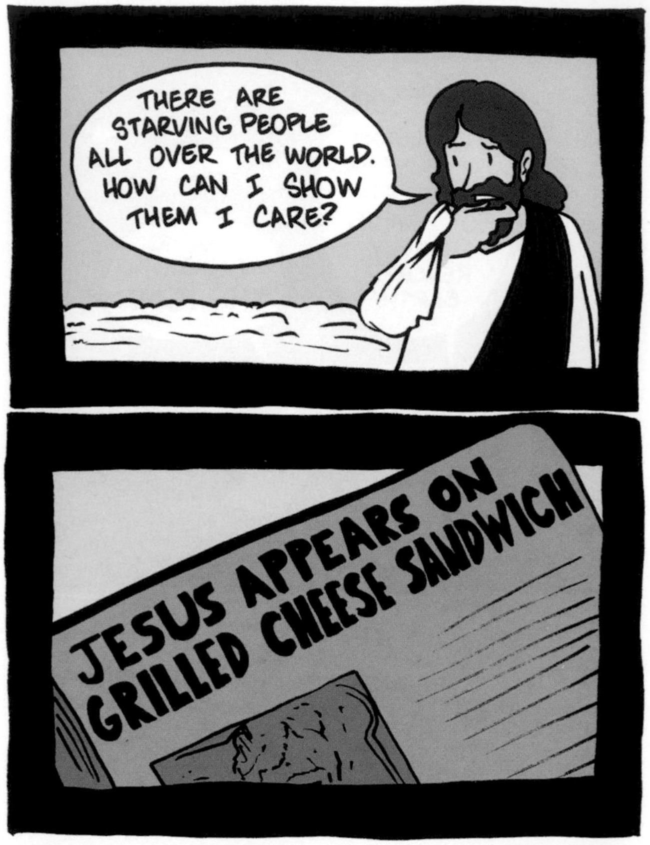
THERE ARE STARVING PEOPLE ALL OVER THE WORLD. HOW CAN I SHOW THEM I CARE?
JESUS APPEARS ON GRILLED CHEESE SANDWICH

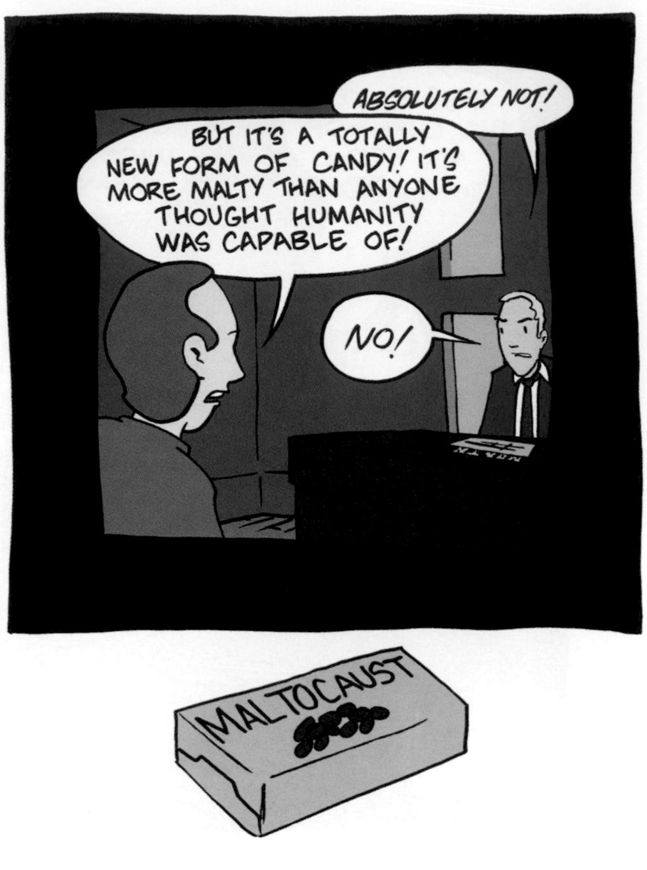
ABSOLUTELY NOT!
BUT IT'S A TOTALLY NEW FORM OF CANDY! IT'S MORE MALTY THAN ANYONE THOUGHT HUMANITY WAS CAPABLE OF!
NO!
MALTOCAUST

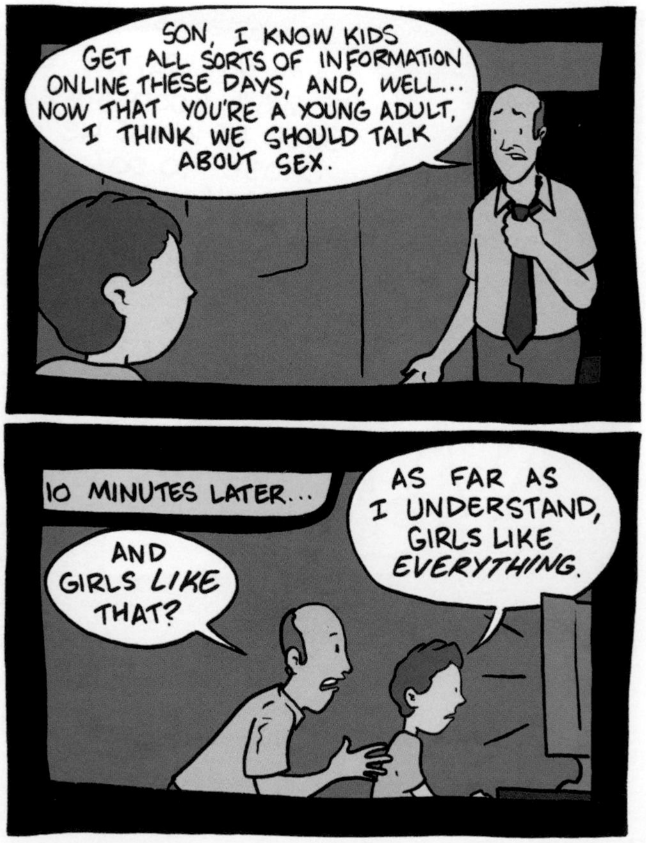
SON, I KNOW KIDS GET ALL SORTS OF INFORMATION ONLINE THESE DAYS, AND, WELL... NOW THAT YOU'RE A YOUNG ADULT, I THINK WE SHOULD TALK ABOUT SEX.
10 MINUTES LATER...
AND GIRLS *LIKE* THAT?
AS FAR AS I UNDERSTAND, GIRLS LIKE *EVERYTHING*.

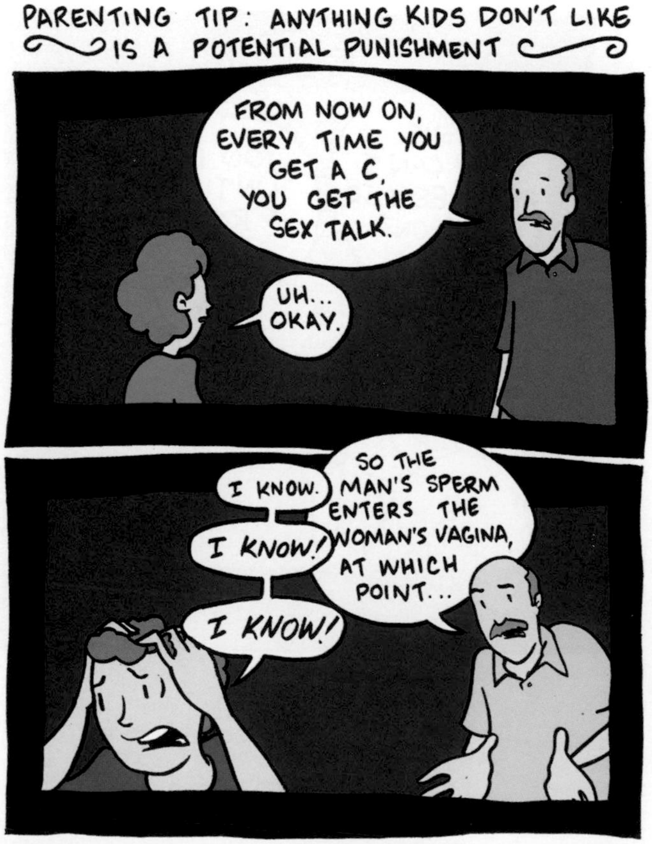
PARENTING TIP: ANYTHING KIDS DON'T LIKE IS A POTENTIAL PUNISHMENT
FROM NOW ON, EVERY TIME YOU GET A C, YOU GET THE SEX TALK.
UH... OKAY.
SO THE MAN'S SPERM ENTERS THE WOMAN'S VAGINA, AT WHICH POINT...
I KNOW.
I KNOW!
I KNOW!

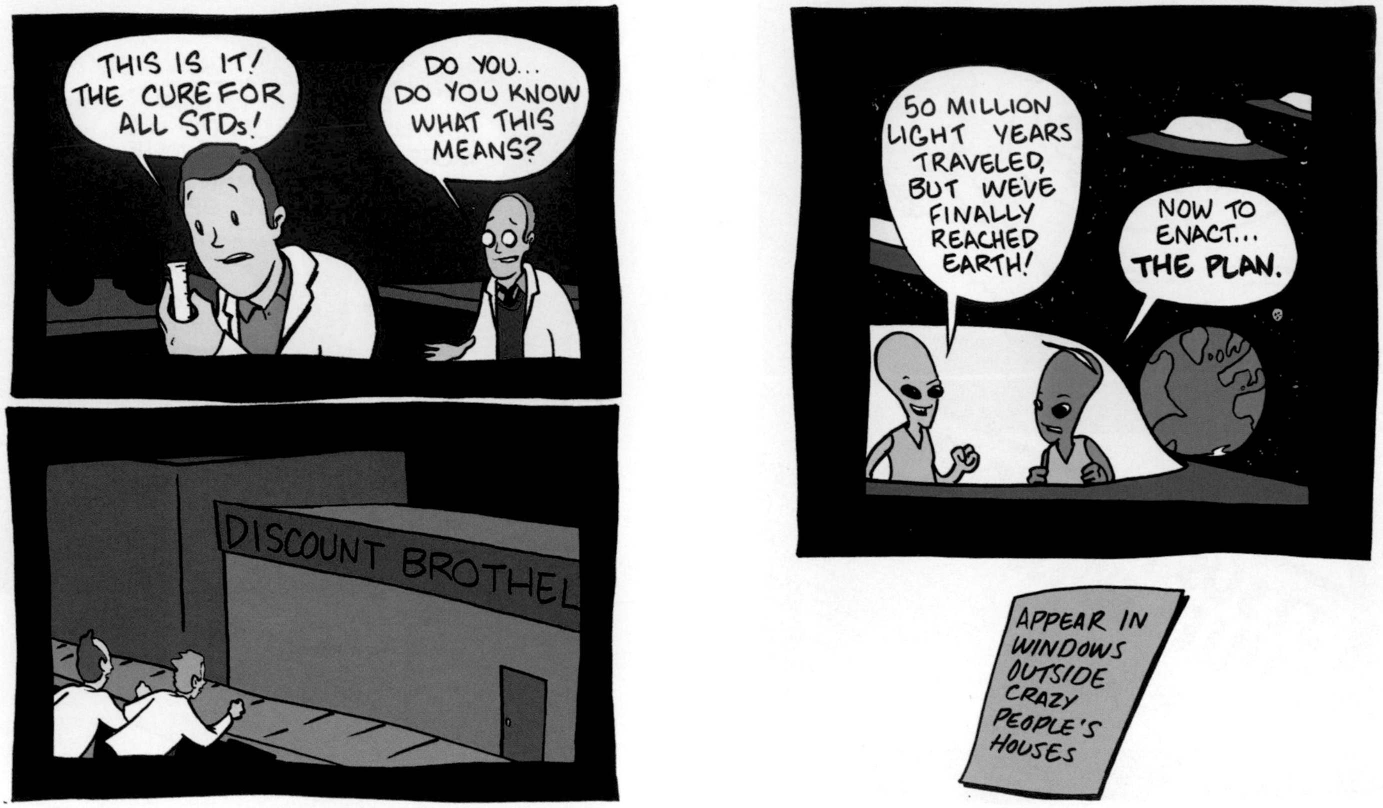
THIS IS IT! THE CURE FOR ALL STDs!
DO YOU... DO YOU KNOW WHAT THIS MEANS?
DISCOUNT BROTHEL
50 MILLION LIGHT YEARS TRAVELED, BUT WE'VE FINALLY REACHED EARTH!
NOW TO ENACT... **THE PLAN.**
APPEAR IN WINDOWS OUTSIDE CRAZY PEOPLE'S HOUSES

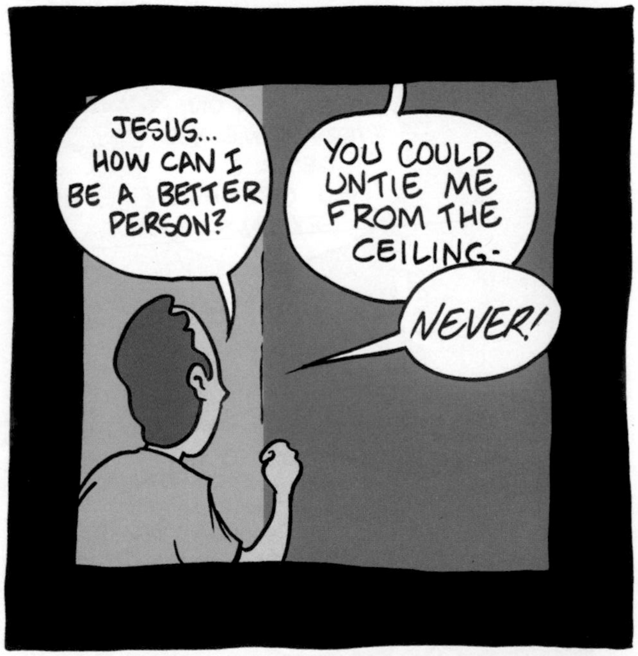
JESUS... HOW CAN I BE A BETTER PERSON?
YOU COULD UNTIE ME FROM THE CEILING-
NEVER!

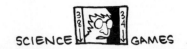

Still waiting for that second coming?

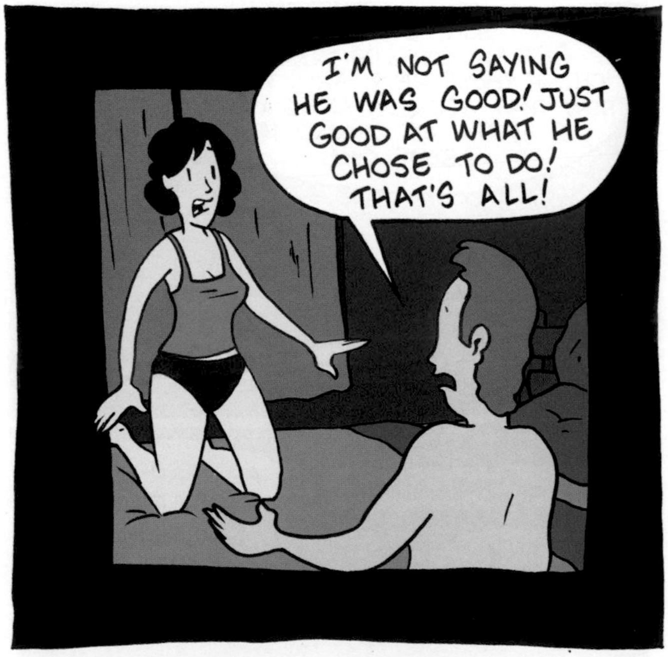
I'M NOT SAYING HE WAS GOOD! JUST GOOD AT WHAT HE CHOSE TO DO! THAT'S ALL!

Sally doesn't feel that I'm "the Hitler of snuggling."

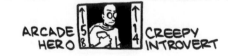

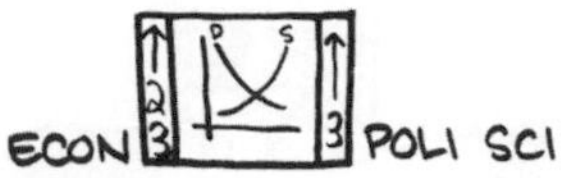

ECON
POLI SCI

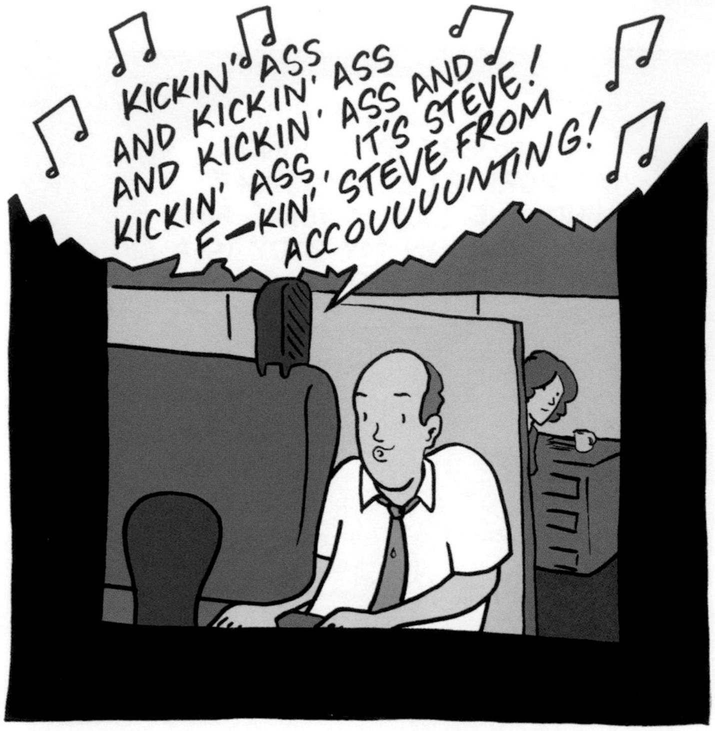

KICKIN' ASS AND KICKIN' ASS AND KICKIN' ASS AND KICKIN' ASS, IT'S STEVE! F—KIN' STEVE FROM ACCOUUUUNTING!

Bring Your Own Theme Song day
ended up being a one-time event.

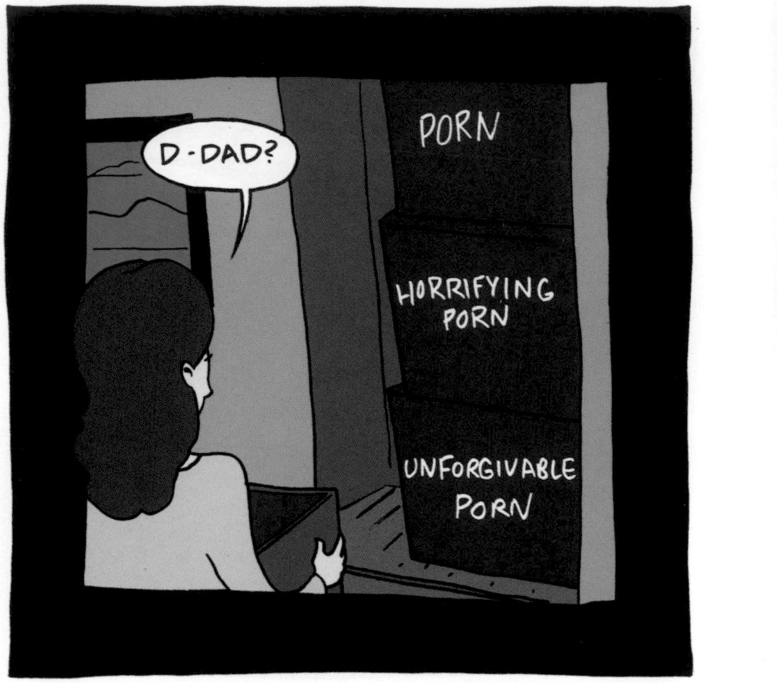

D-DAD?
PORN
HORRIFYING PORN
UNFORGIVABLE PORN

Life Tip:
Before you die, have a friend clean out your stuff.

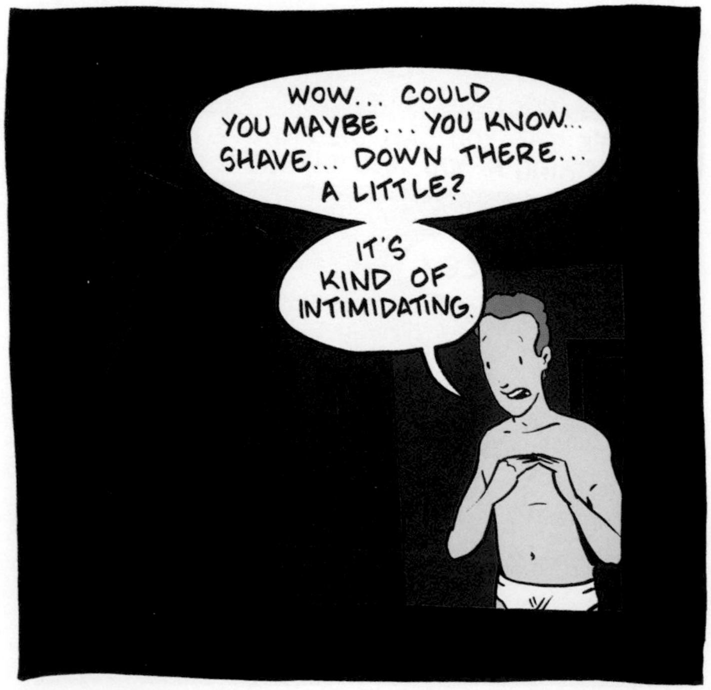

WOW... COULD YOU MAYBE... YOU KNOW... SHAVE... DOWN THERE... A LITTLE?
IT'S KIND OF INTIMIDATING.

My relationship with Medusa was short-lived.

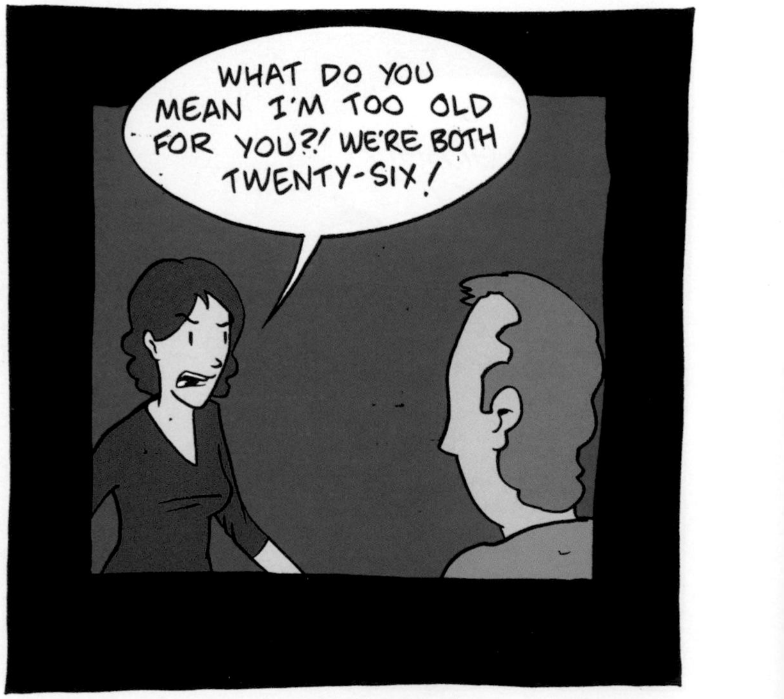

WHAT DO YOU MEAN I'M TOO OLD FOR YOU?! WE'RE BOTH TWENTY-SIX!

Charles explained that this was 43 in girl years.

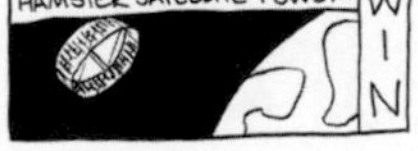

HAMSTER SATELLITE POWER
WIN

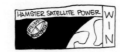

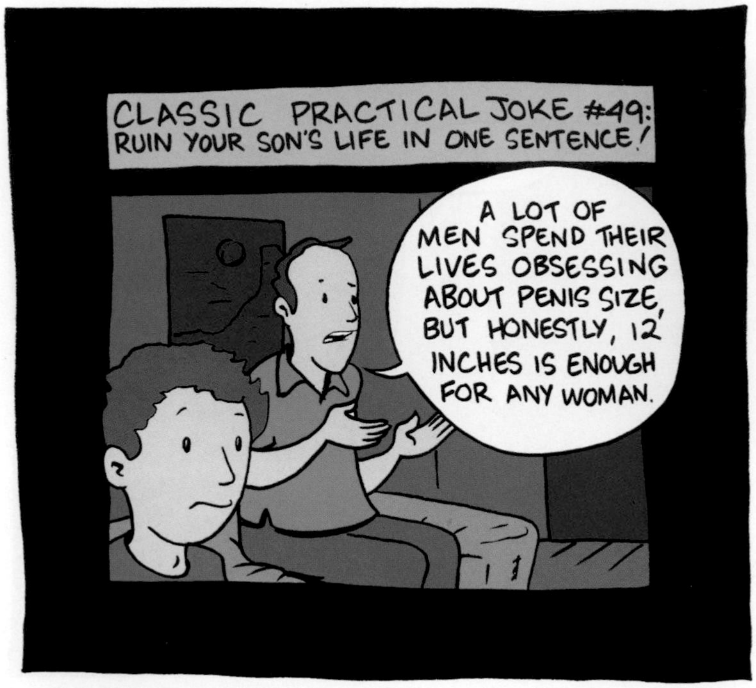
CLASSIC PRACTICAL JOKE #49: RUIN YOUR SON'S LIFE IN ONE SENTENCE!
A LOT OF MEN SPEND THEIR LIVES OBSESSING ABOUT PENIS SIZE, BUT HONESTLY, 12 INCHES IS ENOUGH FOR ANY WOMAN.

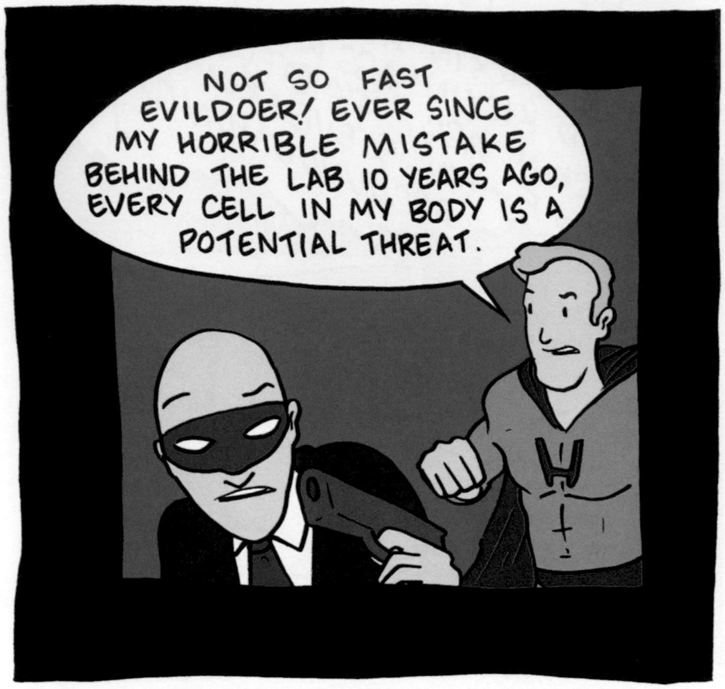
NOT SO FAST EVILDOER! EVER SINCE MY HORRIBLE MISTAKE BEHIND THE LAB 10 YEARS AGO, EVERY CELL IN MY BODY IS A POTENTIAL THREAT.
H

Life tip:
Hepatitis is not a superpower.

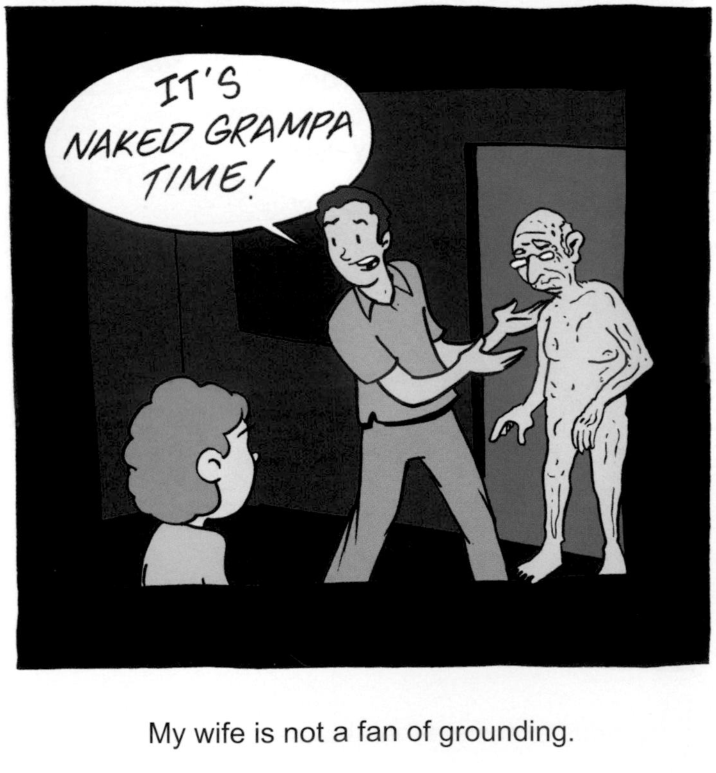
IT'S NAKED GRAMPA TIME!

My wife is not a fan of grounding.

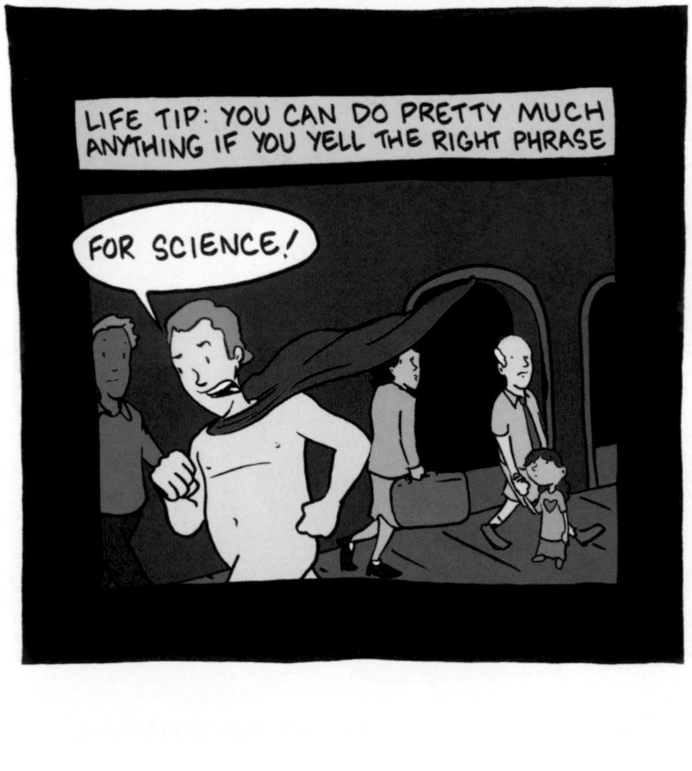
LIFE TIP: YOU CAN DO PRETTY MUCH ANYTHING IF YOU YELL THE RIGHT PHRASE
FOR SCIENCE!

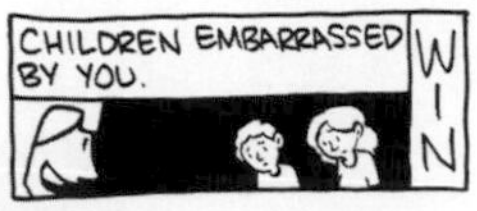
CHILDREN EMBARRASSED BY YOU.
WIN

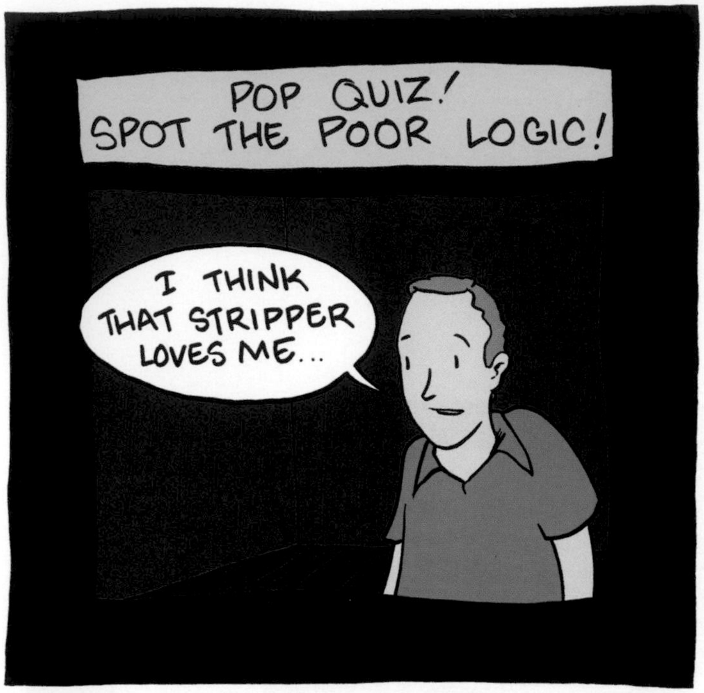
POP QUIZ! SPOT THE POOR LOGIC!
I THINK THAT STRIPPER LOVES ME...

Answer: A corpse can't love.

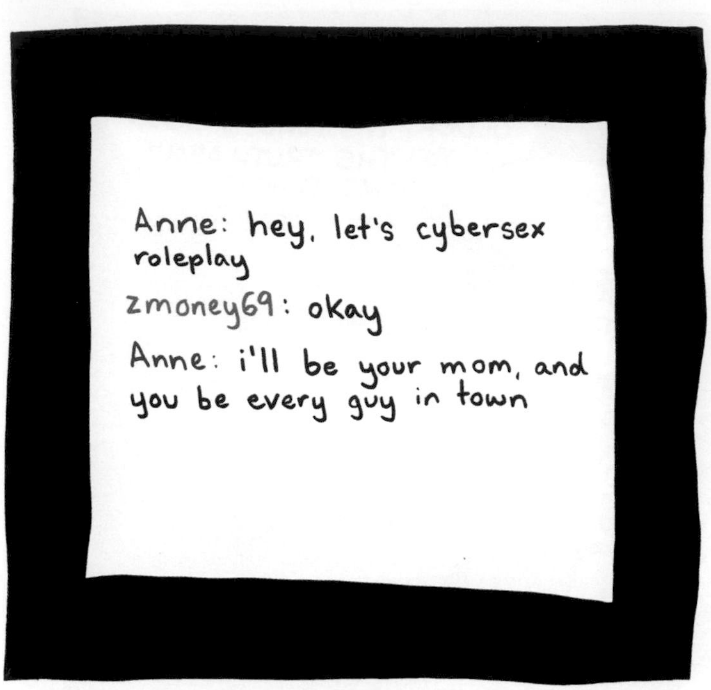
Anne: hey, let's cybersex roleplay
zmoney69: okay
Anne: i'll be your mom, and you be every guy in town

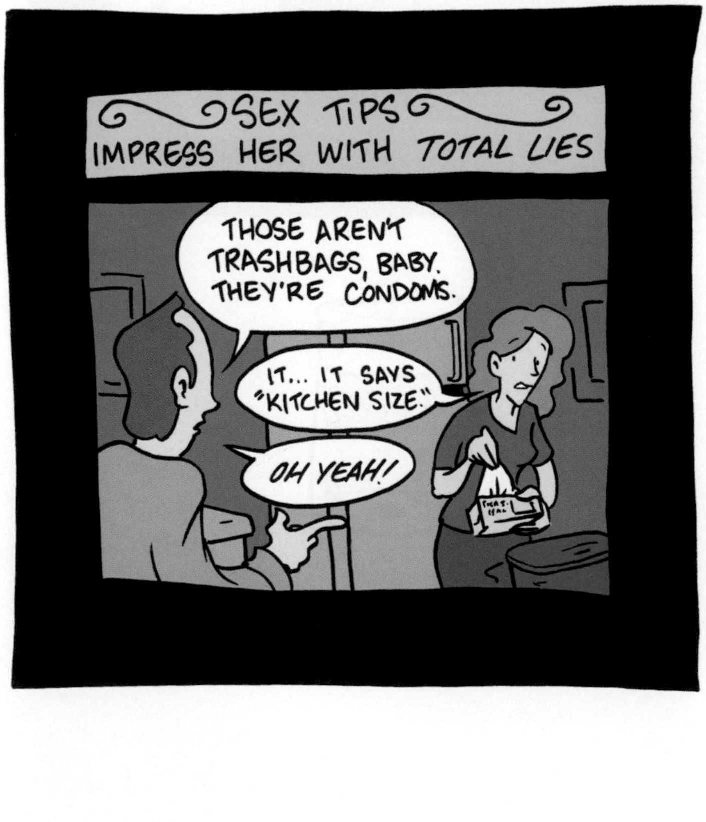
SEX TIPS
IMPRESS HER WITH TOTAL LIES
THOSE AREN'T TRASHBAGS, BABY. THEY'RE CONDOMS.
IT... IT SAYS "KITCHEN SIZE."
OH YEAH!

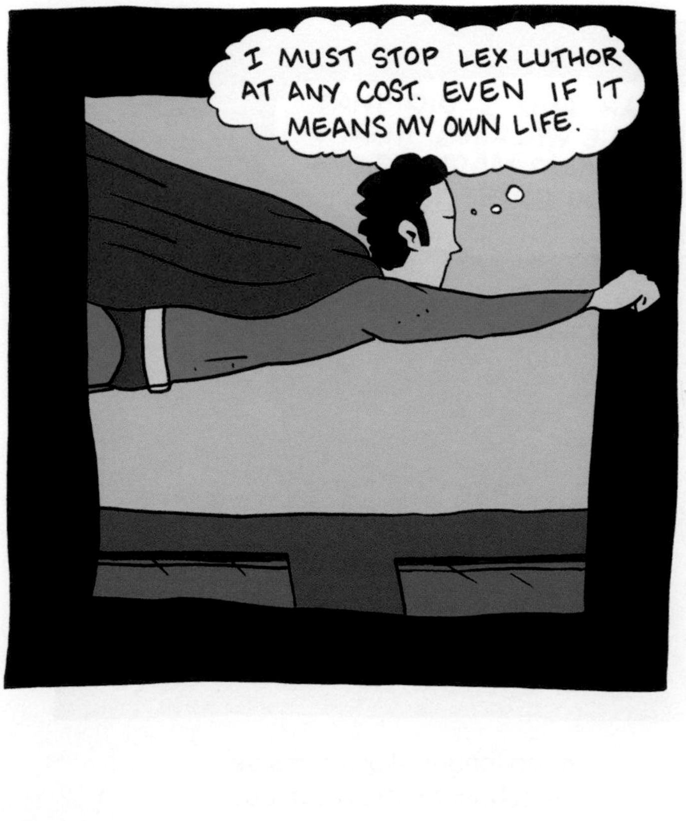
I MUST STOP LEX LUTHOR AT ANY COST. EVEN IF IT MEANS MY OWN LIFE.

The costume made my suicide way more fun.

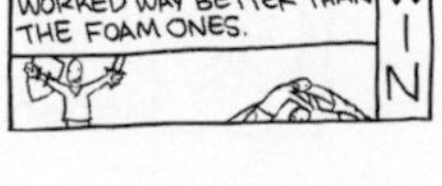
"WOW, THIS METAL SWORD WORKED WAY BETTER THAN THE FOAM ONES."
WIN

OBEY ME!
WIN

SON, NOW THAT YOU'RE GETTING A BIT OLDER, IT'S TIME I TOLD YOU THE TRUTH ABOUT SOME THINGS.
L-LIKE SANTA CLAUS?
GRAMPA IN A COSTUME.
THE TOOTH FAIRY?
MOM. WHILE YOU WERE ASLEEP.
UNICORNS?
RACISTS.

I WISH YOU WOULDN'T SHAKE THAT AROUND AFTER WE MAKE LOVE.

YEAH, AND I DID THAT WHILE WALKING. THAT'S LIKE TWO MAGIC TRICKS TO YOU GUYS.

I'm no longer allowed inside
the school for the disabled.

TIPS

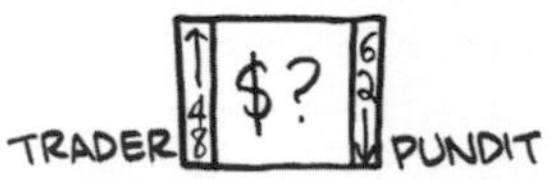
TRADER
$?
148
621
PUNDIT

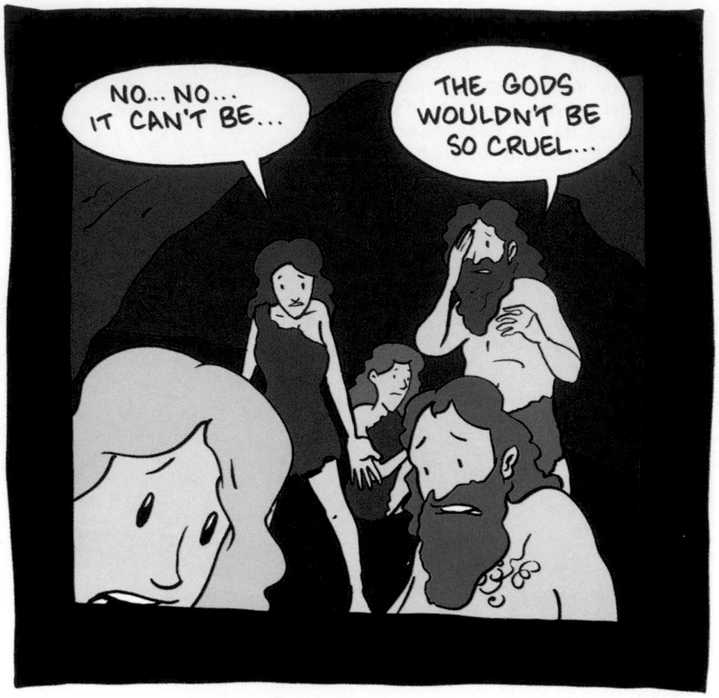
NO... NO... IT CAN'T BE...
THE GODS WOULDN'T BE SO CRUEL...

12,242 B.C.:
The sex-pregnancy connection is discovered

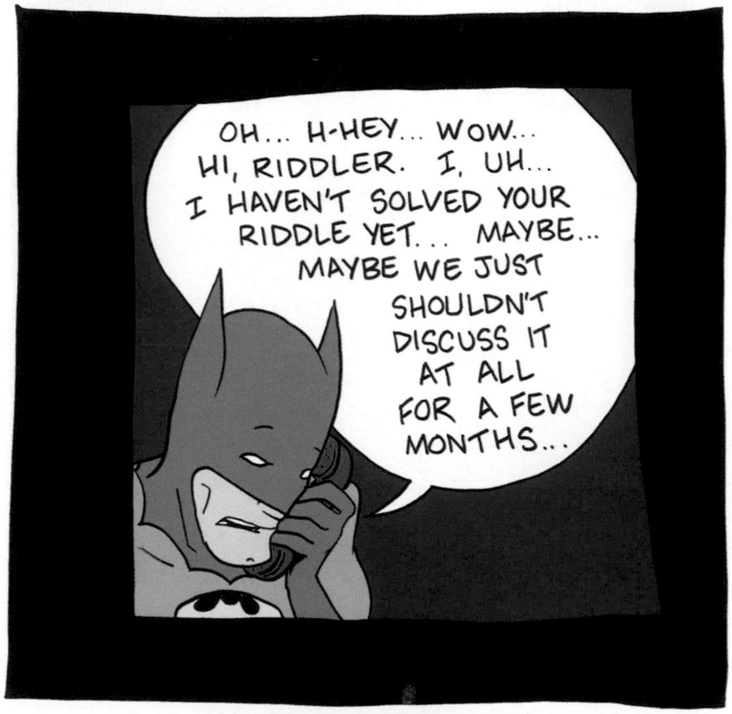
OH... H-HEY... WOW... HI, RIDDLER. I, UH... I HAVEN'T SOLVED YOUR RIDDLE YET... MAYBE... MAYBE WE JUST SHOULDN'T DISCUSS IT AT ALL FOR A FEW MONTHS...

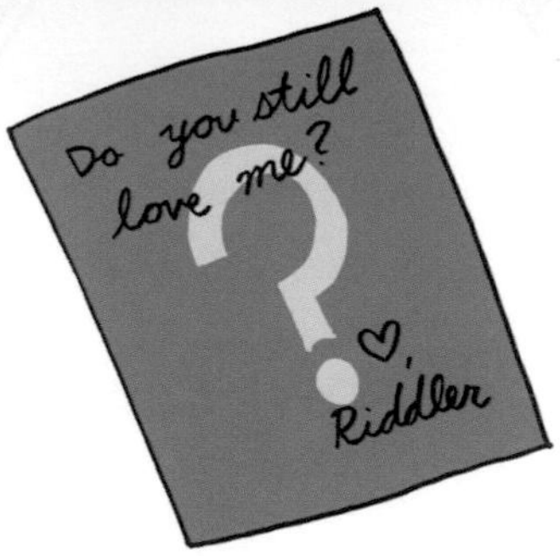
Do you still love me?
?
♡, Riddler

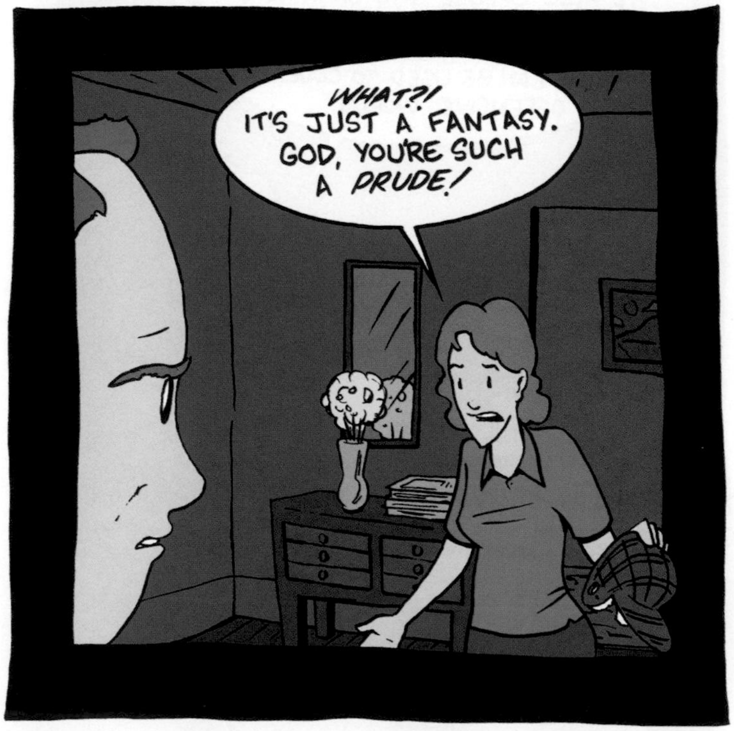
WHAT?! IT'S JUST A FANTASY. GOD, YOU'RE SUCH A PRUDE!

Ted refused to roleplay the guy I cheated with.

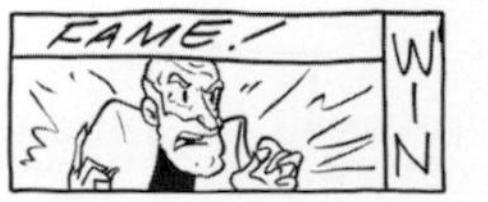
FAME!
WIN

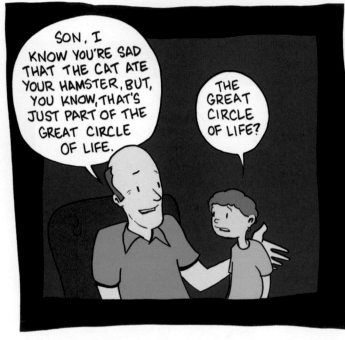

BOOM!
W
I
N

MOM, DAD, I HAVE A CONFESSION! NONE OF THIS IS REAL! YOU'RE BOTH IN A VIRTUAL REALITY MACHINE IN MY BASEMENT! I'M USING YOUR BODY HEAT AS A POWER SOURCE! I'M A MONSTER! A MONSTER!
UH... THAT'S... THAT'S HORRIBLE, SON...

SON, I KNOW YOU'RE SAD THAT THE CAT ATE YOUR HAMSTER, BUT, YOU KNOW, THAT'S JUST PART OF THE GREAT CIRCLE OF LIFE.
THE GREAT CIRCLE OF LIFE?

CRAPPY STUFF HAPPENS TO YOU
BIRTH
DEATH

WE'RE TIRED OF THIS LIBRARY KEEPING SMUTTY ROMANCE NOVELS, BUT WE ALSO OPPOSE THE BANNING OF BOOKS, SO AS A COMPROMISE WE'RE PASSING OUT THESE STICKERS THAT CAN BE USED TO COVER OFFENSIVE WORDS.
He removed his breeches, displaying his enormous
Helen loosened her bodice to reveal her heaving
She suddenly found her in his powerful grip,
and before she could he placed his on her
of soft

MONKEY STYLE
16
52
DRUNK STYLE

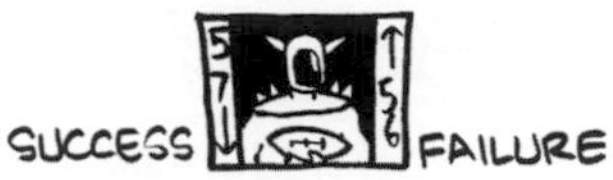
SUCCESS
FAILURE

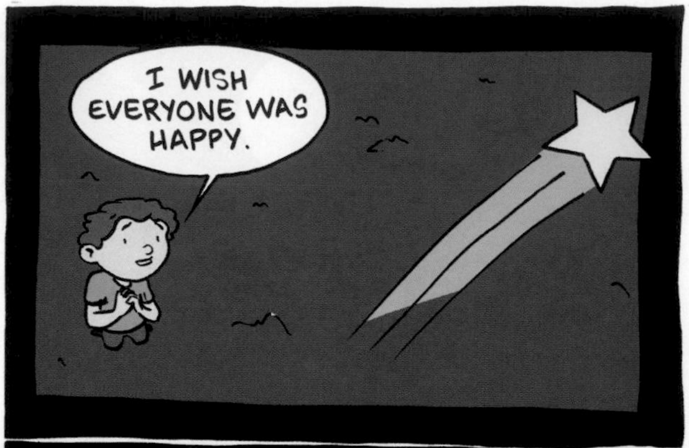
I WISH EVERYONE WAS HAPPY.

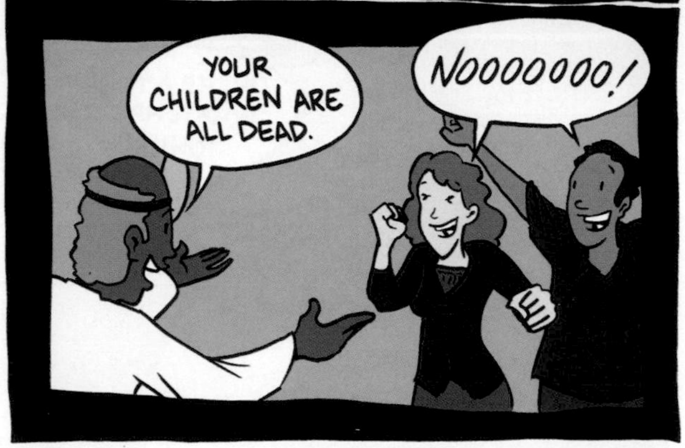
YOUR CHILDREN ARE ALL DEAD.
NOOOOOOO!

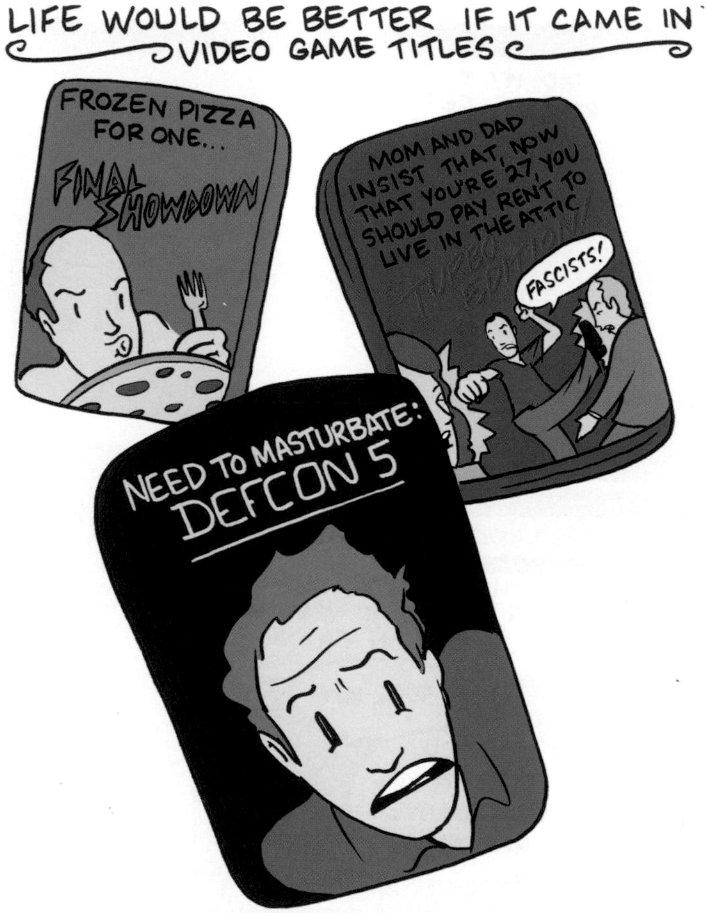
LIFE WOULD BE BETTER IF IT CAME IN VIDEO GAME TITLES
FROZEN PIZZA FOR ONE...
FINAL SHOWDOWN
MOM AND DAD INSIST THAT, NOW THAT YOU'RE 27, YOU SHOULD PAY RENT TO LIVE IN THE ATTIC
TURBO EDITION!
FASCISTS!
NEED TO MASTURBATE:
DEFCON 5

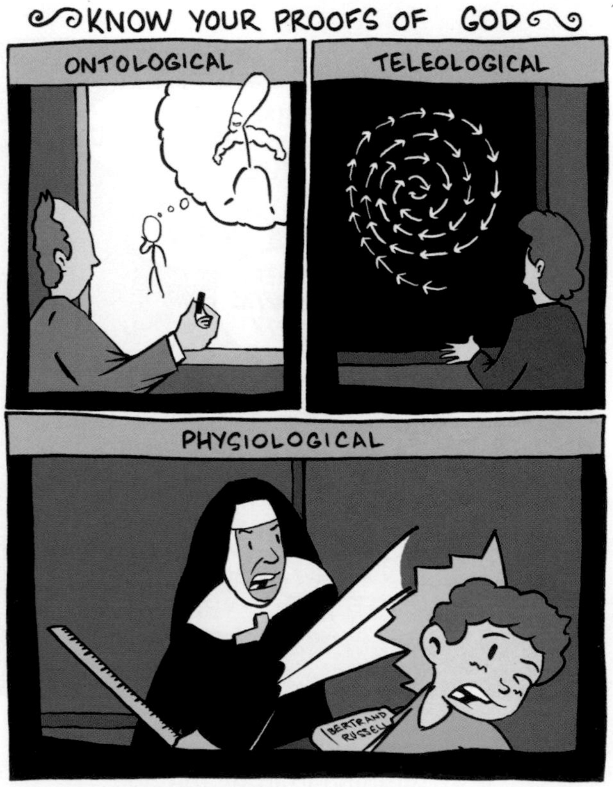
KNOW YOUR PROOFS OF GOD
ONTOLOGICAL
TELEOLOGICAL
PHYSIOLOGICAL
BERTRAND RUSSELL

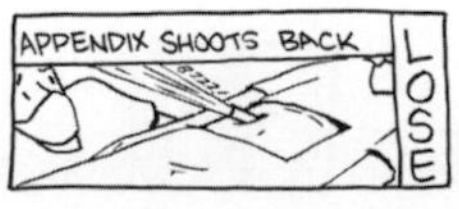
APPENDIX SHOOTS BACK
LOSE

MASSIVE ROYALTIES FOR "REAGAN: AWESOME."
WIN

ADAM... WHY HAVE YOU COVERED YOURSELF?
UH... I, UH... I WAS ASHAMED OF MY NUDITY.
EARLIER...
OH, HEY THERE... WHATCHA DOIN' TONIGHT?

I DID IT! I GOT HERE FIRST! I GET TO LIVE! TO LIVE!
30 YEARS LATER...
THE EMPLOYEE HANDBOOK SAYS THERE'S NO NEED TO WEAR A TIE ON FRIDAY.
SURE, BUT-
DID YOU EVEN READ THE EMPLOYEE HANDBOOK?

HA! THAT'S NOTHIN'! YOU GUYS EVER HAD HOT WAX MELTED LOVINGLY OVER THE SMALL OF YOUR BACK?
N-NO...
WELL, NEITHER HAD I... UNTIL LAST NIGHT!

Todd's masturbation stories are really starting to freak me out.

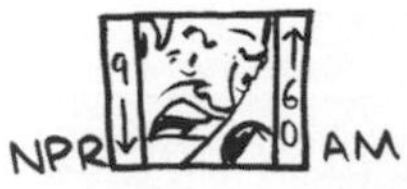
NPR
9
60
AM

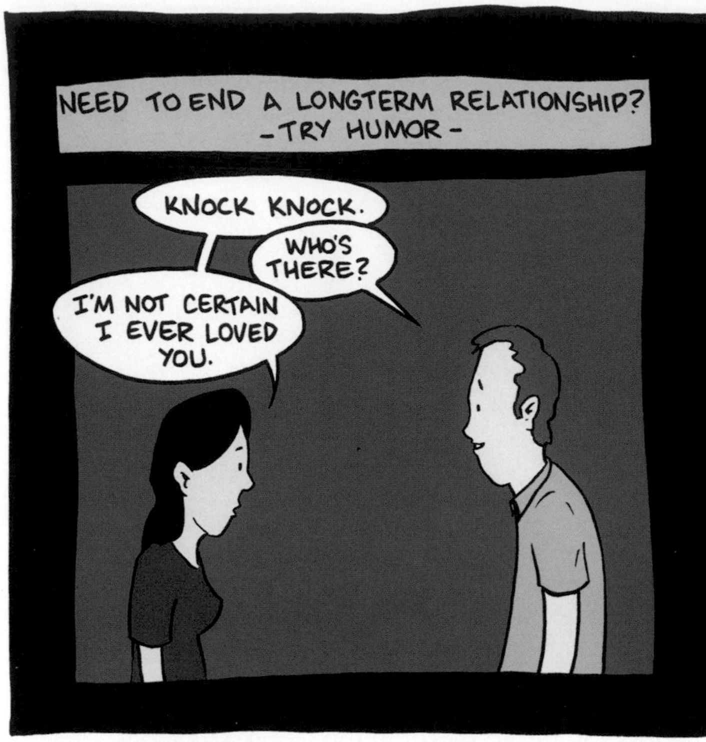
NEED TO END A LONGTERM RELATIONSHIP?
-TRY HUMOR-
KNOCK KNOCK.
WHO'S THERE?
I'M NOT CERTAIN I EVER LOVED YOU.

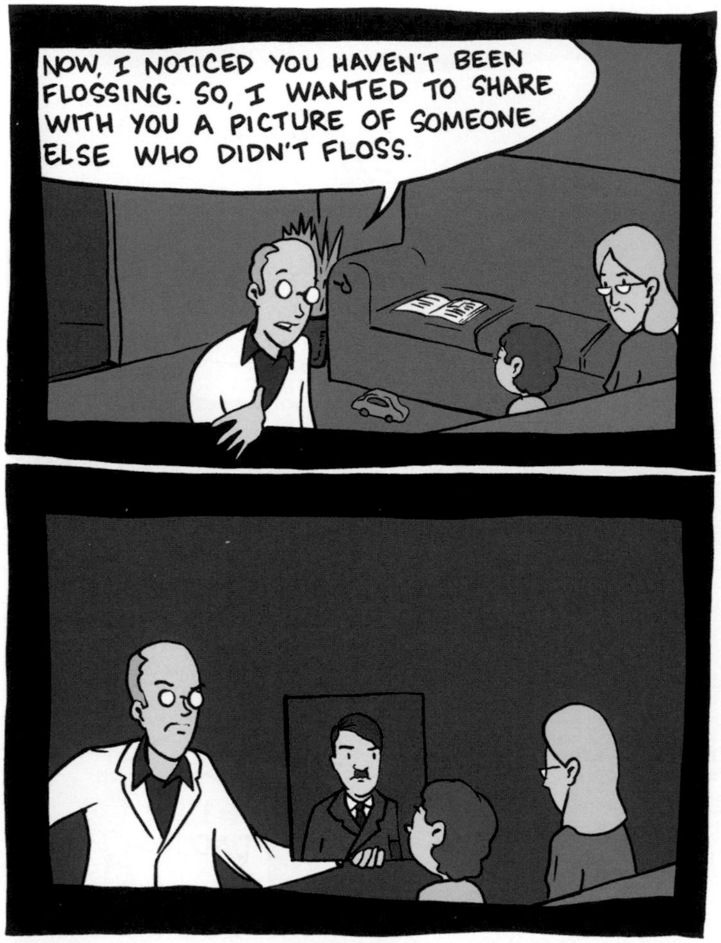
NOW, I NOTICED YOU HAVEN'T BEEN FLOSSING. SO, I WANTED TO SHARE WITH YOU A PICTURE OF SOMEONE ELSE WHO DIDN'T FLOSS.

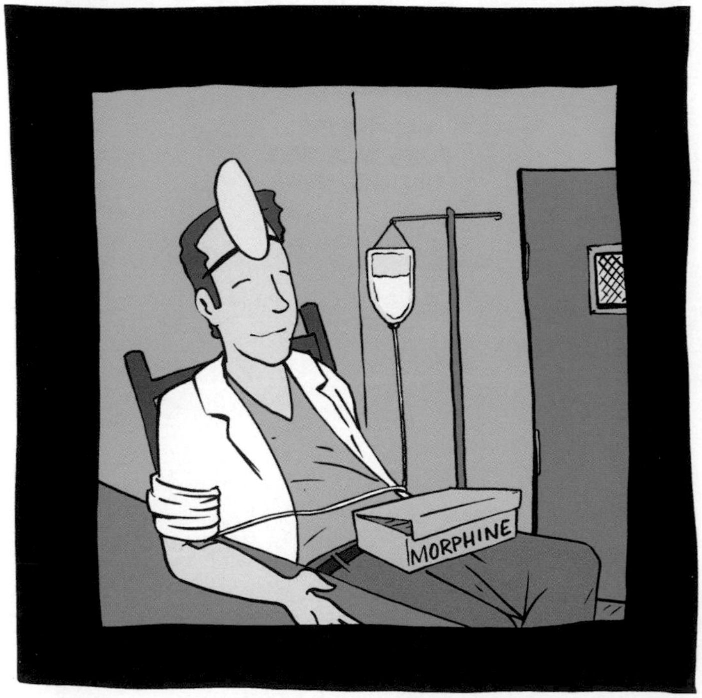
MORPHINE

I didn't become a doctor for the money.

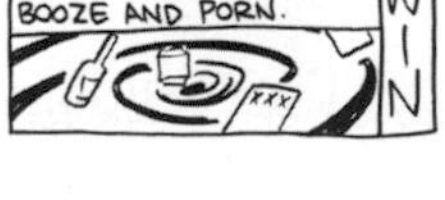
DOWNWARD SPIRAL OF BOOZE AND PORN.
WIN

FOREGO WORLDLY DELIGHTS FOR LOVE OF FELLOW MAN
LOSE

HEY! WHO'S OVER THERE LOOKING SEXY! IT'S ILLEGAL TO LOOK THAT SEXY IN THE VATICAN! WE HAVE RULES! STOP! STOP IT!

We were eventually compelled to remove the full-length mirror in the Pope's hallway.

YOU UH... YOU DECIDED TO KEEP TWO KINDS OF EACH SCORPION?
THE TSETSE FLIES WILL HAVE FRIENDS NOW!

MOMENTS PRIOR...
#1 DAD
#1 DAD

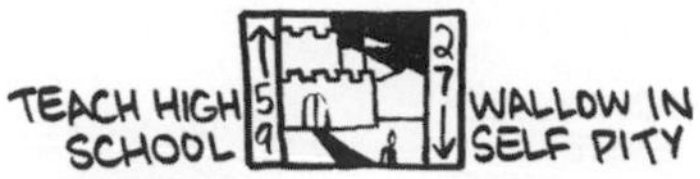

TEACH HIGH SCHOOL
5 9
2 7
WALLOW IN SELF PITY

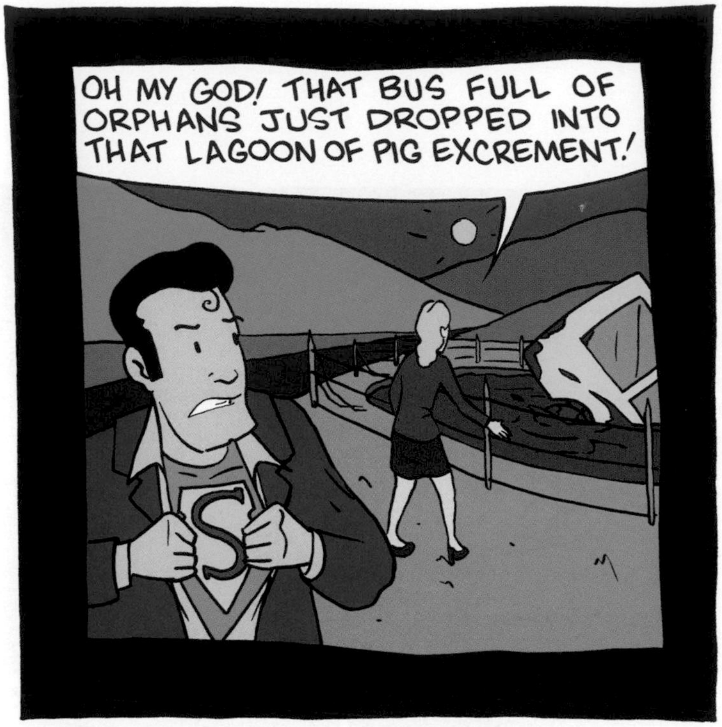

OH MY GOD! THAT BUS FULL OF ORPHANS JUST DROPPED INTO THAT LAGOON OF PIG EXCREMENT!

I managed to get my shirt back on just before she turned around.

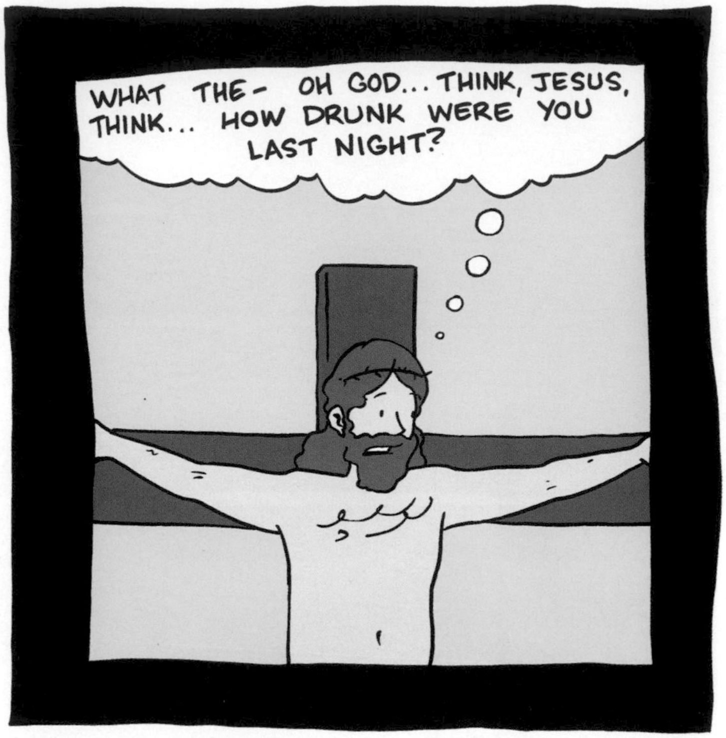

WHAT THE- OH GOD... THINK, JESUS, THINK... HOW DRUNK WERE YOU LAST NIGHT?

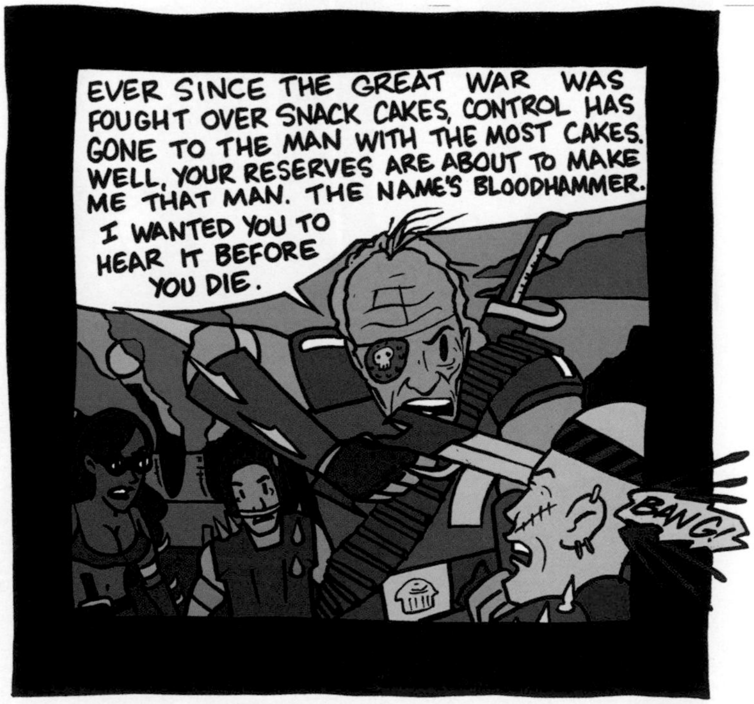

EVER SINCE THE GREAT WAR WAS FOUGHT OVER SNACK CAKES, CONTROL HAS GONE TO THE MAN WITH THE MOST CAKES. WELL, YOUR RESERVES ARE ABOUT TO MAKE ME THAT MAN. THE NAME'S BLOODHAMMER.
I WANTED YOU TO HEAR IT BEFORE YOU DIE.
BANG!

There were some significant unintended consequences to legalizing pot.

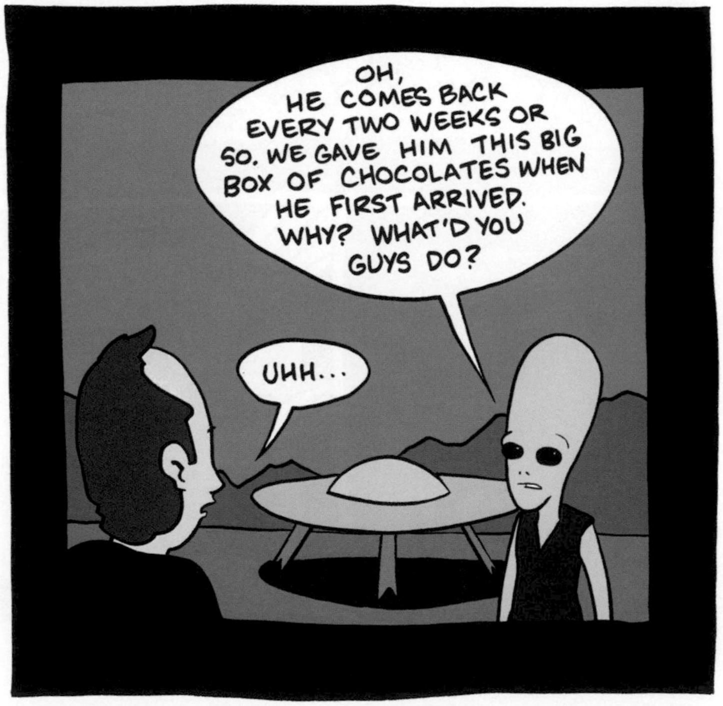

OH, HE COMES BACK EVERY TWO WEEKS OR SO. WE GAVE HIM THIS BIG BOX OF CHOCOLATES WHEN HE FIRST ARRIVED. WHY? WHAT'D YOU GUYS DO?
UHH...

Well, the good news is that we found out Jesus is worshipped on other planets.

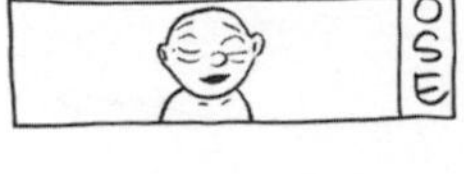

MIRACLE OF CHILDBIRTH
LOSE

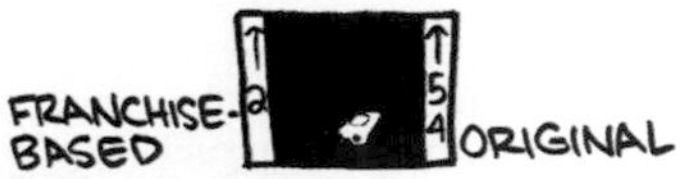
FRANCHISE-BASED
ORIGINAL

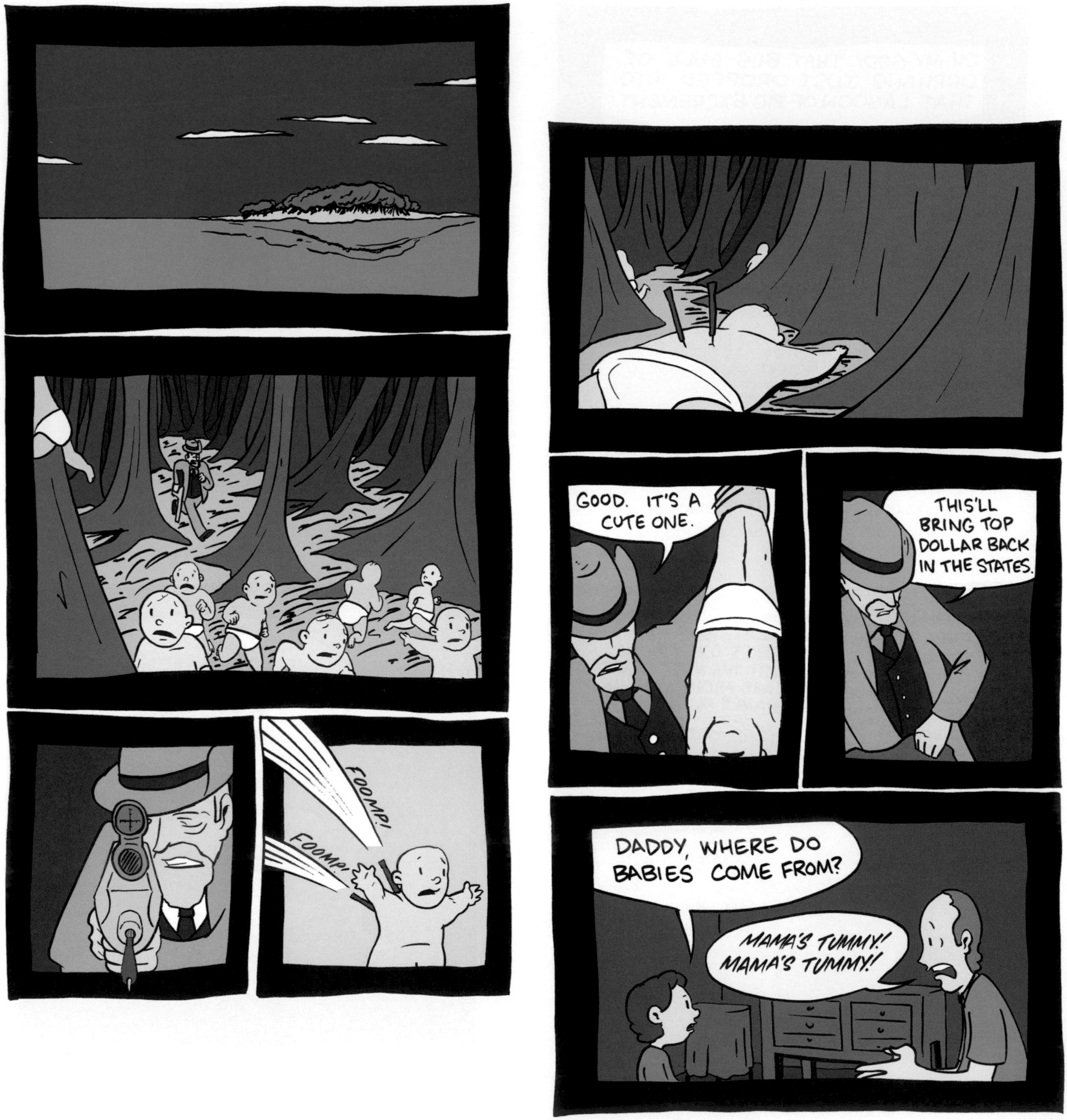
FOOMP!
FOOMP!
GOOD. IT'S A CUTE ONE.
THIS'LL BRING TOP DOLLAR BACK IN THE STATES.
DADDY, WHERE DO BABIES COME FROM?
MAMA'S TUMMY! MAMA'S TUMMY!

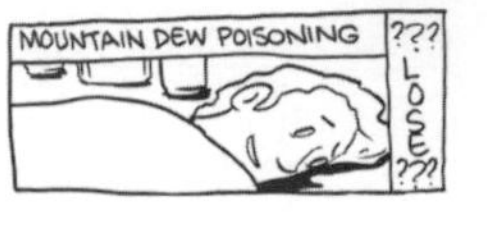
MOUNTAIN DEW POISONING
LOSE

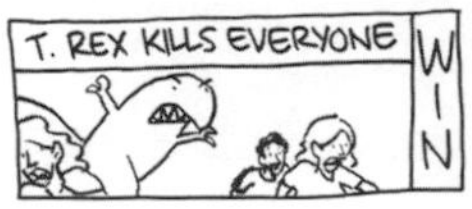
T. REX KILLS EVERYONE
WIN

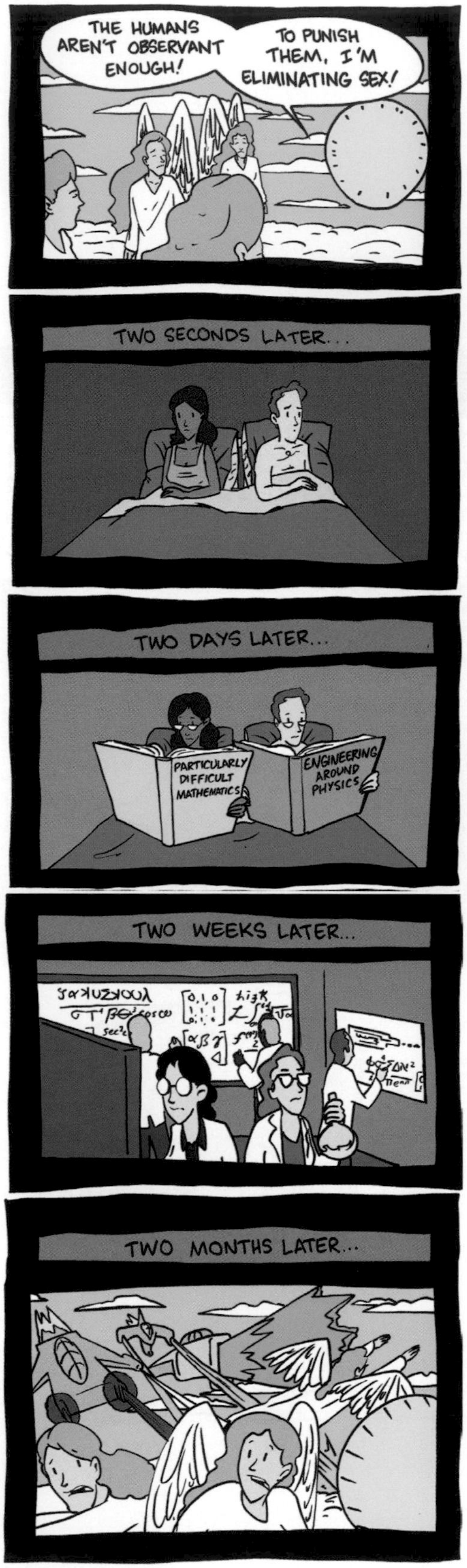
THE HUMANS AREN'T OBSERVANT ENOUGH!
TO PUNISH THEM, I'M ELIMINATING SEX!
TWO SECONDS LATER...
TWO DAYS LATER...
PARTICULARLY DIFFICULT MATHEMATICS
ENGINEERING AROUND PHYSICS
TWO WEEKS LATER...
TWO MONTHS LATER...

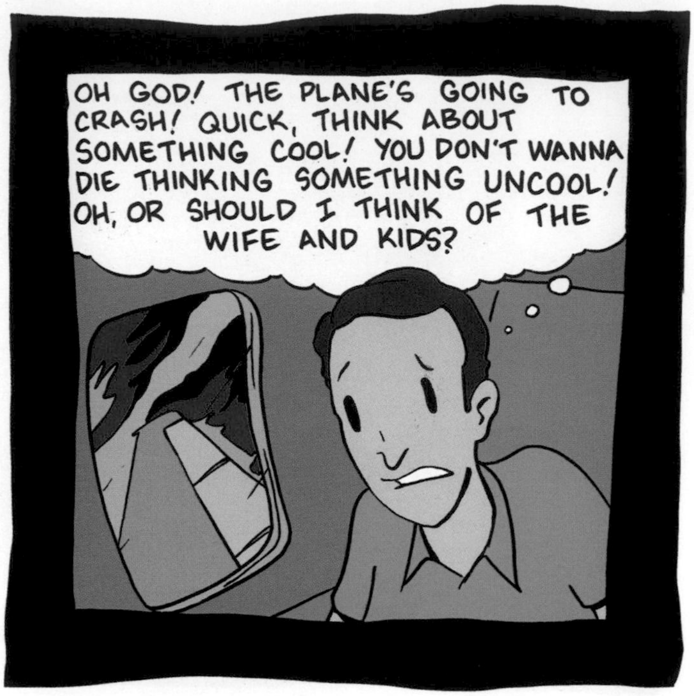
OH GOD! THE PLANE'S GOING TO CRASH! QUICK, THINK ABOUT SOMETHING COOL! YOU DON'T WANNA DIE THINKING SOMETHING UNCOOL! OH, OR SHOULD I THINK OF THE WIFE AND KIDS?

Fun fact:
95% of men die thinking of Batman.

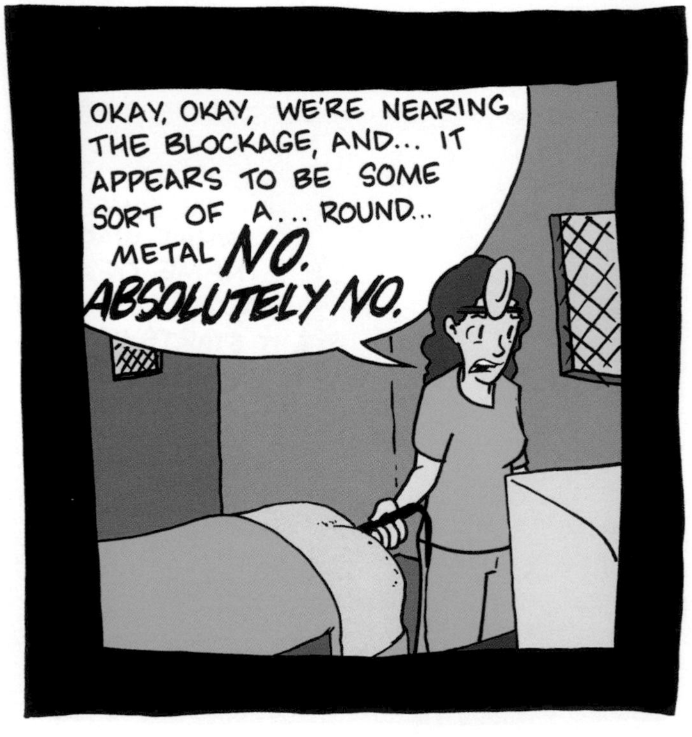
OKAY, OKAY, WE'RE NEARING THE BLOCKAGE, AND... IT APPEARS TO BE SOME SORT OF A... ROUND... METAL NO. ABSOLUTELY NO.

Candice didn't appreciate my
creative marriage poposal.

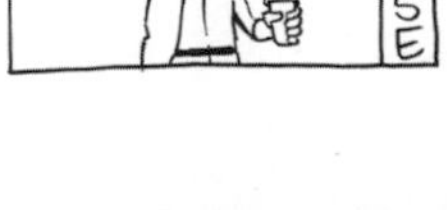
LOSE

sex = awesome
online roleplaying games = awesome
∴ online roleplaying games = sex

Math says I'm not a virgin.

I HAVE A CONFESSION... REMEMBER WHEN I USED TO SAY "I'M GOING TO THE GARAGE," THEN RETURN THREE HOURS LATER, SMELLING OF BEER, WITH LIPSTICK ALL OVER MY FACE?
Y-YES.
WELL...

THE WORST DEATH IMAGINABLE:
OH, COME ON, WHAT WAS THE NAME OF THAT ACTOR?! I KNOW IT STARTS WITH A J... COME ON. COME ON!

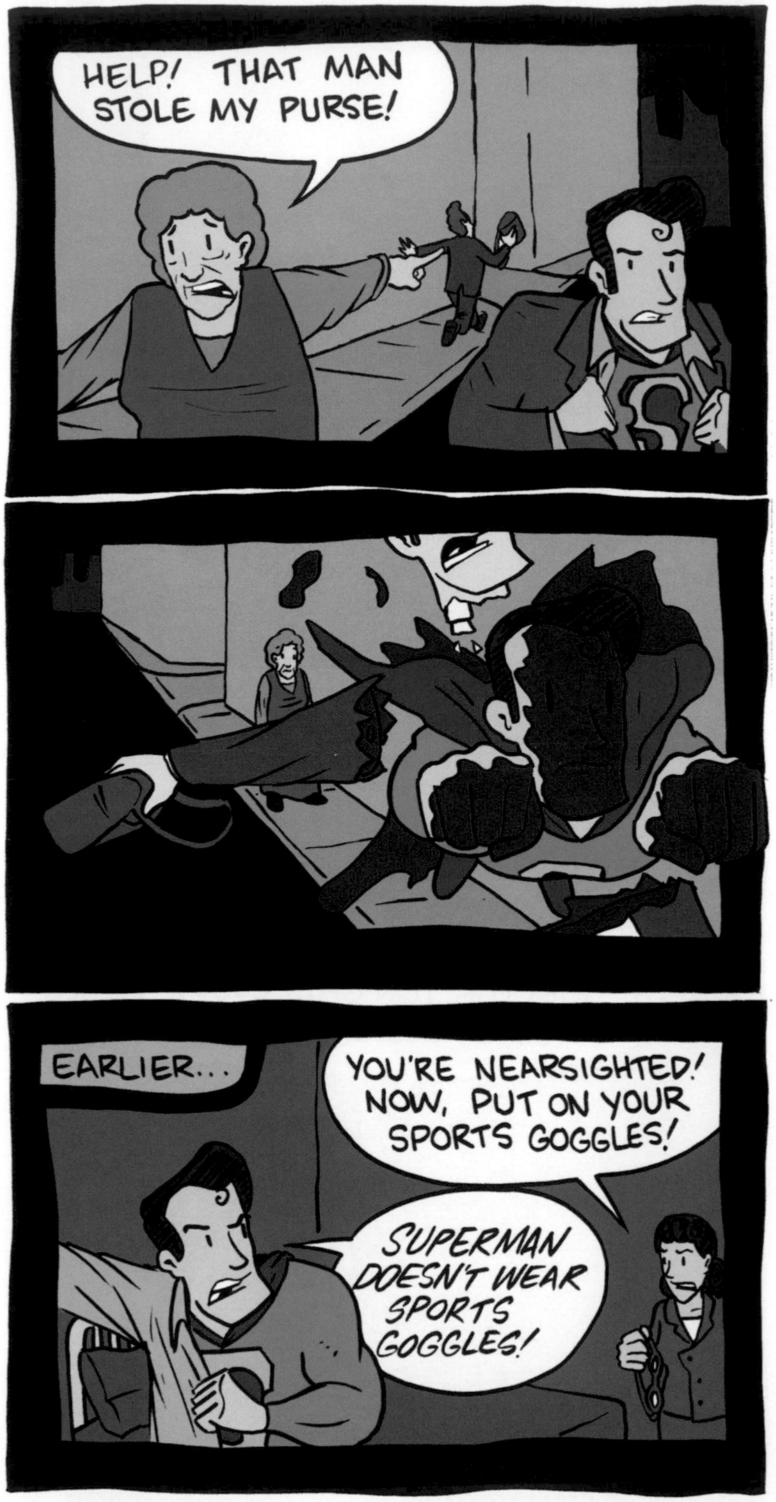
HELP! THAT MAN STOLE MY PURSE!
EARLIER...
YOU'RE NEARSIGHTED! NOW, PUT ON YOUR SPORTS GOGGLES!
SUPERMAN DOESN'T WEAR SPORTS GOGGLES!

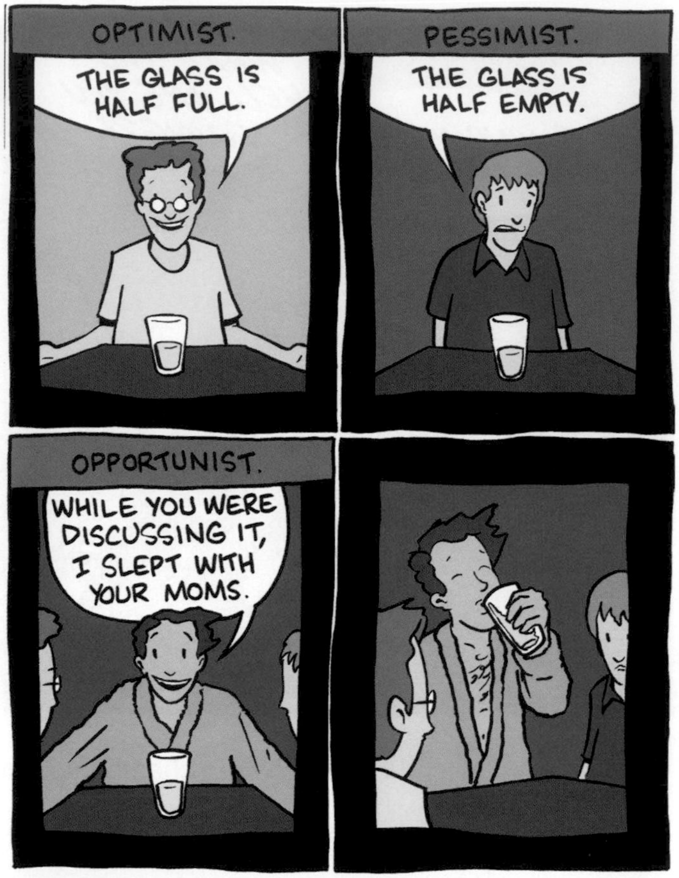
OPTIMIST.
THE GLASS IS HALF FULL.
PESSIMIST.
THE GLASS IS HALF EMPTY.
OPPORTUNIST.
WHILE YOU WERE DISCUSSING IT, I SLEPT WITH YOUR MOMS.

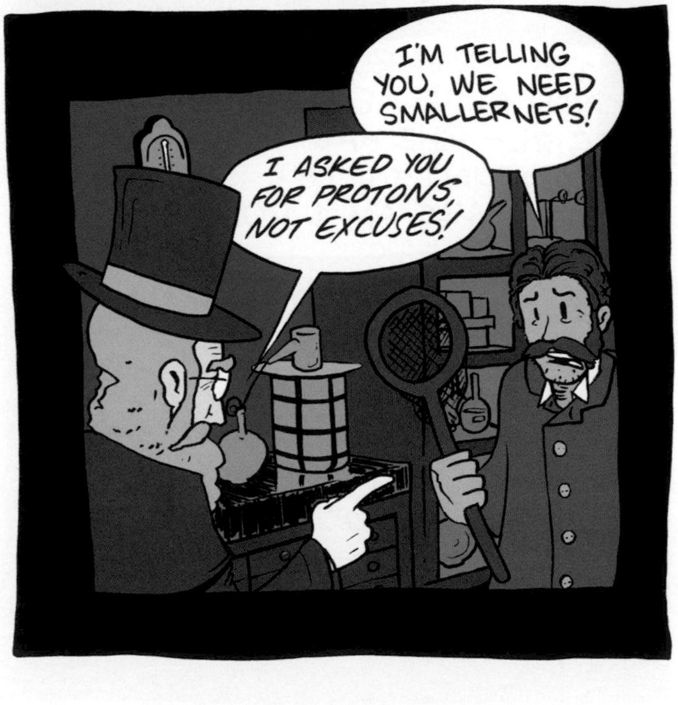
I'M TELLING YOU, WE NEED SMALLERNETS!
I ASKED YOU FOR PROTONS, NOT EXCUSES!

Particle physics has come a long way since the 1700s.

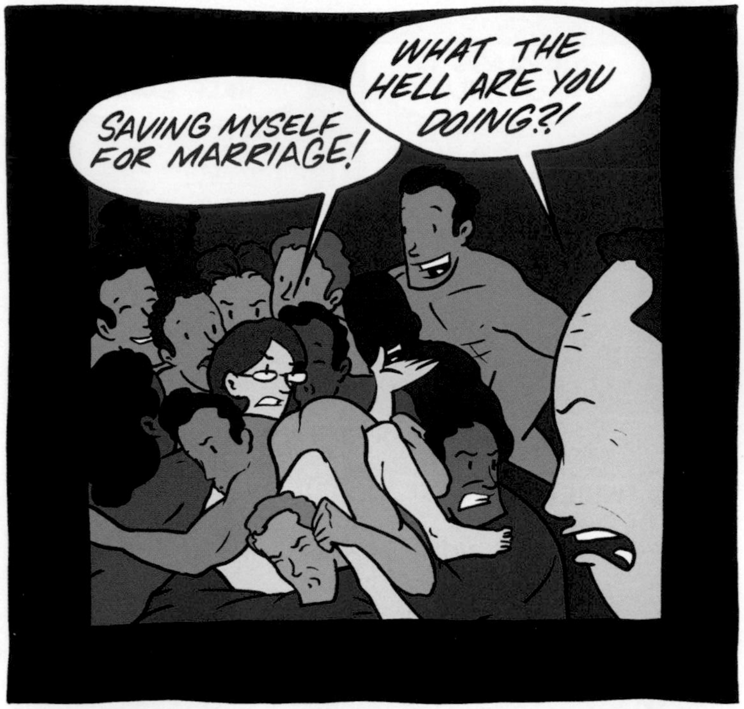
SAVING MYSELF FOR MARRIAGE!
WHAT THE HELL ARE YOU DOING?!

Dad doesn't let me in the hologram chamber anymore.

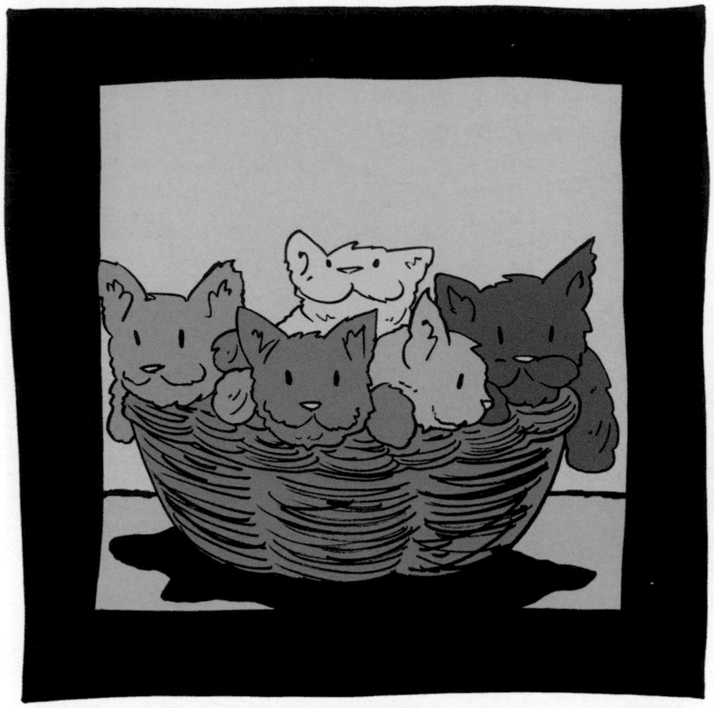

Sad fact:
Nazi kittens are just as cute as regular kittens.

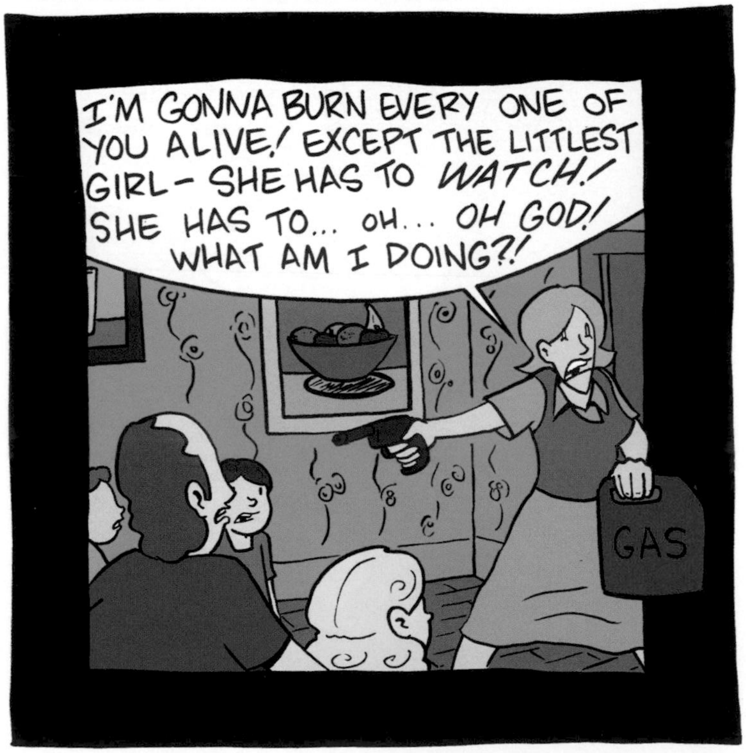
I'M GONNA BURN EVERY ONE OF YOU ALIVE! EXCEPT THE LITTLEST GIRL– SHE HAS TO WATCH! SHE HAS TO... OH... OH GOD! WHAT AM I DOING?!
GAS

At some point in every woman's life,
she realizes that she's become her mother.

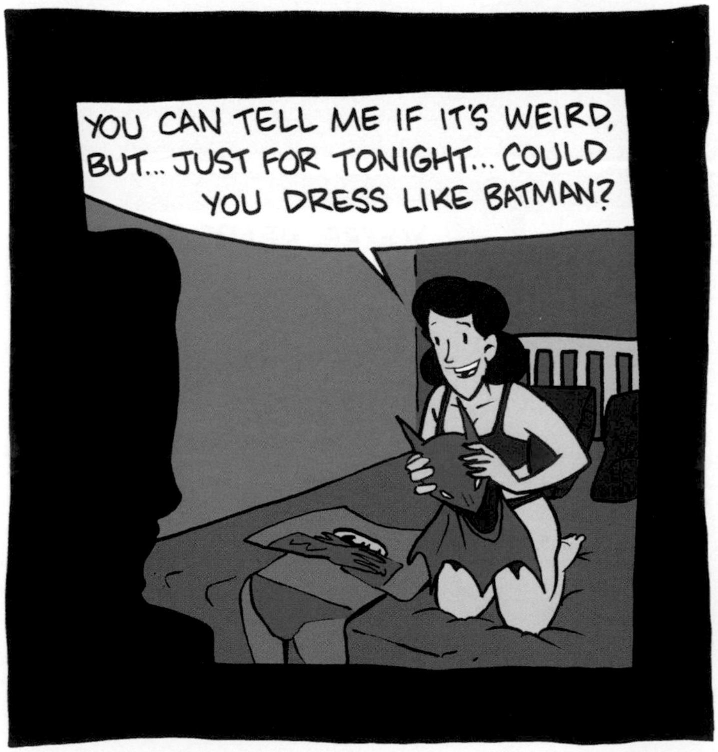
YOU CAN TELL ME IF IT'S WEIRD, BUT... JUST FOR TONIGHT... COULD YOU DRESS LIKE BATMAN?

Clark Kent's honeymoon began on a down note.

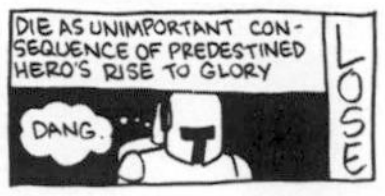
DIE AS UNIMPORTANT CON-
SEQUENCE OF PREDESTINED
HERO'S RISE TO GLORY
DANG.
LOSE

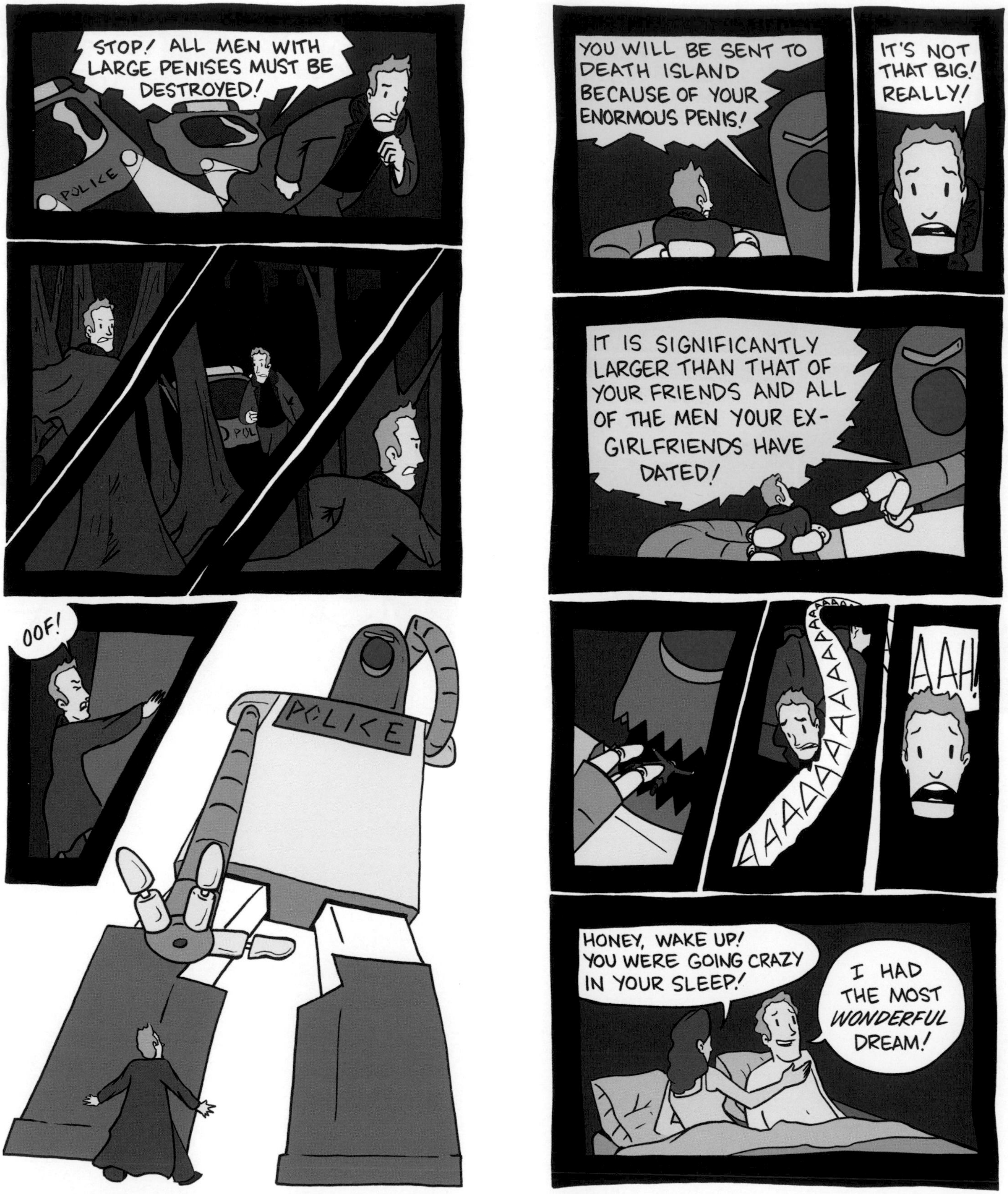
STOP! ALL MEN WITH LARGE PENISES MUST BE DESTROYED!
POLICE
POL
OOF!
POLICE
YOU WILL BE SENT TO DEATH ISLAND BECAUSE OF YOUR ENORMOUS PENIS!
IT'S NOT THAT BIG! REALLY!
IT IS SIGNIFICANTLY LARGER THAN THAT OF YOUR FRIENDS AND ALL OF THE MEN YOUR EX-GIRLFRIENDS HAVE DATED!
AAAAAAAAAAAAAAAAAA
AAH!
HONEY, WAKE UP! YOU WERE GOING CRAZY IN YOUR SLEEP!
I HAD THE MOST *WONDERFUL* DREAM!

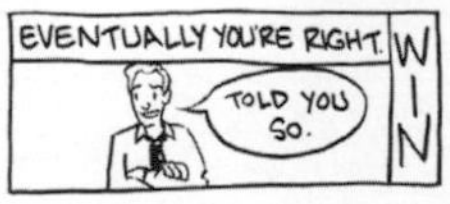
EVENTUALLY YOU'RE RIGHT.
TOLD YOU SO.
WIN

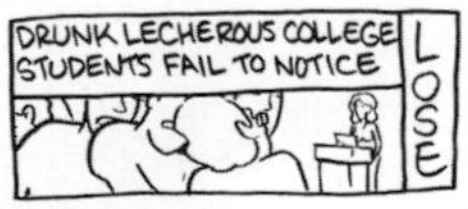
DRUNK LECHEROUS COLLEGE STUDENTS FAIL TO NOTICE
LOSE

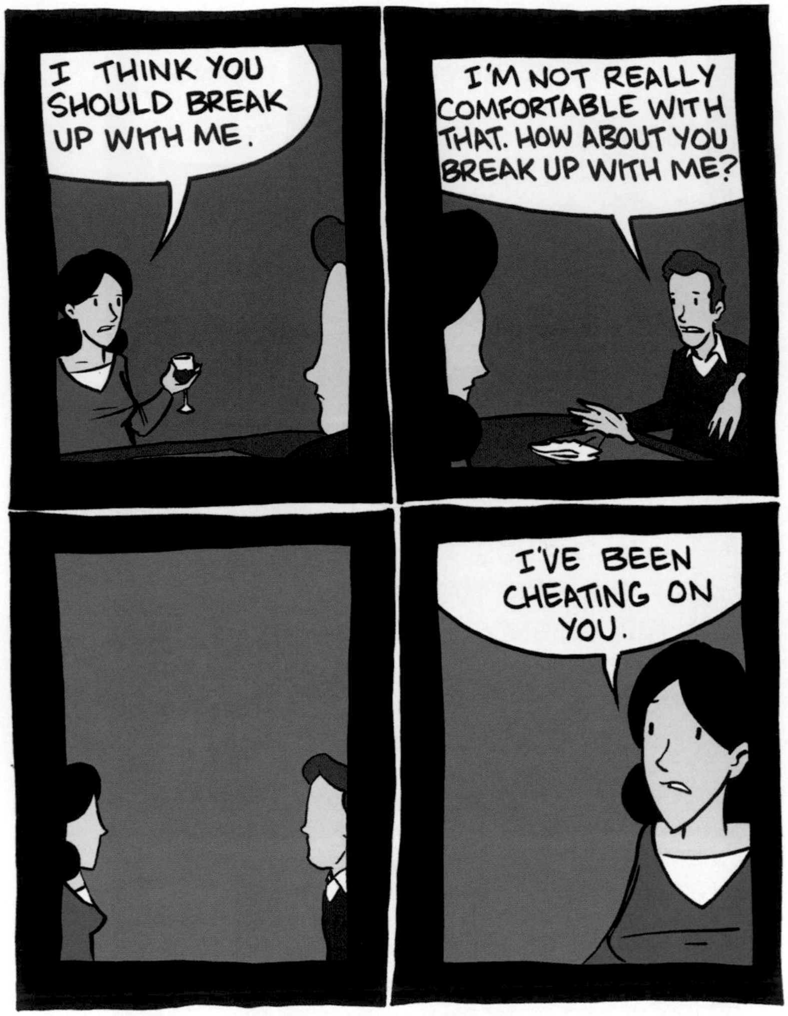
I THINK YOU SHOULD BREAK UP WITH ME.
I'M NOT REALLY COMFORTABLE WITH THAT. HOW ABOUT YOU BREAK UP WITH ME?
I'VE BEEN CHEATING ON YOU.

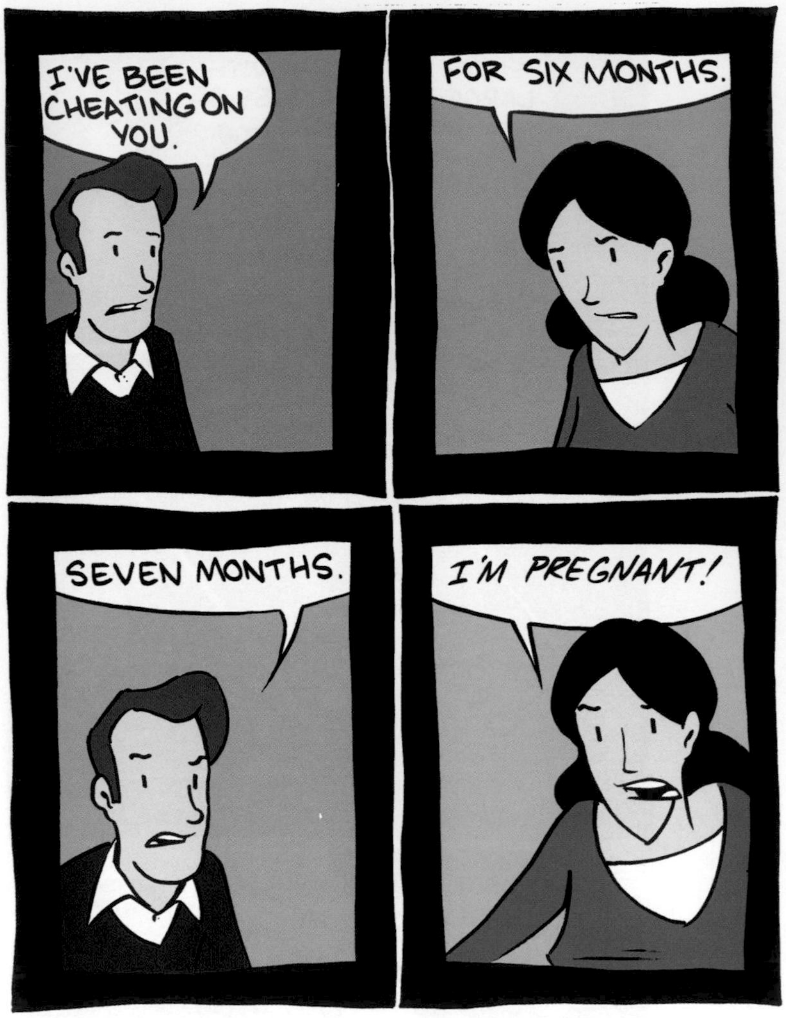
I'VE BEEN CHEATING ON YOU.
FOR SIX MONTHS.
SEVEN MONTHS.
I'M PREGNANT!

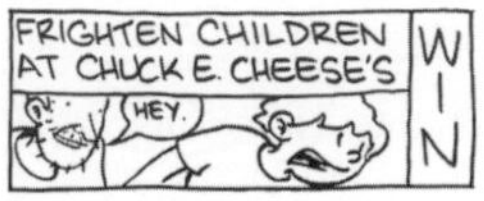
FRIGHTEN CHILDREN AT CHUCK E. CHEESE'S
HEY.
WIN

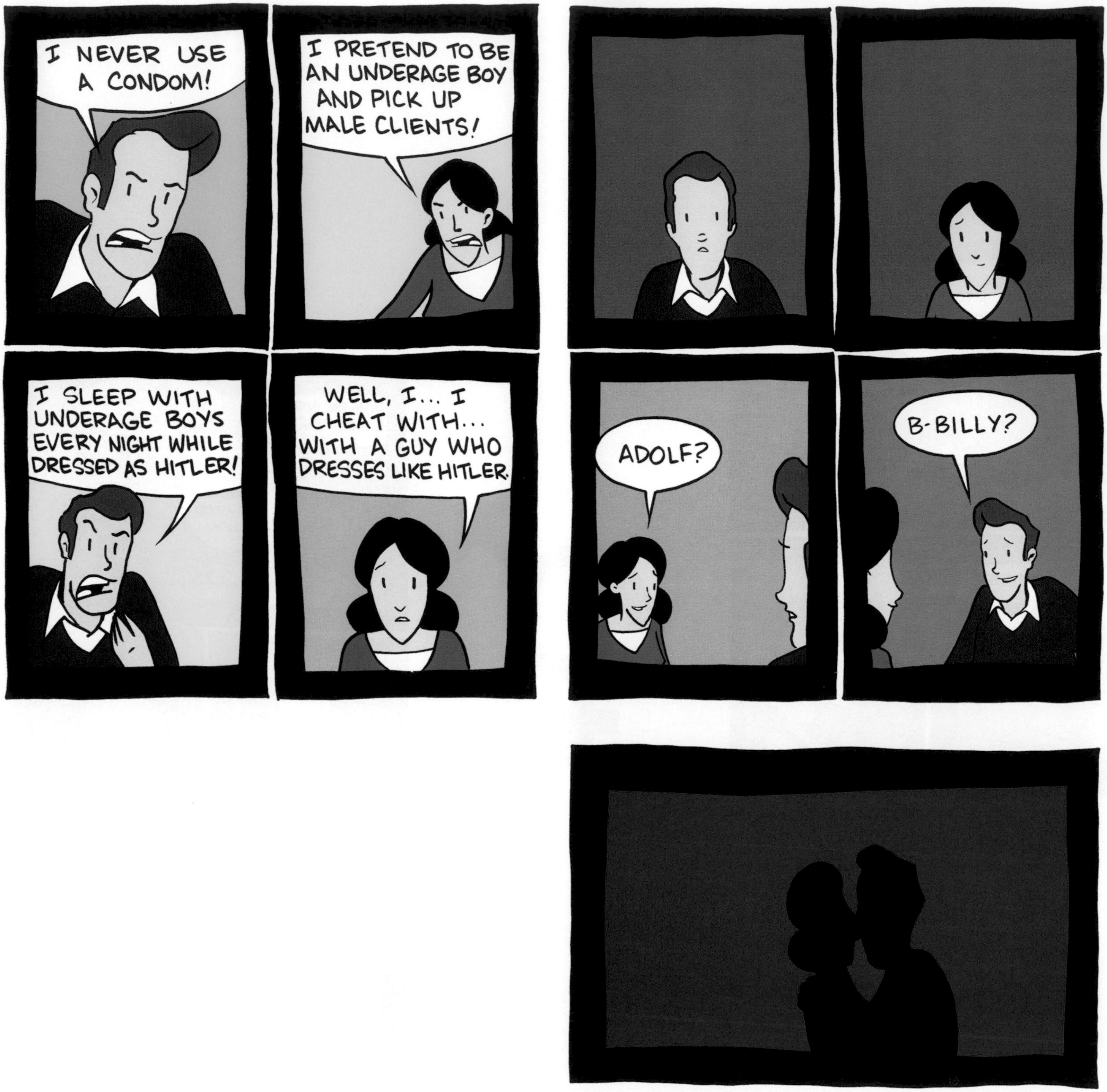
I NEVER USE A CONDOM!
I PRETEND TO BE AN UNDERAGE BOY AND PICK UP MALE CLIENTS!
I SLEEP WITH UNDERAGE BOYS EVERY NIGHT WHILE DRESSED AS HITLER!
WELL, I... I CHEAT WITH... WITH A GUY WHO DRESSES LIKE HITLER.
ADOLF?
B-BILLY?

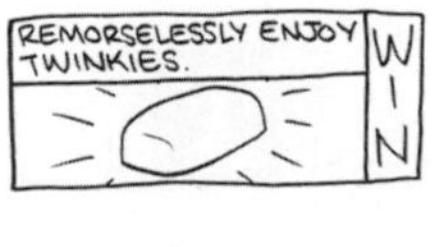
REMORSELESSLY ENJOY TWINKIES.
WIN

BAT-BASED 6 3 NON-BAT-BASED

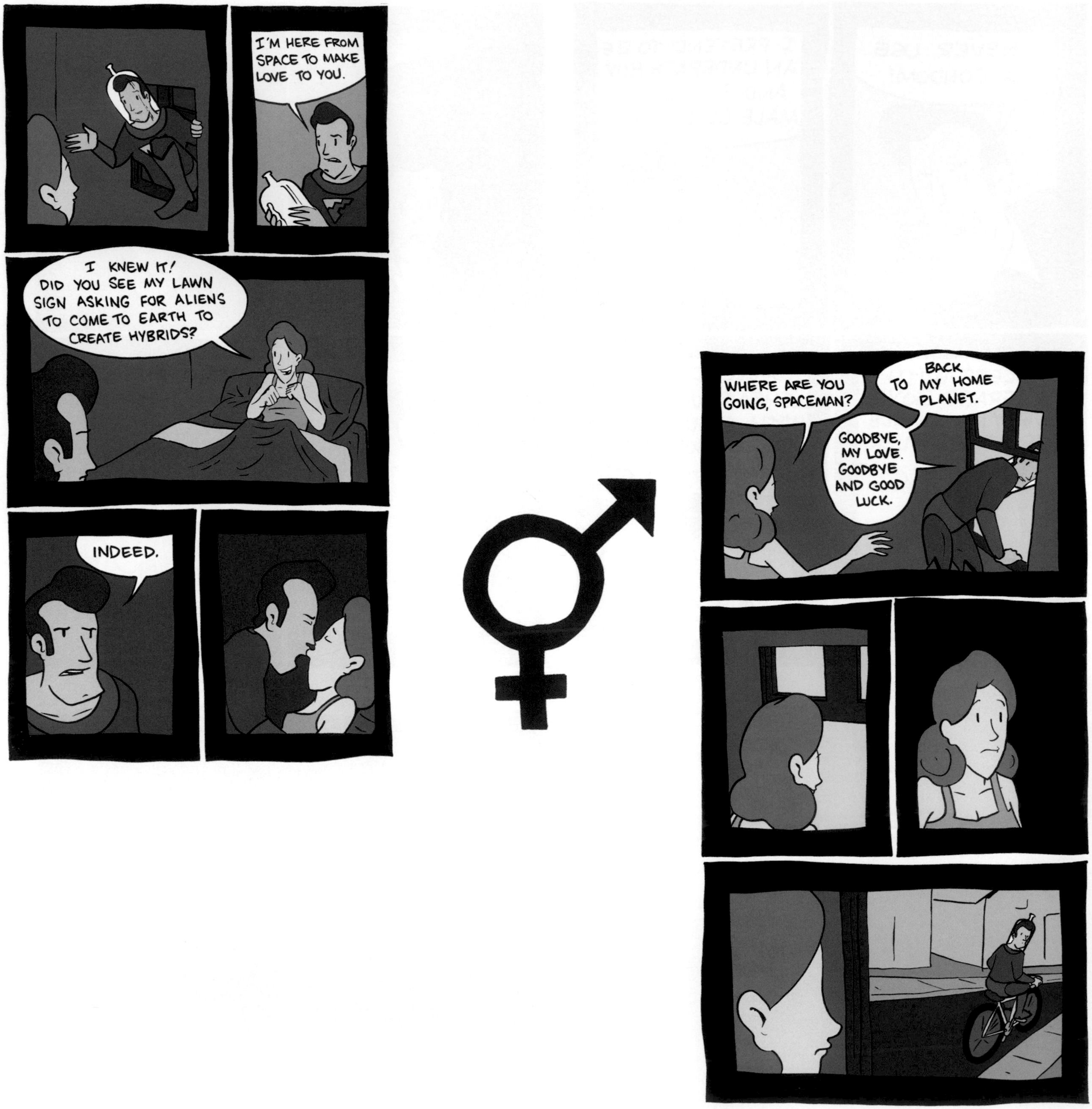
I'M HERE FROM SPACE TO MAKE LOVE TO YOU.
I KNEW IT! DID YOU SEE MY LAWN SIGN ASKING FOR ALIENS TO COME TO EARTH TO CREATE HYBRIDS?
INDEED.
WHERE ARE YOU GOING, SPACEMAN?
BACK TO MY HOME PLANET.
GOODBYE, MY LOVE. GOODBYE AND GOOD LUCK.

GOOD 1 3 EVIL

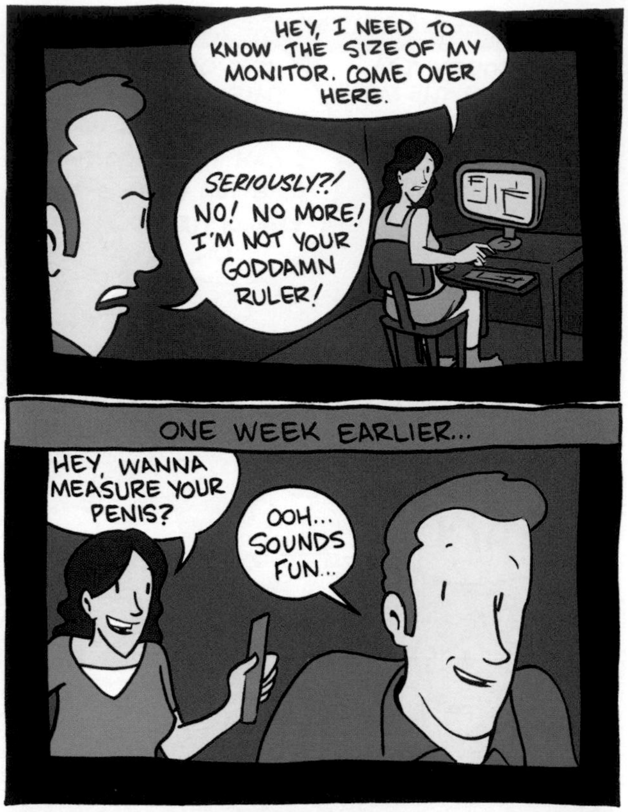
HEY, I NEED TO KNOW THE SIZE OF MY MONITOR. COME OVER HERE.
SERIOUSLY?! NO! NO MORE! I'M NOT YOUR GODDAMN RULER!
ONE WEEK EARLIER...
HEY, WANNA MEASURE YOUR PENIS?
OOH... SOUNDS FUN...

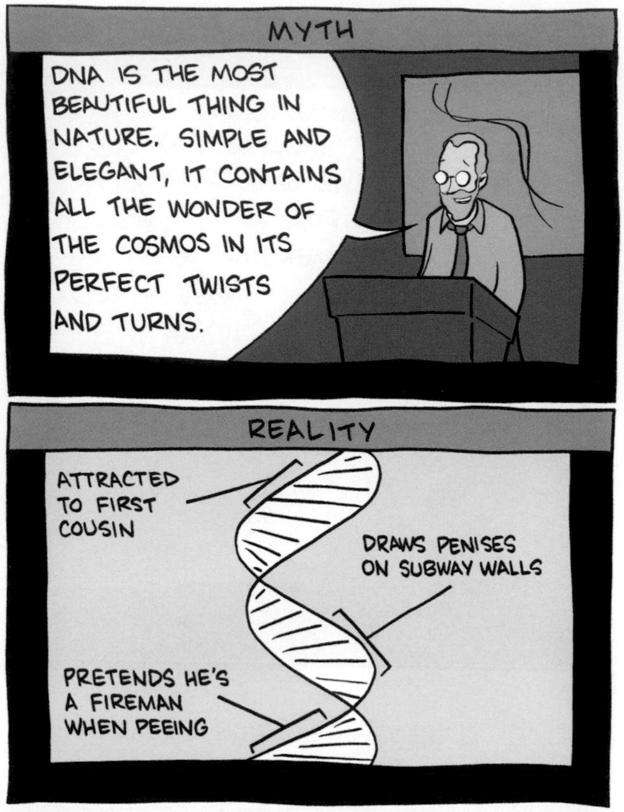
MYTH
DNA IS THE MOST BEAUTIFUL THING IN NATURE. SIMPLE AND ELEGANT, IT CONTAINS ALL THE WONDER OF THE COSMOS IN ITS PERFECT TWISTS AND TURNS.
REALITY
ATTRACTED TO FIRST COUSIN
DRAWS PENISES ON SUBWAY WALLS
PRETENDS HE'S A FIREMAN WHEN PEEING

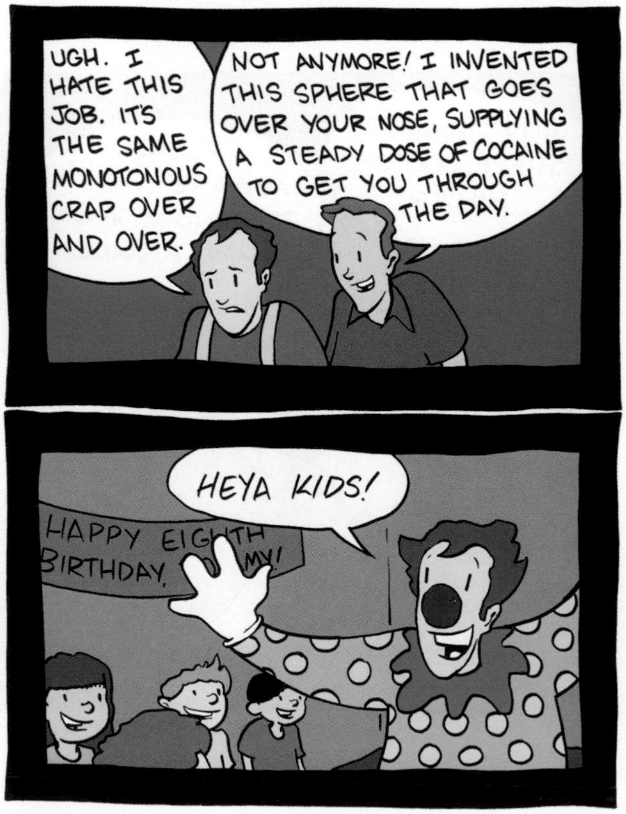
UGH. I HATE THIS JOB. IT'S THE SAME MONOTONOUS CRAP OVER AND OVER.
NOT ANYMORE! I INVENTED THIS SPHERE THAT GOES OVER YOUR NOSE, SUPPLYING A STEADY DOSE OF COCAINE TO GET YOU THROUGH THE DAY.
HEYA KIDS!
HAPPY EIGHTH
BIRTHDAY,
MY!

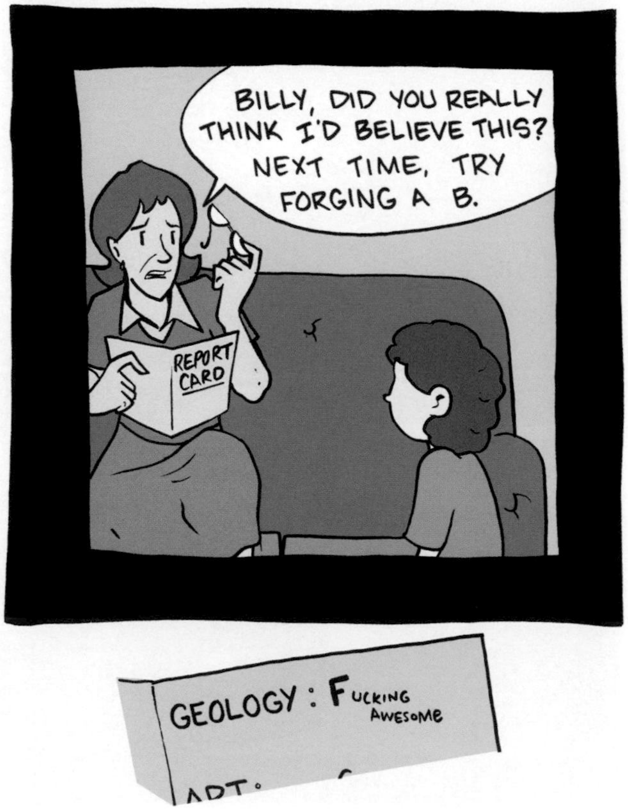
BILLY, DID YOU REALLY THINK I'D BELIEVE THIS? NEXT TIME, TRY FORGING A B.
REPORT CARD
GEOLOGY : Fucking Awesome
ART:

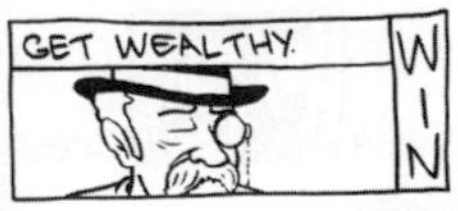
GET WEALTHY.
WIN

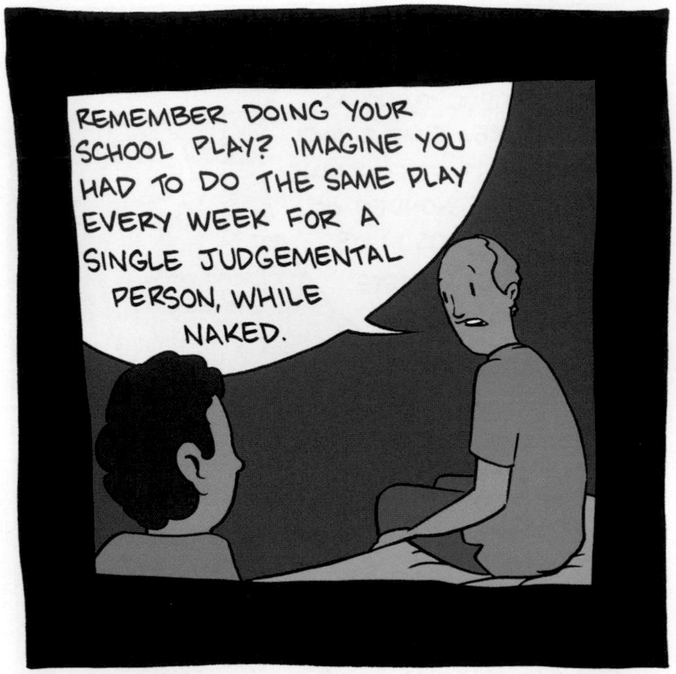
REMEMBER DOING YOUR SCHOOL PLAY? IMAGINE YOU HAD TO DO THE SAME PLAY EVERY WEEK FOR A SINGLE JUDGEMENTAL PERSON, WHILE NAKED.

Dad gave his usual sex talk.

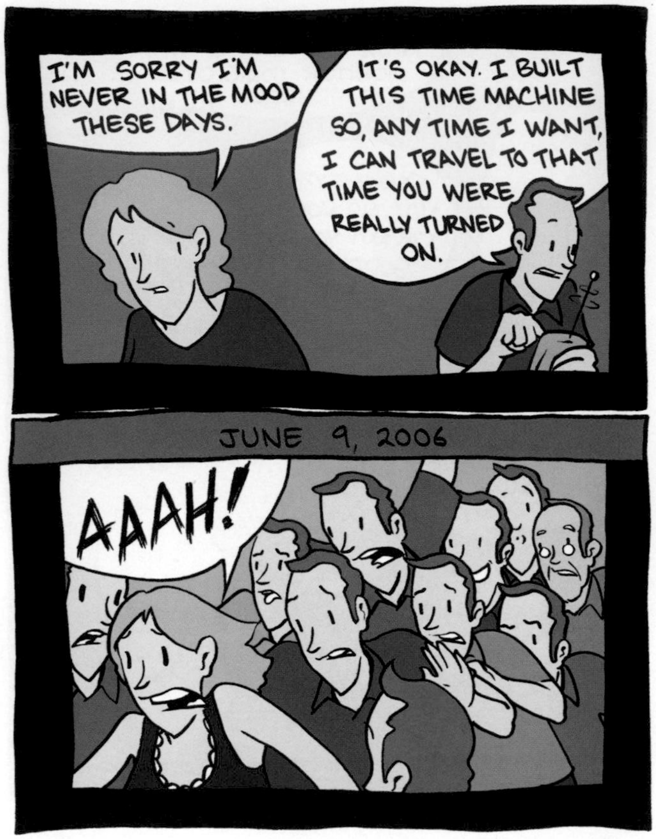
I'M SORRY I'M NEVER IN THE MOOD THESE DAYS.
IT'S OKAY. I BUILT THIS TIME MACHINE SO, ANY TIME I WANT, I CAN TRAVEL TO THAT TIME YOU WERE REALLY TURNED ON.
JUNE 9, 2006
AAAH!

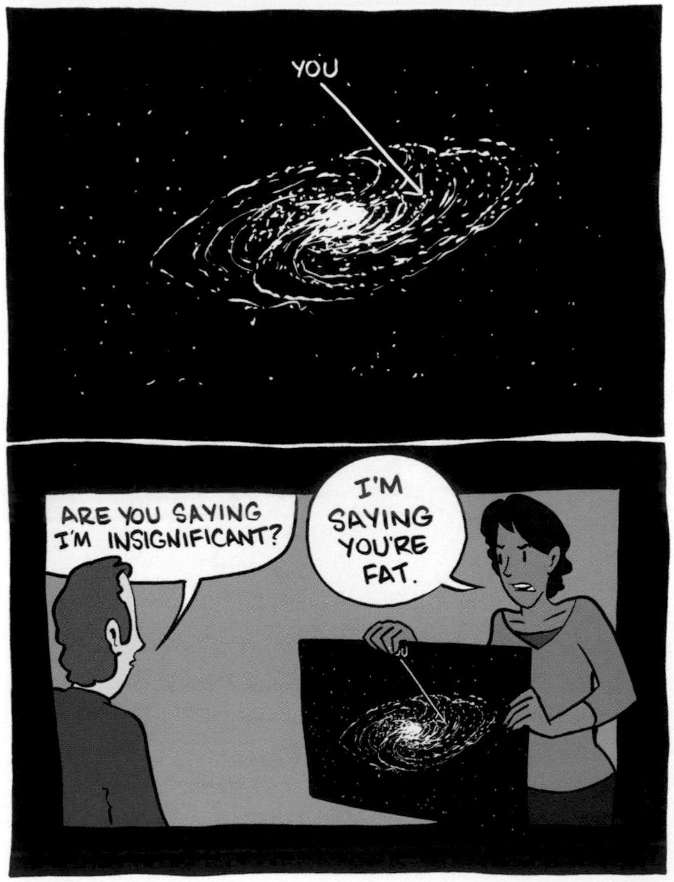
YOU
ARE YOU SAYING I'M INSIGNIFICANT?
I'M SAYING YOU'RE FAT.

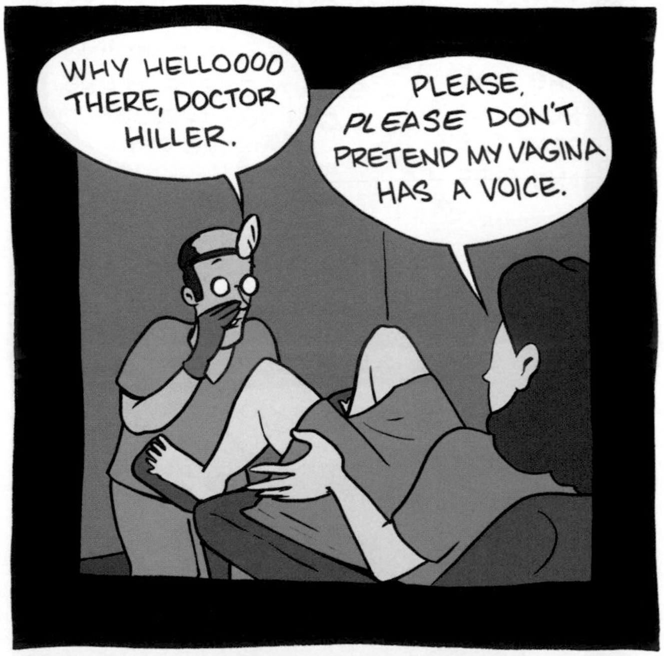
WHY HELLOOOO THERE, DOCTOR HILLER.
PLEASE, PLEASE DON'T PRETEND MY VAGINA HAS A VOICE.

It's not the ventriloquism that bothers me.
It's the baritone.

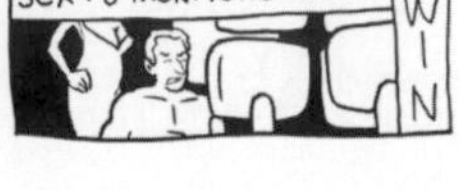
SEX + 8 MONITORS = WIN
WIN

GET WEALTHY.
WIN

MOM, DAD! I HAVE ENNUI!
WELL, YOU SHOULD'VE MADE PEACE WITH THE ABSURDITY OF HUMAN EXISTENCE BEFORE WE STARTED DRIVING!

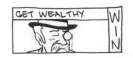

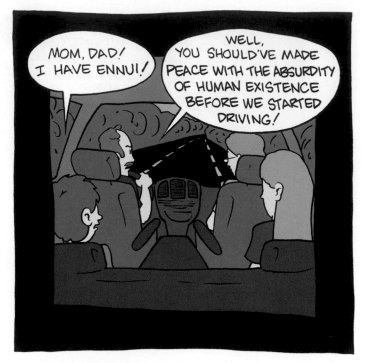

Dad eventually pulled over at a frozen lake, which represented the sublime beauty of impermanence, but he was pretty annoyed about it.

A KISS FROM A PRINCE! THE WITCH'S SPELL IS BROKEN!

Dear diary,
Today I was kissing dead chicks, and you'll never believe what happened!

JUST SHOOT OFF THEIR HEADS! JUST SHOOT!
I DID! THEY KEEP COMING!

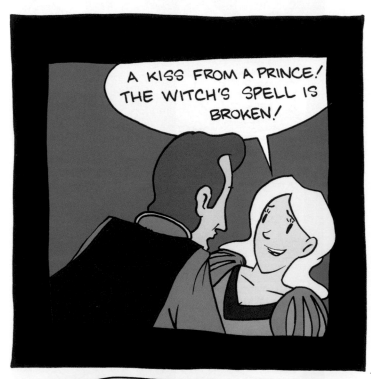

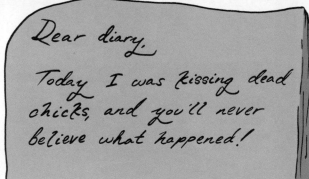

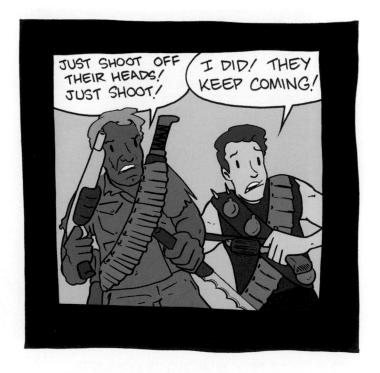

Once the chickens became zombies, the war was lost.

KATANATONSILECTOMY
SAY "AH."
WIN

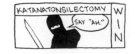

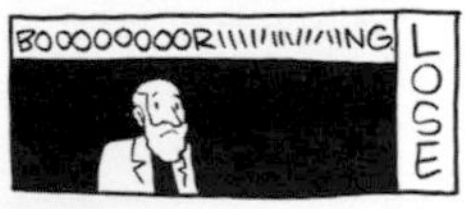
BOOOOOOOORIIIIIIIIIING
LOSE

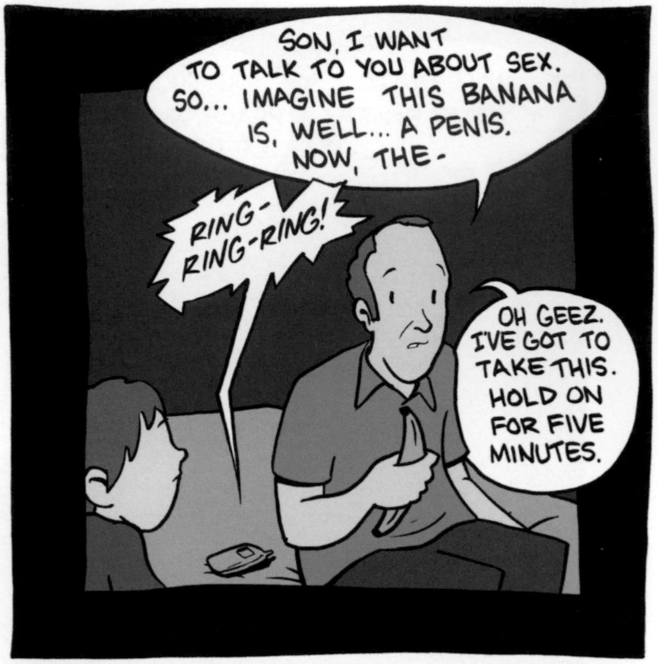
SON, I WANT TO TALK TO YOU ABOUT SEX. SO... IMAGINE THIS BANANA IS, WELL... A PENIS. NOW, THE-
RING-RING-RING!
OH GEEZ. I'VE GOT TO TAKE THIS. HOLD ON FOR FIVE MINUTES.

It was a bad time to be absent-minded.

It was a worse time to be hungry.

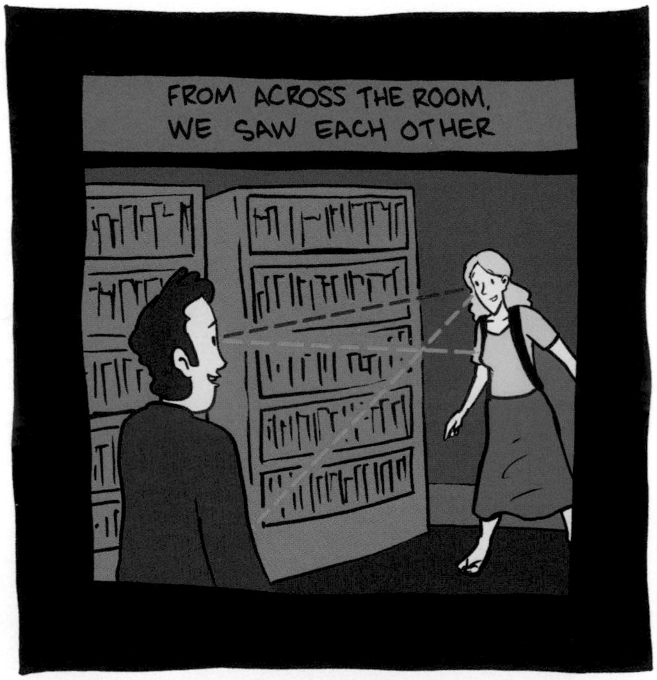
FROM ACROSS THE ROOM, WE SAW EACH OTHER

- What you told your kids.
- What really happened.

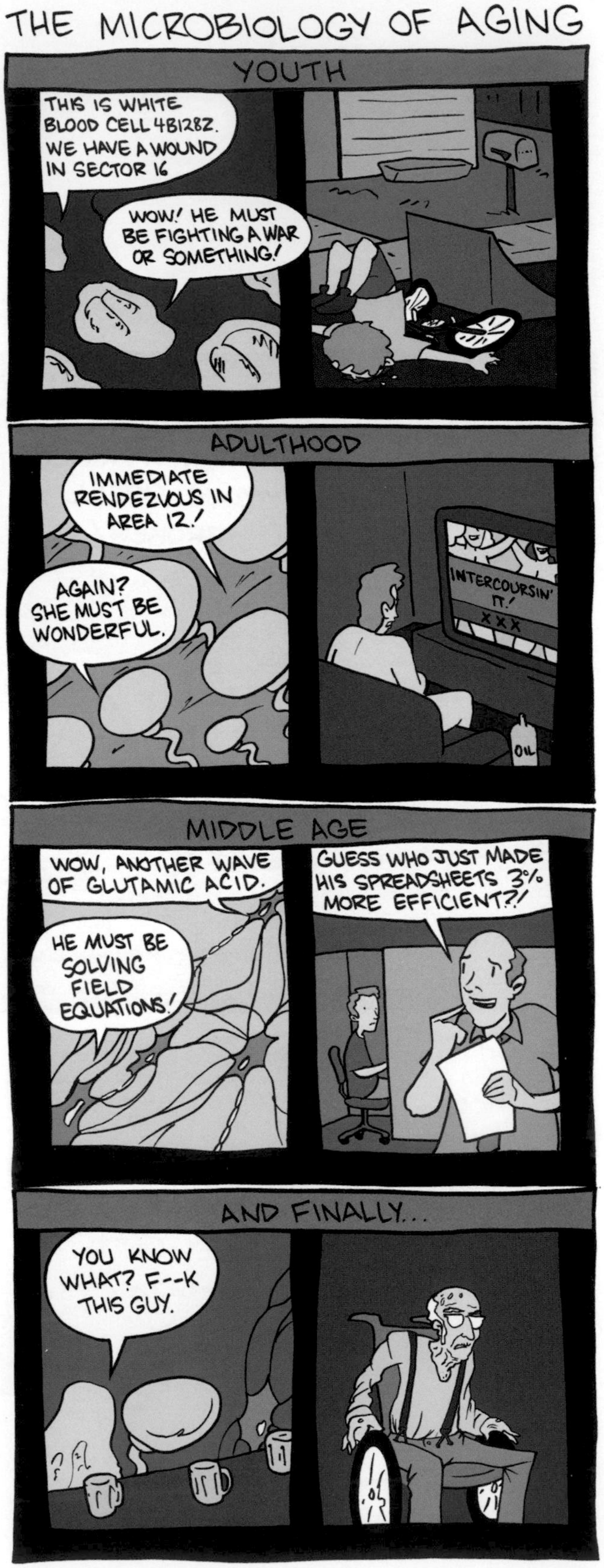
THE MICROBIOLOGY OF AGING
YOUTH
THIS IS WHITE BLOOD CELL 4B1282. WE HAVE A WOUND IN SECTOR 16
WOW! HE MUST BE FIGHTING A WAR OR SOMETHING!
ADULTHOOD
IMMEDIATE RENDEZVOUS IN AREA 12!
AGAIN? SHE MUST BE WONDERFUL.
INTERCOURSIN' IT!
XXX
OIL
MIDDLE AGE
WOW, ANOTHER WAVE OF GLUTAMIC ACID.
HE MUST BE SOLVING FIELD EQUATIONS!
GUESS WHO JUST MADE HIS SPREADSHEETS 3% MORE EFFICIENT?!
AND FINALLY...
YOU KNOW WHAT? F--K THIS GUY.

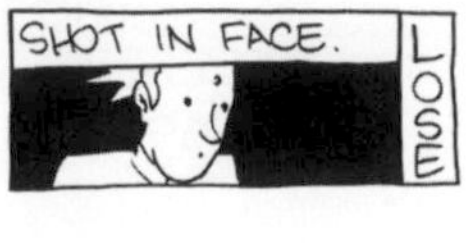
SHOT IN FACE.
LOSE

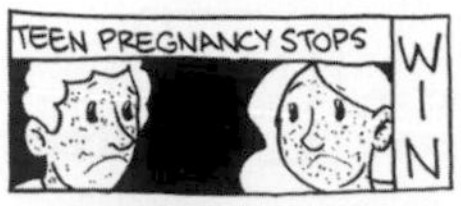
TEEN PREGNANCY STOPS
W I N

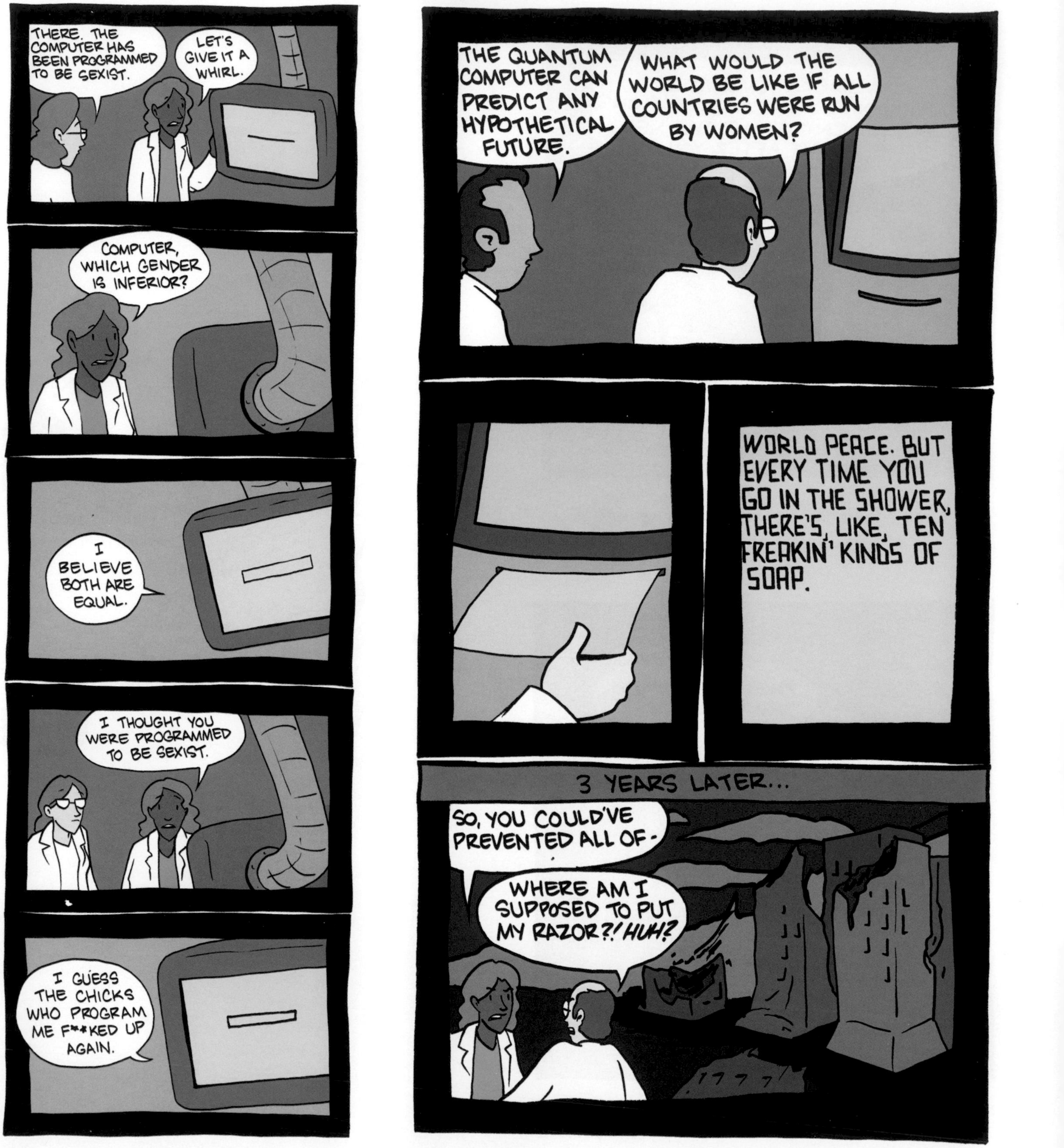
THERE. THE COMPUTER HAS BEEN PROGRAMMED TO BE SEXIST.
LET'S GIVE IT A WHIRL.
COMPUTER, WHICH GENDER IS INFERIOR?
I BELIEVE BOTH ARE EQUAL.
I THOUGHT YOU WERE PROGRAMMED TO BE SEXIST.
I GUESS THE CHICKS WHO PROGRAM ME F**KED UP AGAIN.
THE QUANTUM COMPUTER CAN PREDICT ANY HYPOTHETICAL FUTURE.
WHAT WOULD THE WORLD BE LIKE IF ALL COUNTRIES WERE RUN BY WOMEN?
WORLD PEACE. BUT EVERY TIME YOU GO IN THE SHOWER, THERE'S, LIKE, TEN FREAKIN' KINDS OF SOAP.
3 YEARS LATER...
SO, YOU COULD'VE PREVENTED ALL OF-
WHERE AM I SUPPOSED TO PUT MY RAZOR?! HUH?

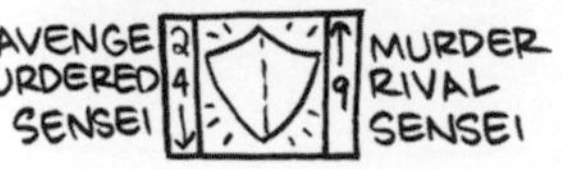
AVENGE MURDERED SENSEI
24
19
MURDER RIVAL SENSEI

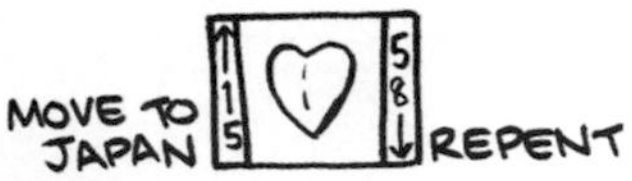

MOVE TO JAPAN
115
58
REPENT

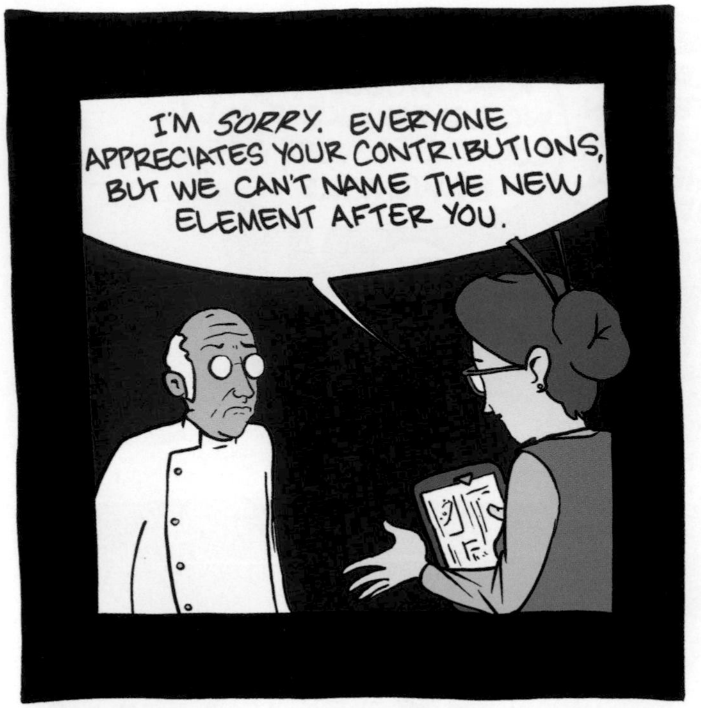

I'M SORRY. EVERYONE APPRECIATES YOUR CONTRIBUTIONS, BUT WE CAN'T NAME THE NEW ELEMENT AFTER YOU.

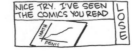

Another sad day for Professor Hitlerballs.

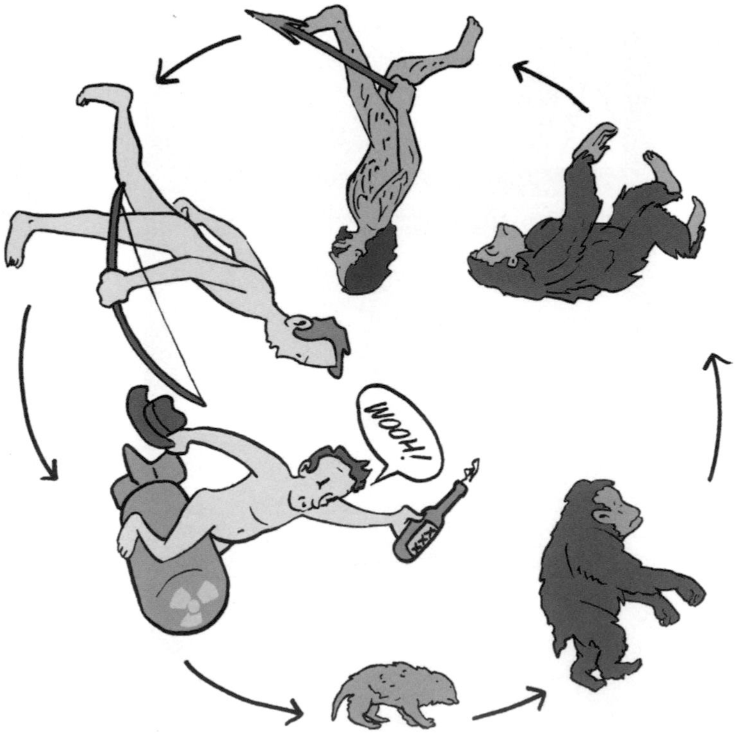

WOOH!

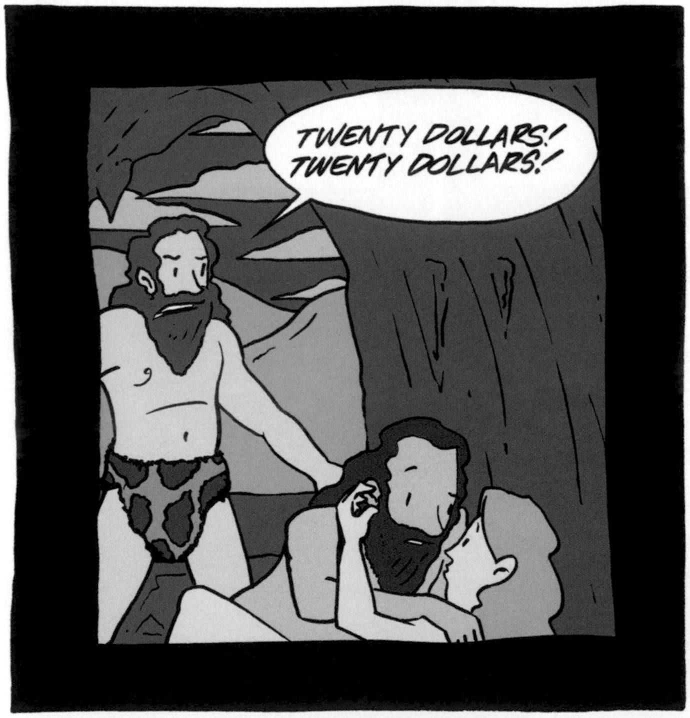

TWENTY DOLLARS! TWENTY DOLLARS!

Fortunately, sex was invented before copyright law.

NICE TRY. I'VE SEEN THE COMICS YOU READ
LOSE

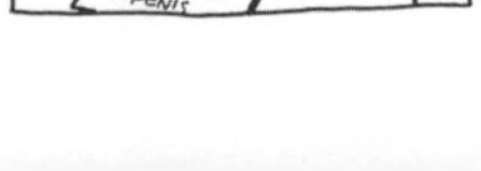

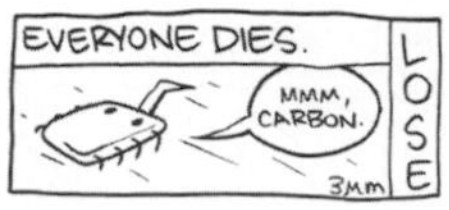
EVERYONE DIES.
MMM, CARBON.
LOSE

HOW SCIENCE REPORTING WORKS:

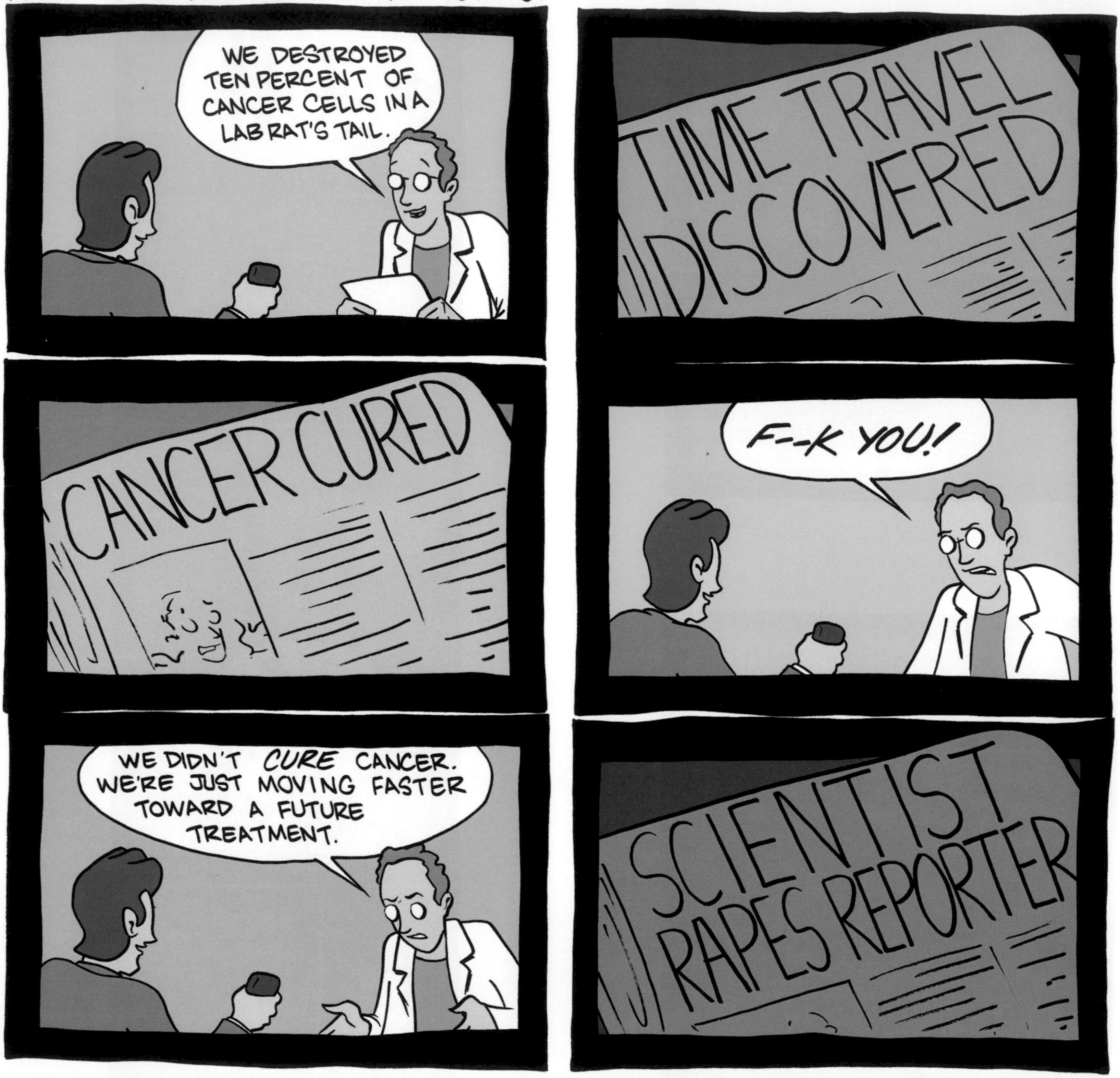
WE DESTROYED TEN PERCENT OF CANCER CELLS IN A LAB RAT'S TAIL.
CANCER CURED
WE DIDN'T *CURE* CANCER. WE'RE JUST MOVING FASTER TOWARD A FUTURE TREATMENT.
TIME TRAVEL DISCOVERED
F--K YOU!
SCIENTIST RAPES REPORTER

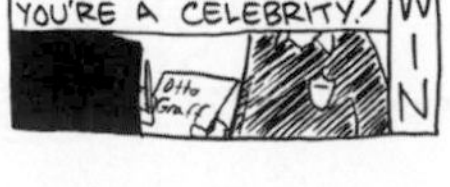
GO TO JAIL. JUST KIDDING! YOU'RE A CELEBRITY!
WIN

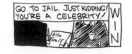

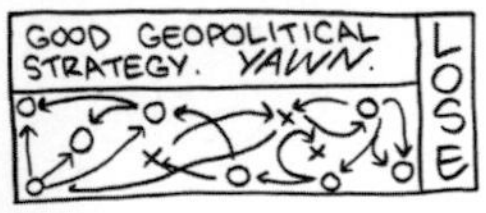
GOOD GEOPOLITICAL STRATEGY. YAWN.
LOSE

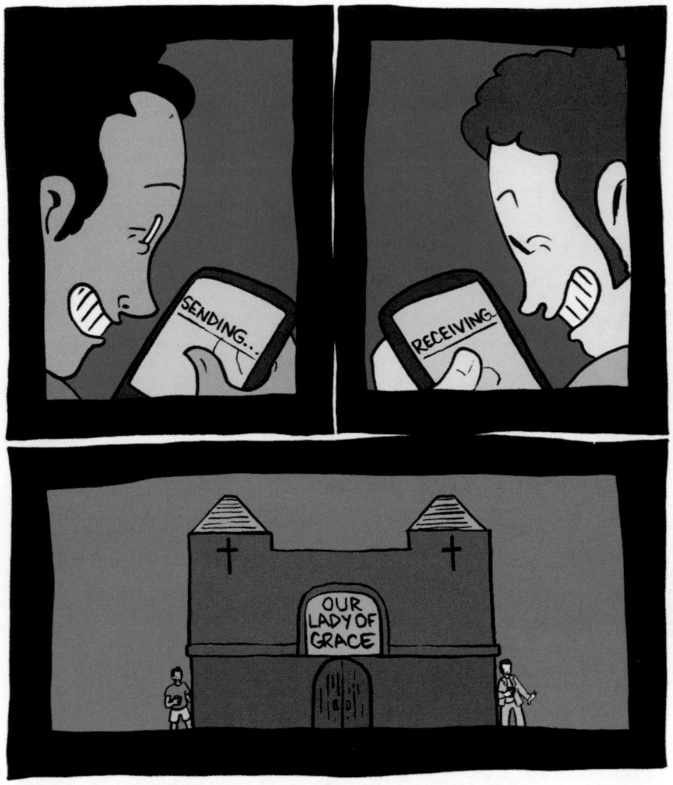
SENDING...
RECEIVING...
OUR LADY OF GRACE

Improper use of the Internet #86:
beaming porn through nuns.

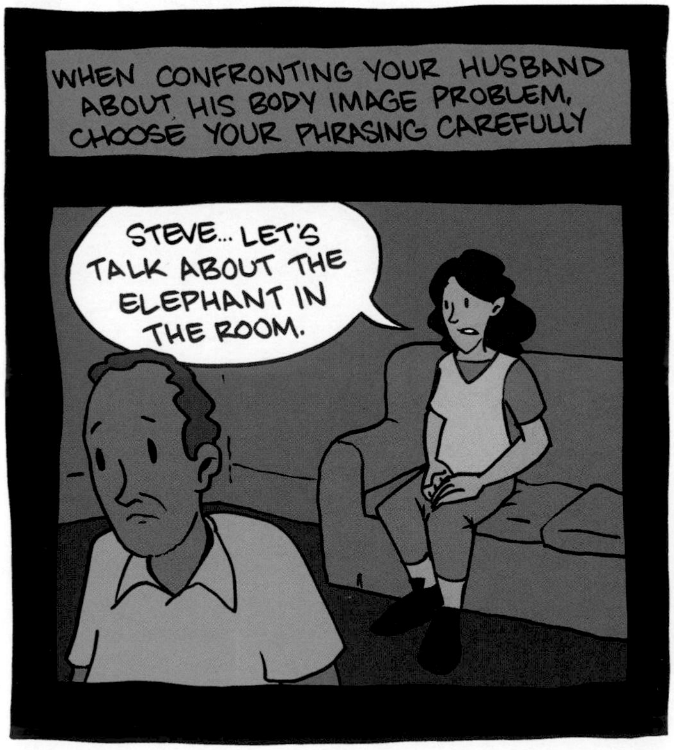
WHEN CONFRONTING YOUR HUSBAND ABOUT HIS BODY IMAGE PROBLEM, CHOOSE YOUR PHRASING CAREFULLY
STEVE... LET'S TALK ABOUT THE ELEPHANT IN THE ROOM.

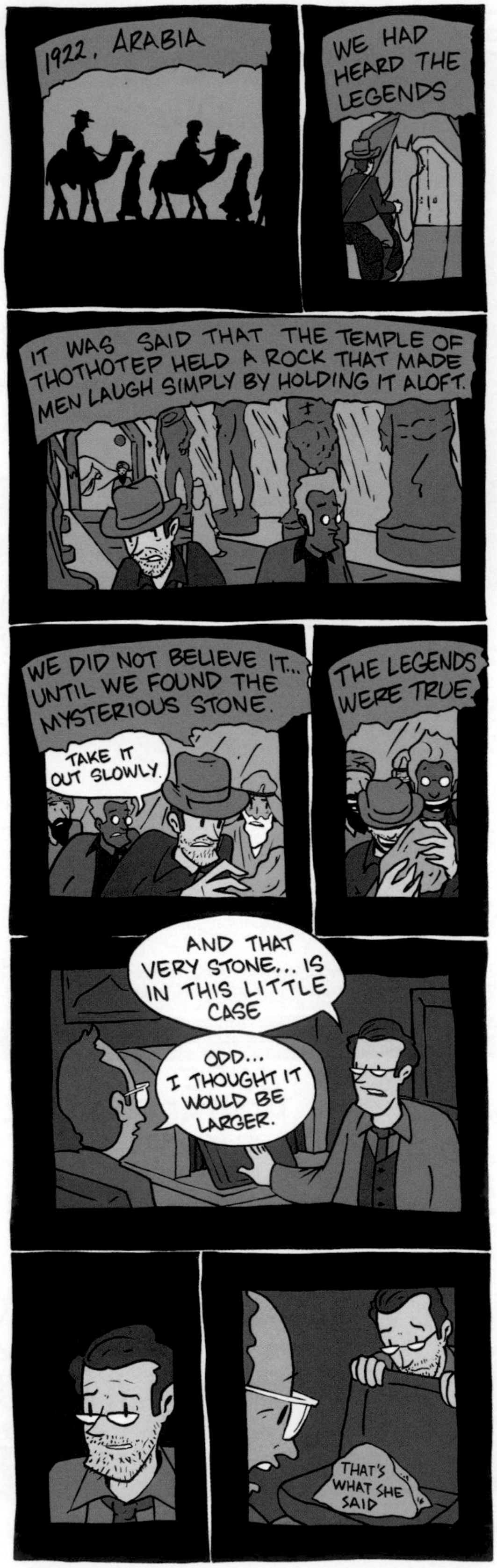
1922, ARABIA
WE HAD HEARD THE LEGENDS
IT WAS SAID THAT THE TEMPLE OF THOTHOTEP HELD A ROCK THAT MADE MEN LAUGH SIMPLY BY HOLDING IT ALOFT.
WE DID NOT BELIEVE IT... UNTIL WE FOUND THE MYSTERIOUS STONE.
TAKE IT OUT SLOWLY.
THE LEGENDS WERE TRUE.
AND THAT VERY STONE... IS IN THIS LITTLE CASE
ODD... I THOUGHT IT WOULD BE LARGER.
THAT'S WHAT SHE SAID

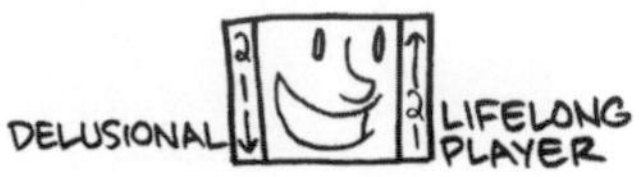
DELUSIONAL
LIFELONG PLAYER

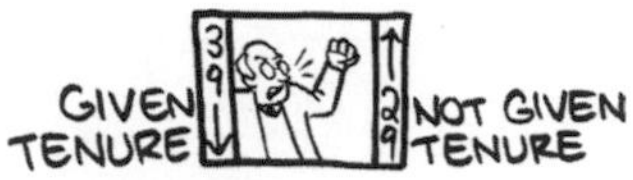
GIVEN TENURE
39
29
NOT GIVEN TENURE

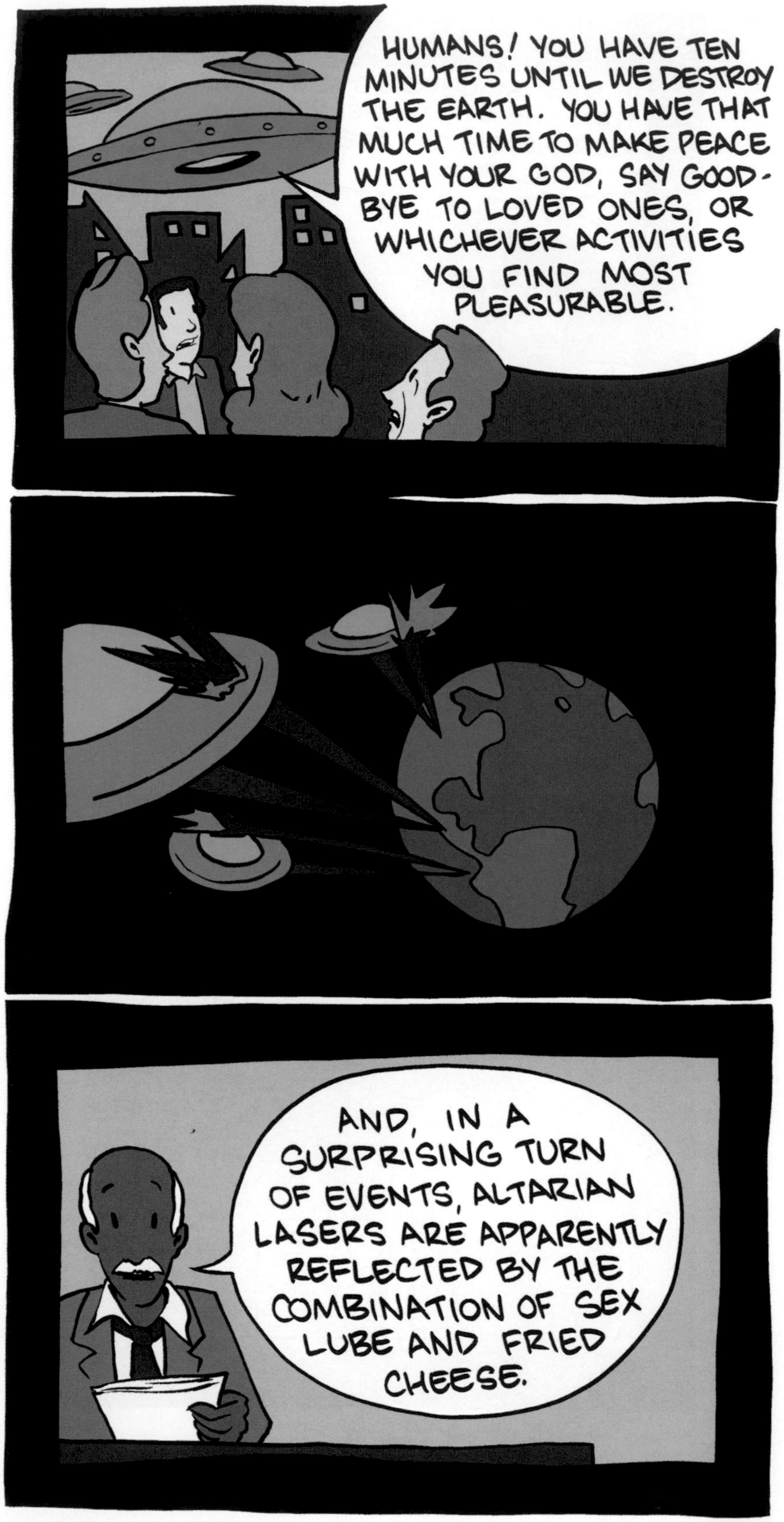
HUMANS! YOU HAVE TEN MINUTES UNTIL WE DESTROY THE EARTH. YOU HAVE THAT MUCH TIME TO MAKE PEACE WITH YOUR GOD, SAY GOOD-BYE TO LOVED ONES, OR WHICHEVER ACTIVITIES YOU FIND MOST PLEASURABLE.
AND, IN A SURPRISING TURN OF EVENTS, ALTARIAN LASERS ARE APPARENTLY REFLECTED BY THE COMBINATION OF SEX LUBE AND FRIED CHEESE.

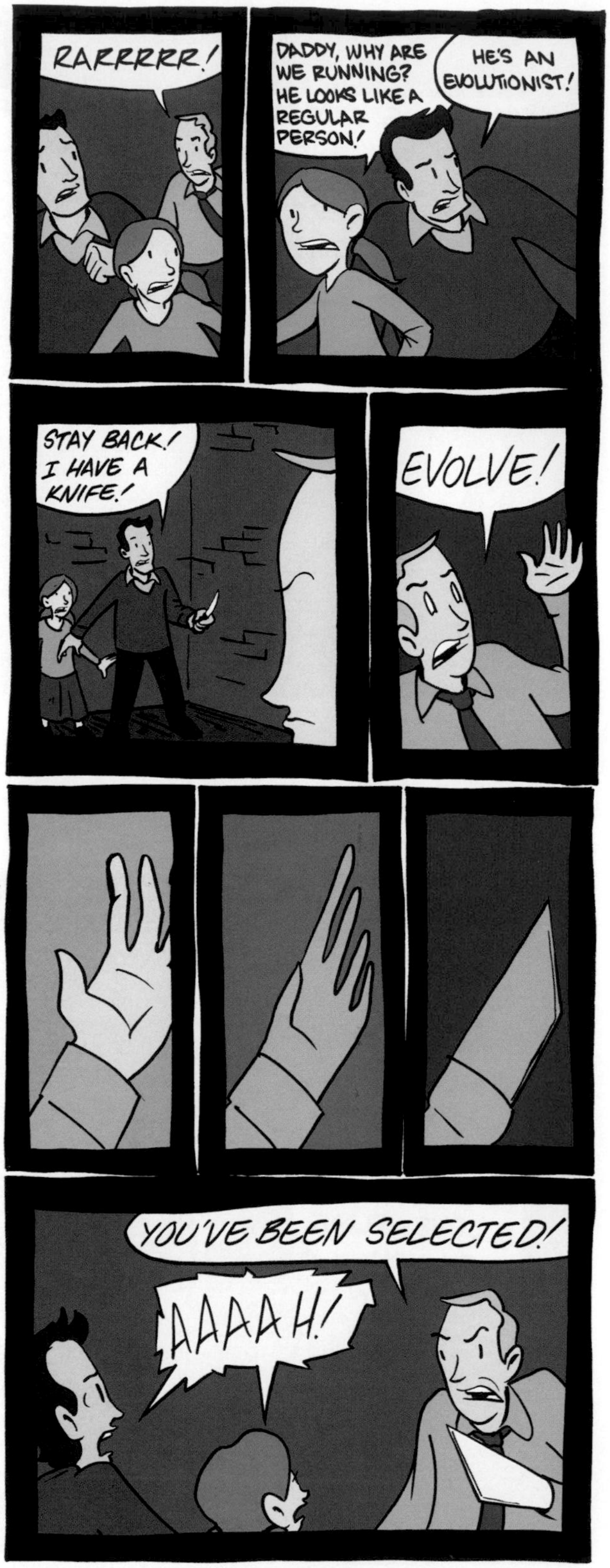
RARRRRR!
DADDY, WHY ARE WE RUNNING? HE LOOKS LIKE A REGULAR PERSON!
HE'S AN EVOLUTIONIST!
STAY BACK! I HAVE A KNIFE!
EVOLVE!
YOU'VE BEEN SELECTED!
AAAAH!

Ironically, only biologists truly appreciate creationist horror films.

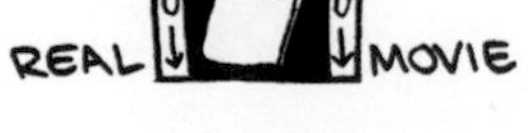
REAL
30
2600
40
MOVIE

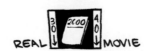

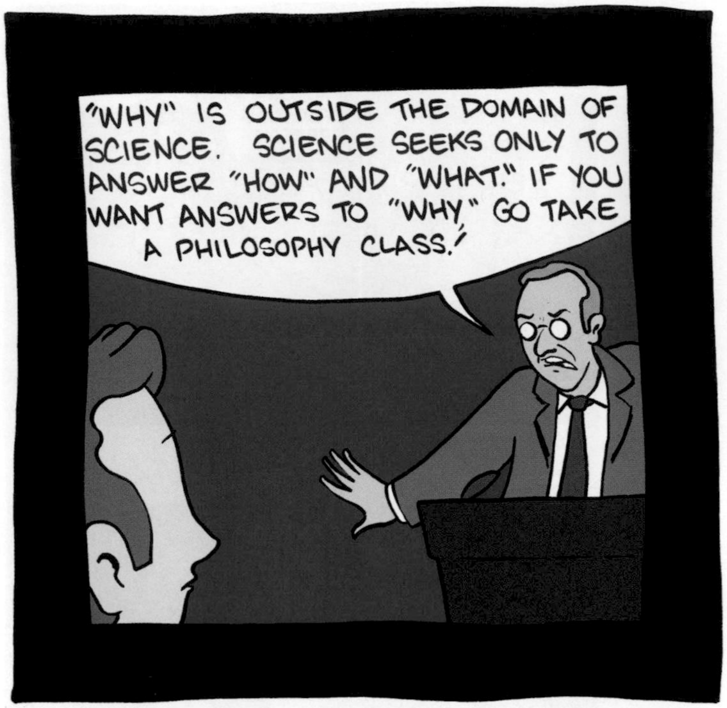
"WHY" IS OUTSIDE THE DOMAIN OF SCIENCE. SCIENCE SEEKS ONLY TO ANSWER "HOW" AND "WHAT." IF YOU WANT ANSWERS TO "WHY," GO TAKE A PHILOSOPHY CLASS.

Professor Beiser gave a brief Q&A as to his experiments on bears flying jetpacks.

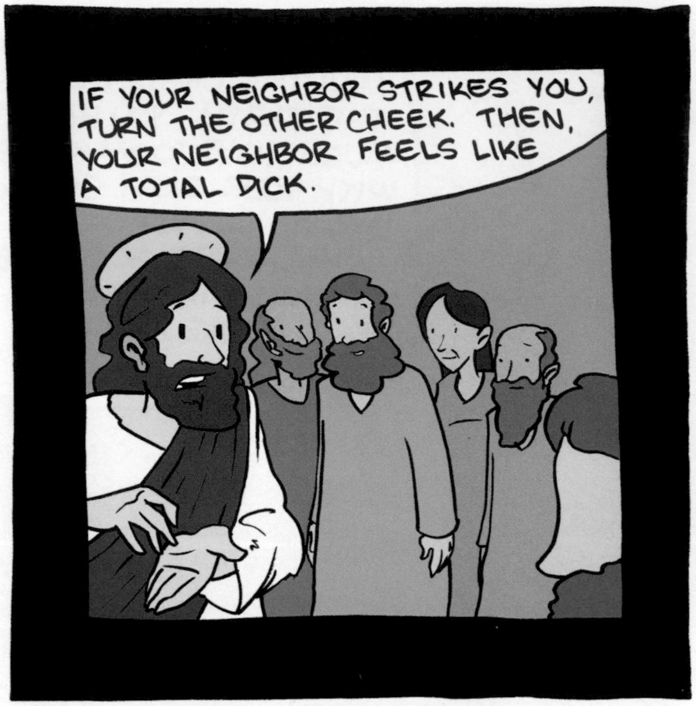
IF YOUR NEIGHBOR STRIKES YOU, TURN THE OTHER CHEEK. THEN, YOUR NEIGHBOR FEELS LIKE A TOTAL DICK.

Jesus' oft-forgotten sermon on passive-aggression.

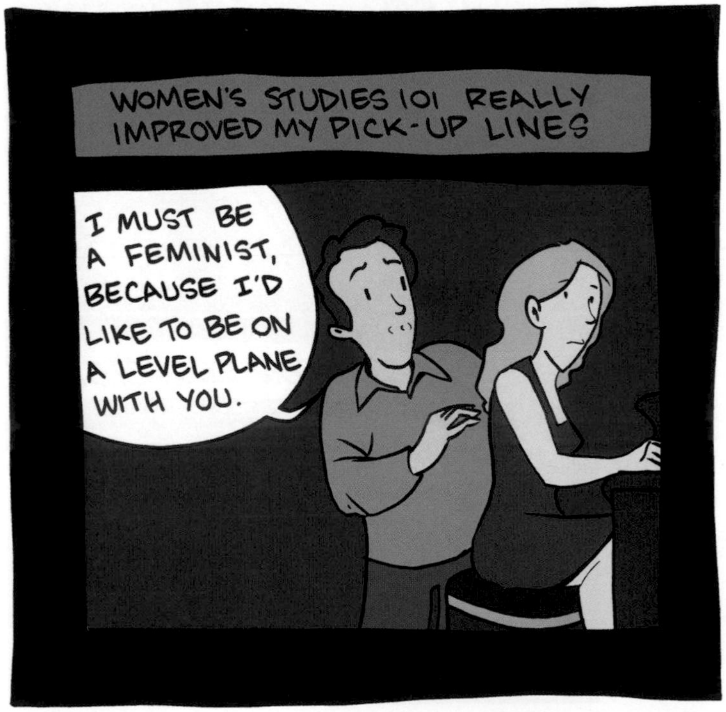
WOMEN'S STUDIES 101 REALLY IMPROVED MY PICK-UP LINES
I MUST BE A FEMINIST, BECAUSE I'D LIKE TO BE ON A LEVEL PLANE WITH YOU.

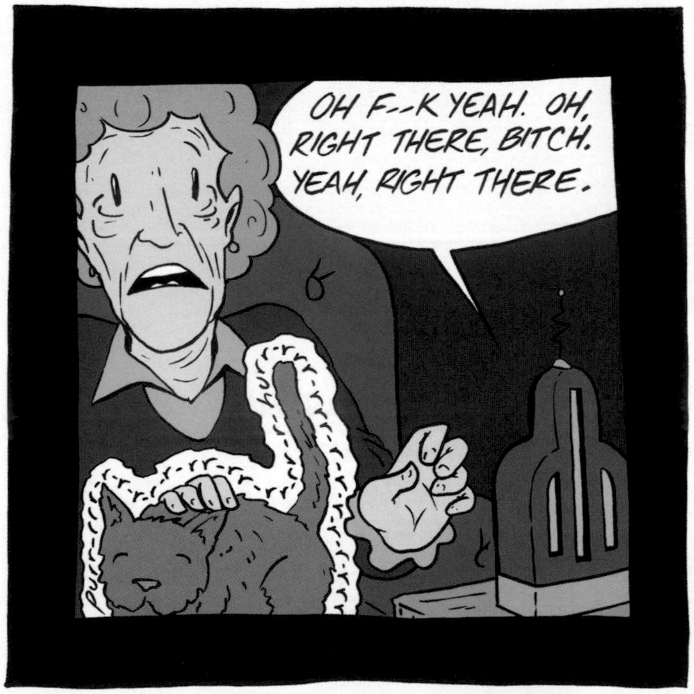
OH F--K YEAH. OH, RIGHT THERE, BITCH. YEAH, RIGHT THERE.

Excitement over the Cat Translator died off quickly.

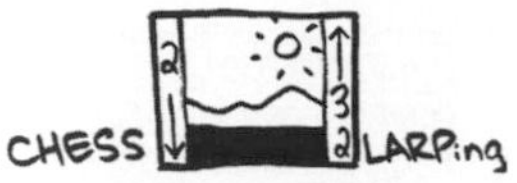
CHESS
LARPing

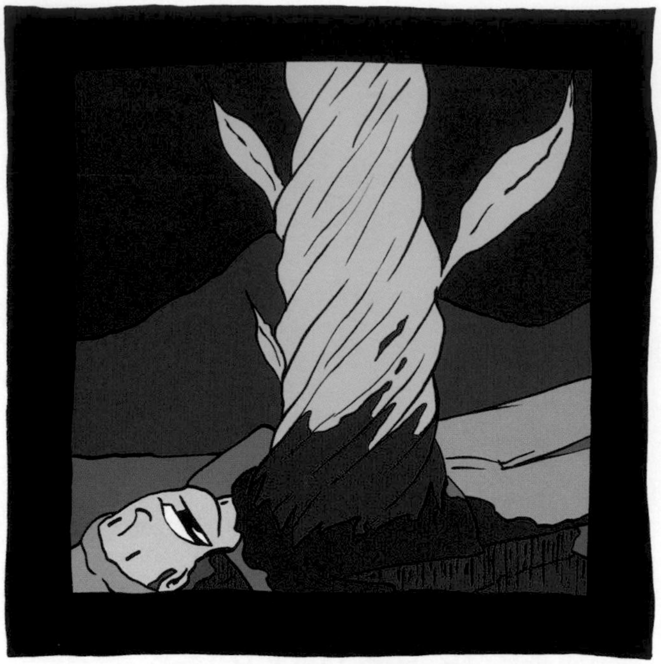

In Jack's defense, "Magic Beans" sounds like an awesome drug.

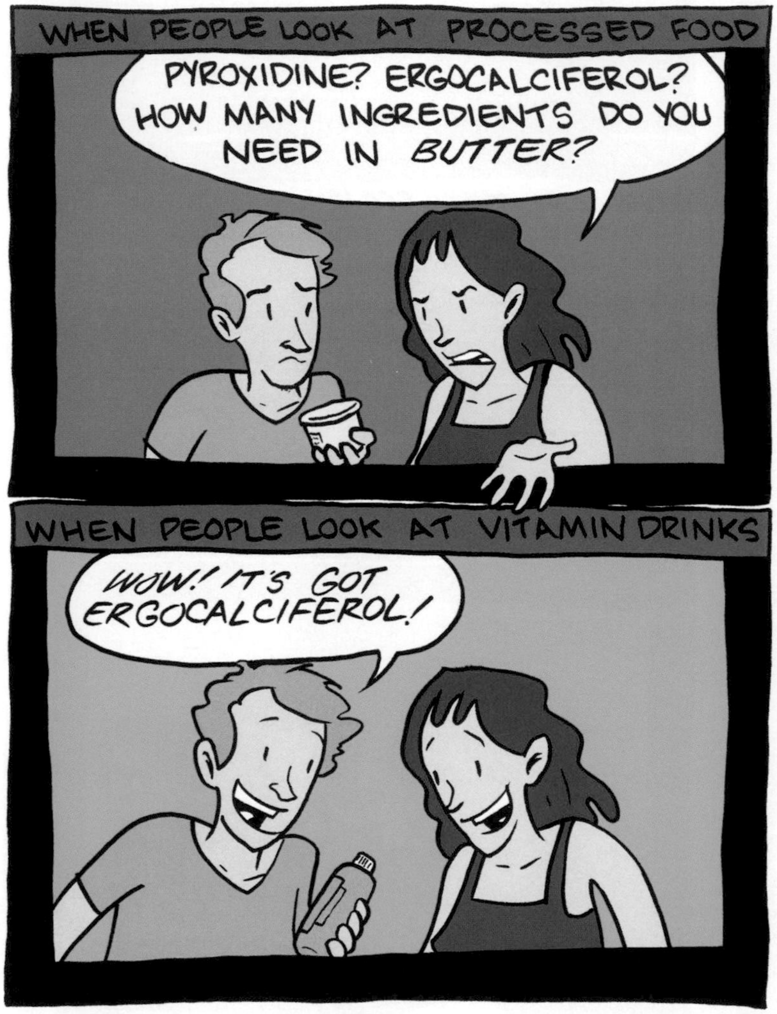
WHEN PEOPLE LOOK AT PROCESSED FOOD
PYROXIDINE? ERGOCALCIFEROL? HOW MANY INGREDIENTS DO YOU NEED IN *BUTTER?*
WHEN PEOPLE LOOK AT VITAMIN DRINKS
WOW! IT'S GOT ERGOCALCIFEROL!

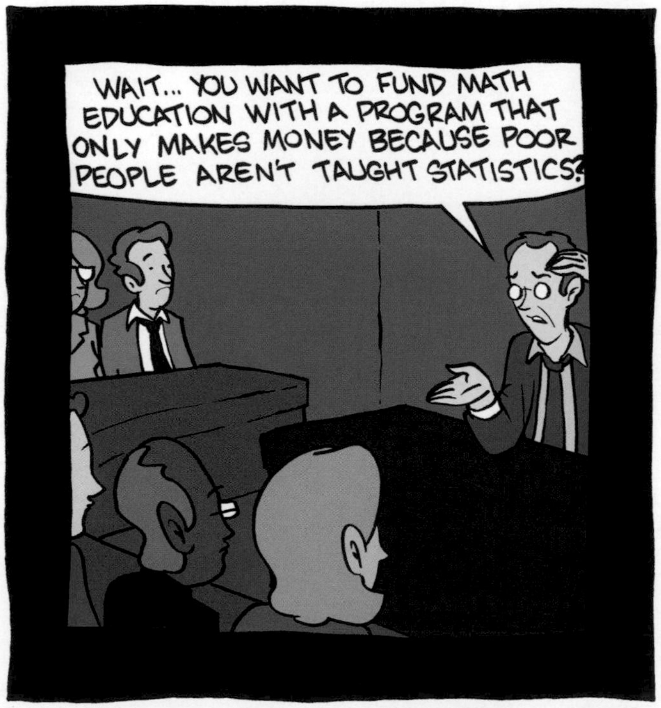
WAIT... YOU WANT TO FUND MATH EDUCATION WITH A PROGRAM THAT ONLY MAKES MONEY BECAUSE POOR PEOPLE AREN'T TAUGHT STATISTICS?

Mathematicians are no longer allowed at the state lottery funds debate.

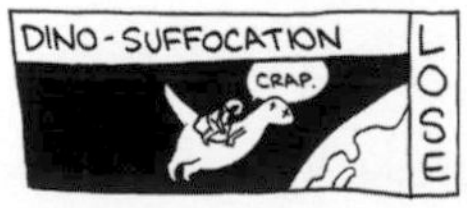
DINO-SUFFOCATION
CRAP.
LOSE

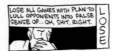

LOSE ALL GAMES WITH PLAN TO LULL OPPONENTS INTO FALSE SENSE OF... OH, SHIT, RIGHT.
LOSE

BAT-ROPE!
MAN, THIS WORKS GREAT. I WONDER IF WE COULD USE IT TO FIGHT CRIME.
EARLIER...
SO, WE NEED TO TALK ABOUT OUR RELATIONSHIP.
PEOPLE OF EARTH! WE BRING YOU A CHALLENGE! IF YOU FAIL, YOUR CIVILIZATION IS FORFEIT!
BEHOLD! MINDLESS POINT-AND-CLICK VIDEO GAMES!
I JUST... I JUST...
WHAT THE HELL DO THEY DO ALL DAY?!
IT'S OKAY, MAN DON'T LET IT UPSET YOU.

ANTISOCIAL POLITE
23
42

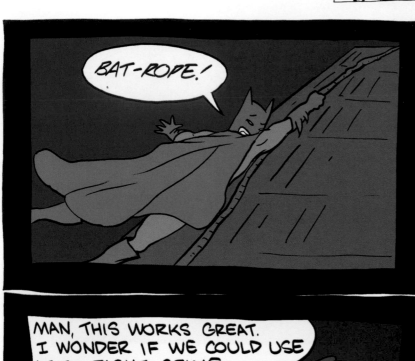

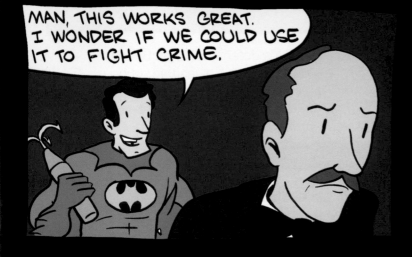

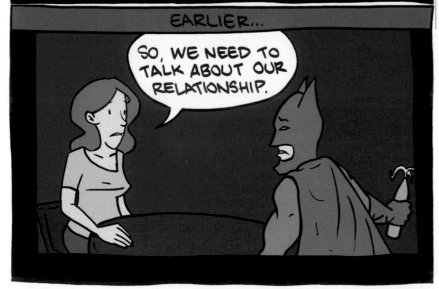

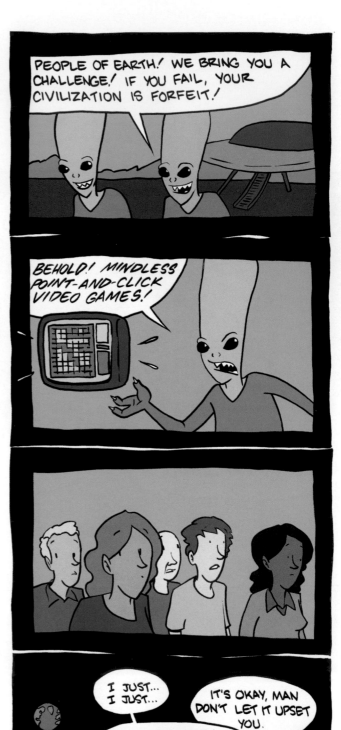

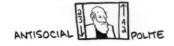

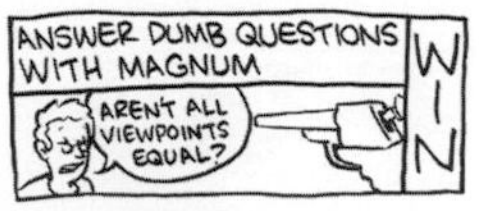
ANSWER DUMB QUESTIONS WITH MAGNUM
AREN'T ALL VIEWPOINTS EQUAL?
WIN

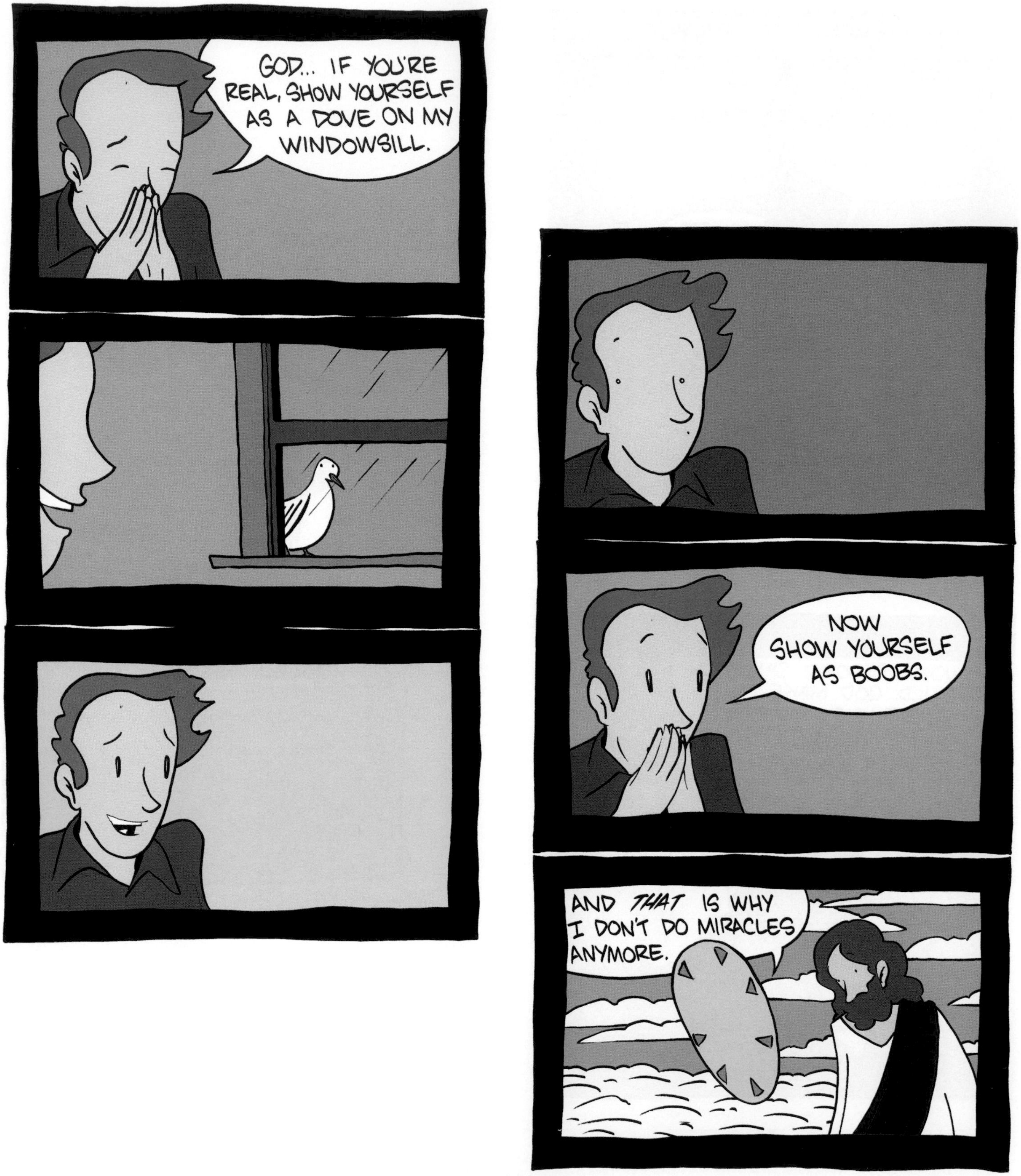
GOD... IF YOU'RE REAL, SHOW YOURSELF AS A DOVE ON MY WINDOWSILL.
NOW SHOW YOURSELF AS BOOBS.
AND *THAT* IS WHY I DON'T DO MIRACLES ANYMORE.

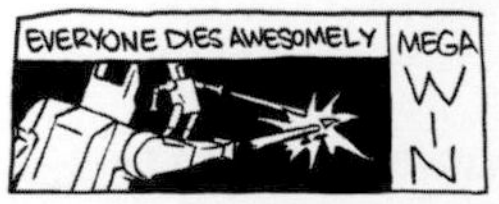
EVERYONE DIES AWESOMELY
MEGA WIN

SUCCEED, LOOK AWESOME
WIN

THE PERCEPTION PROBLEM
SOCIALLY UNACCEPTABLE
SOCIALLY ACCEPTABLE
BILLY, WHY HAVEN'T YOU FINISHED YOUR HOMEWORK.
LAZINESS.
BILLY, WHY HAVEN'T YOU FINISHED YOUR HOMEWORK.
LAZINESS SYNDROME!

AUTOEROTIC ASPHYXIATION KIT: MOST IMPORTANT ITEMS
1) STRONG CORD OR STRING
2) LUBRICANT
MAYO
3) NOTE TO LEAVE OUT IN CASE THINGS GO HORRIBLY WRONG
Oh no! This animated rope has taken my clothes! I must try to stop it or perish in the attempt!

WOW! SECOND QUESTION. COULD GOD MAKE AN ARGUMENT SO CIRCULAR THAT EVEN HE COULDN'T BELIEVE IT?

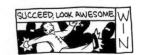

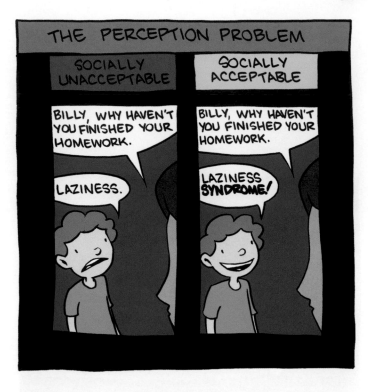

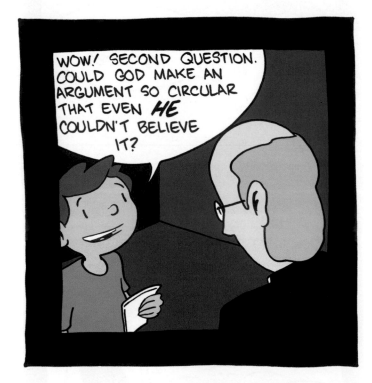

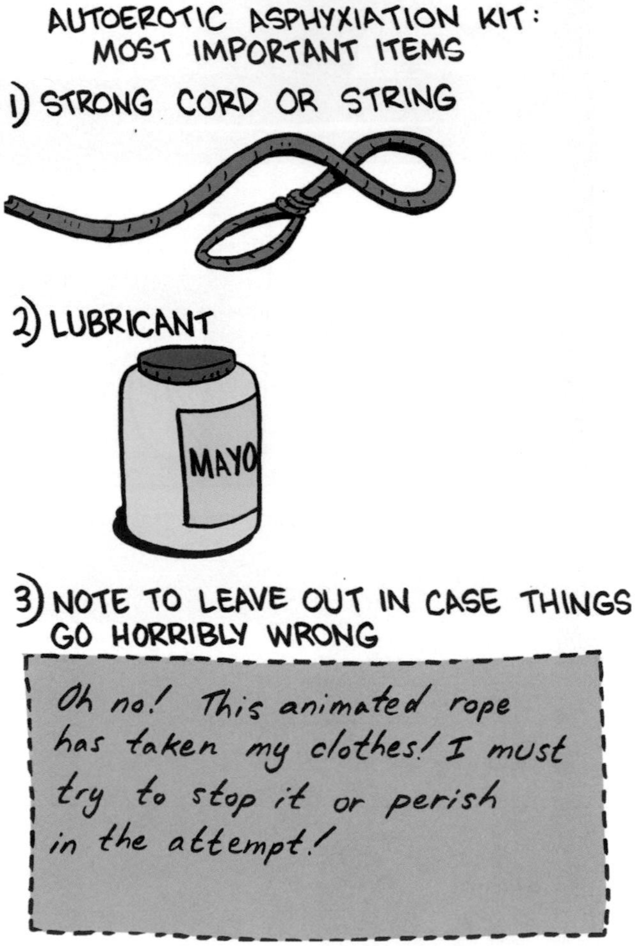

Apparently Bobby didn't appreciate my explanation of the Paradox of the Stone.

NERD
JOCK

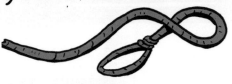

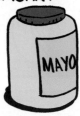

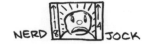

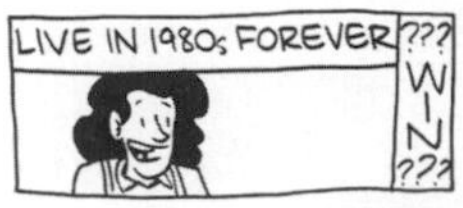
LIVE IN 1980s FOREVER
??? WIN ???

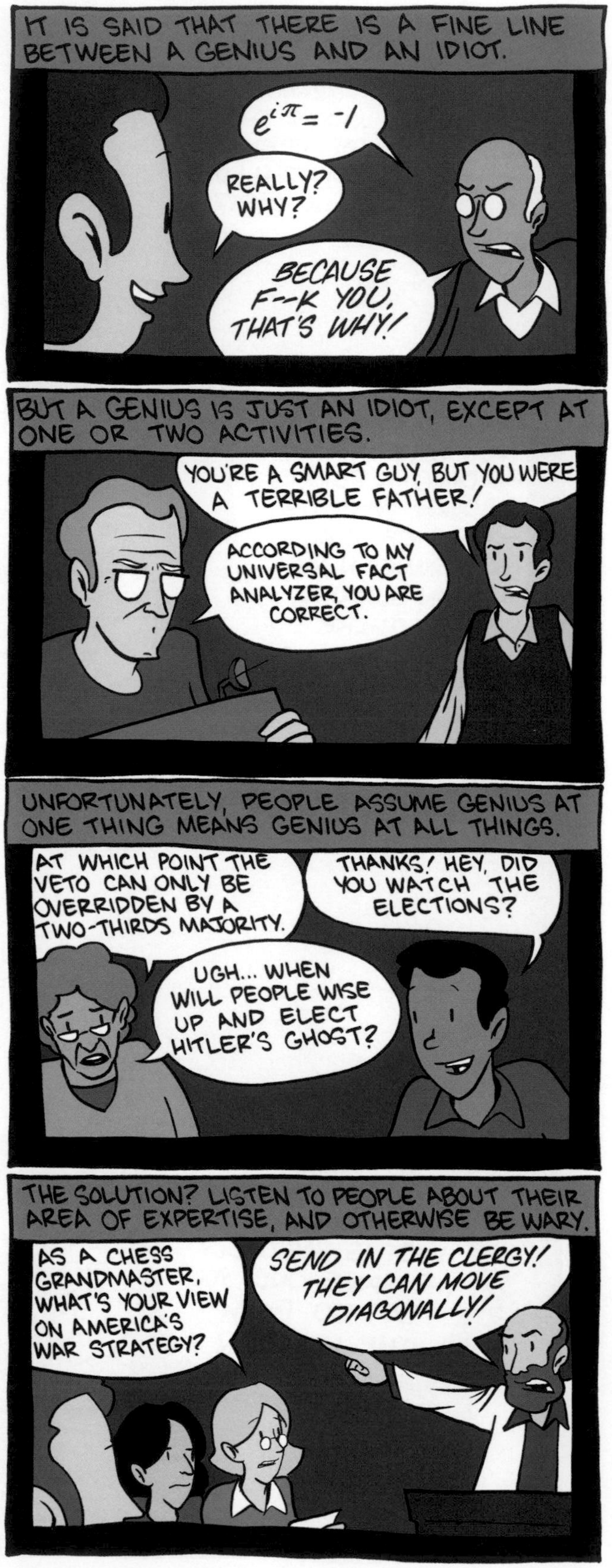
IT IS SAID THAT THERE IS A FINE LINE BETWEEN A GENIUS AND AN IDIOT.
$e^{i\pi} = -1$
REALLY? WHY?
BECAUSE F--K YOU, THAT'S WHY!
BUT A GENIUS IS JUST AN IDIOT, EXCEPT AT ONE OR TWO ACTIVITIES.
YOU'RE A SMART GUY, BUT YOU WERE A TERRIBLE FATHER!
ACCORDING TO MY UNIVERSAL FACT ANALYZER, YOU ARE CORRECT.
UNFORTUNATELY, PEOPLE ASSUME GENIUS AT ONE THING MEANS GENIUS AT ALL THINGS.
AT WHICH POINT THE VETO CAN ONLY BE OVERRIDDEN BY A TWO-THIRDS MAJORITY.
THANKS! HEY, DID YOU WATCH THE ELECTIONS?
UGH... WHEN WILL PEOPLE WISE UP AND ELECT HITLER'S GHOST?
THE SOLUTION? LISTEN TO PEOPLE ABOUT THEIR AREA OF EXPERTISE, AND OTHERWISE BE WARY.
AS A CHESS GRANDMASTER, WHAT'S YOUR VIEW ON AMERICA'S WAR STRATEGY?
SEND IN THE CLERGY! THEY CAN MOVE DIAGONALLY!

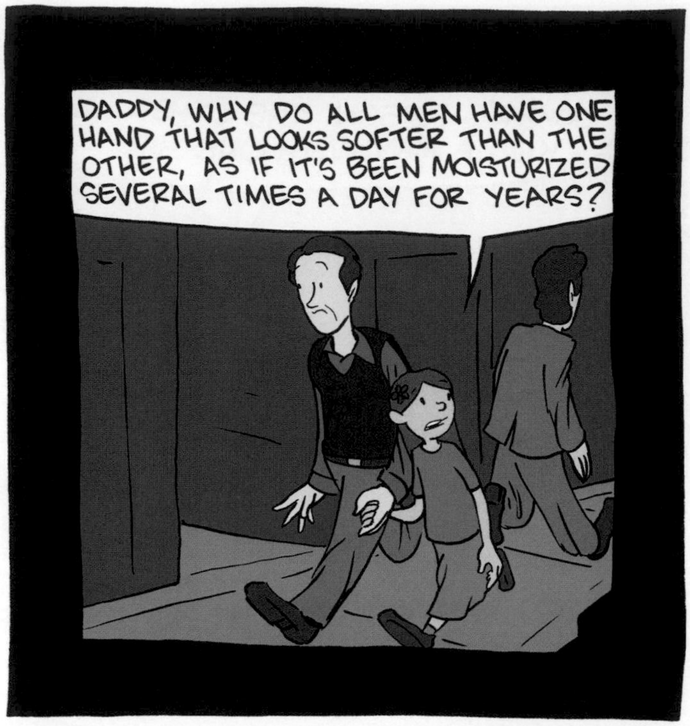
DADDY, WHY DO ALL MEN HAVE ONE HAND THAT LOOKS SOFTER THAN THE OTHER, AS IF IT'S BEEN MOISTURIZED SEVERAL TIMES A DAY FOR YEARS?

I've decided I don't want observant children after all.

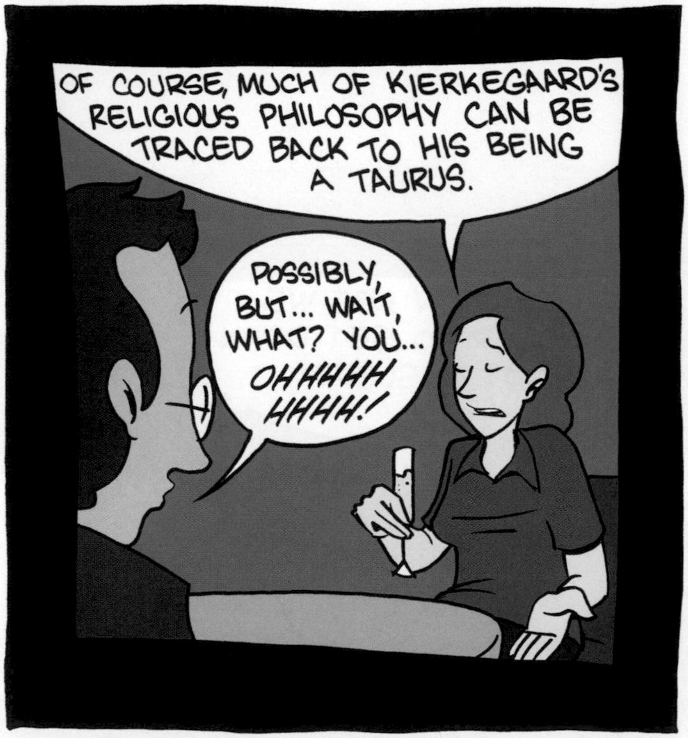
OF COURSE, MUCH OF KIERKEGAARD'S RELIGIOUS PHILOSOPHY CAN BE TRACED BACK TO HIS BEING A TAURUS.
POSSIBLY, BUT... WAIT, WHAT? YOU... OHHHHH HHHH!

Dumbpiphany: The realization that the reason the entire conversation has been difficult to follow is that you're talking to an idiot.

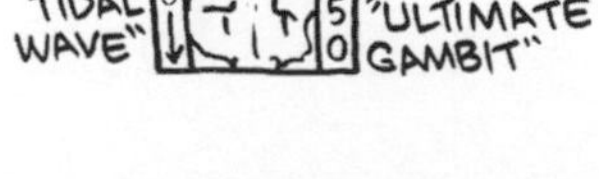
"TIDAL WAVE"
161
A8→B1→C3
150
"ULTIMATE GAMBIT"

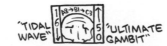

DIE ALONE AND POOR
LOSE

ONE IS AN ANTIDOTE FOR THE JOKER'S POISON. THE OTHER WILL KILL A MAN WITH ONE SIP.
BLAST! IF WE CAN'T FIND A WAY OUT, WE'LL DIE OF STARVATION IN THE NEXT FEW DAYS!
DAMN! HOW ARE WE SUPPOSED TO GET DOWN WITHOUT A SLED?!

Fun Fact:
There have been 4,286 Robins.

GRAMPA, WHAT'S THE DIFFERENCE BETWEEN LOVE AND LUST?
TRUE LOVE IS LIKE FINDING A PERFECT UNICORN, WITH ITS ALABASTER COAT GLISTENING IN AN AUTUMN SUNRISE, WAITING THERE JUST TO BE WITH YOU.
LUST IS BASICALLY THE SAME, ONLY YOU GET TO F—K THE UNICORN.

DEATH BY ULTRAHAMSTER
LOSE

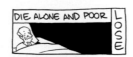

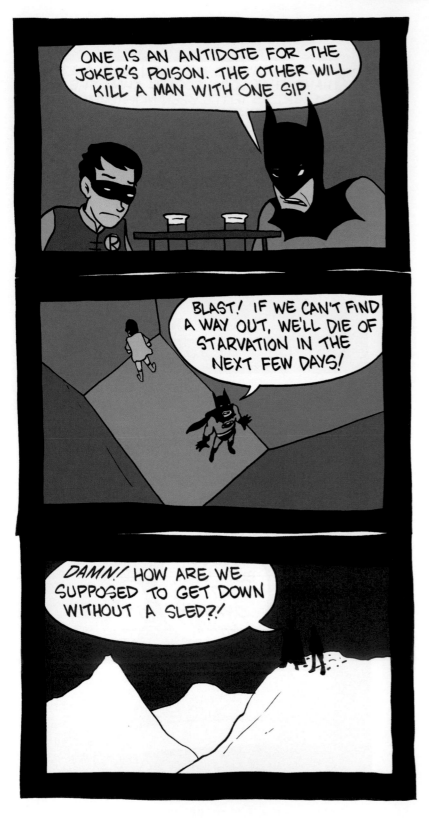

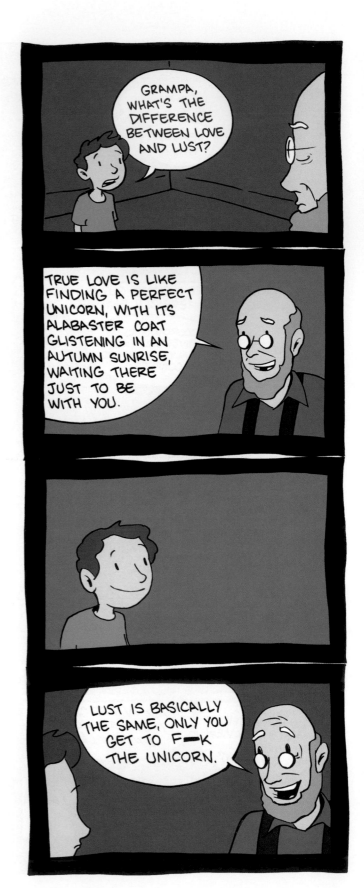

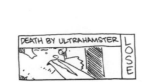

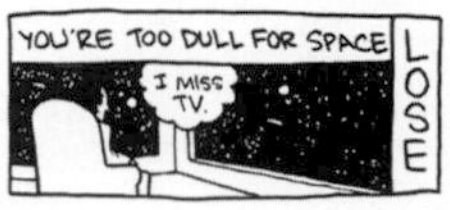

YOU'RE TOO DULL FOR SPACE
I MISS TV.
LOSE

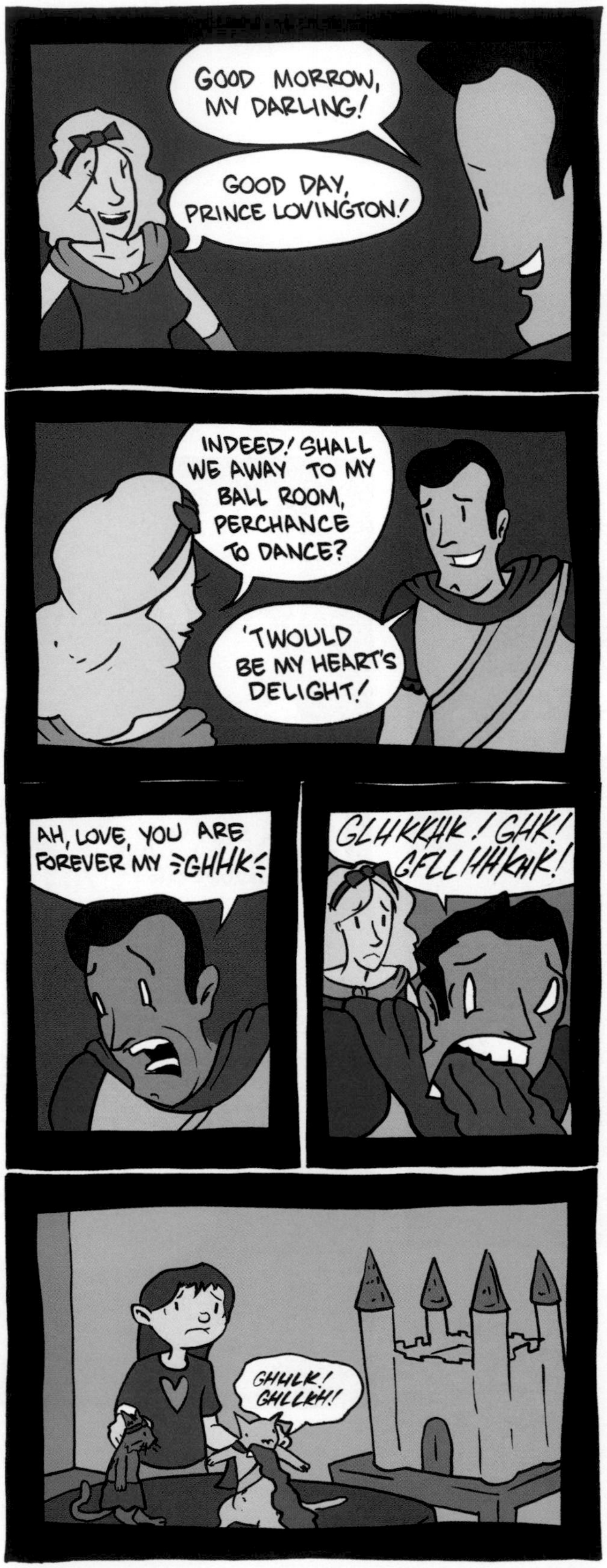

GOOD MORROW, MY DARLING!
GOOD DAY, PRINCE LOVINGTON!
INDEED! SHALL WE AWAY TO MY BALL ROOM, PERCHANCE TO DANCE?
'TWOULD BE MY HEART'S DELIGHT!
AH, LOVE, YOU ARE FOREVER MY ≶GHHK≶
GLHKKHK! GHK! GFLLHHKHK!
GHHLK! GHLLKH!

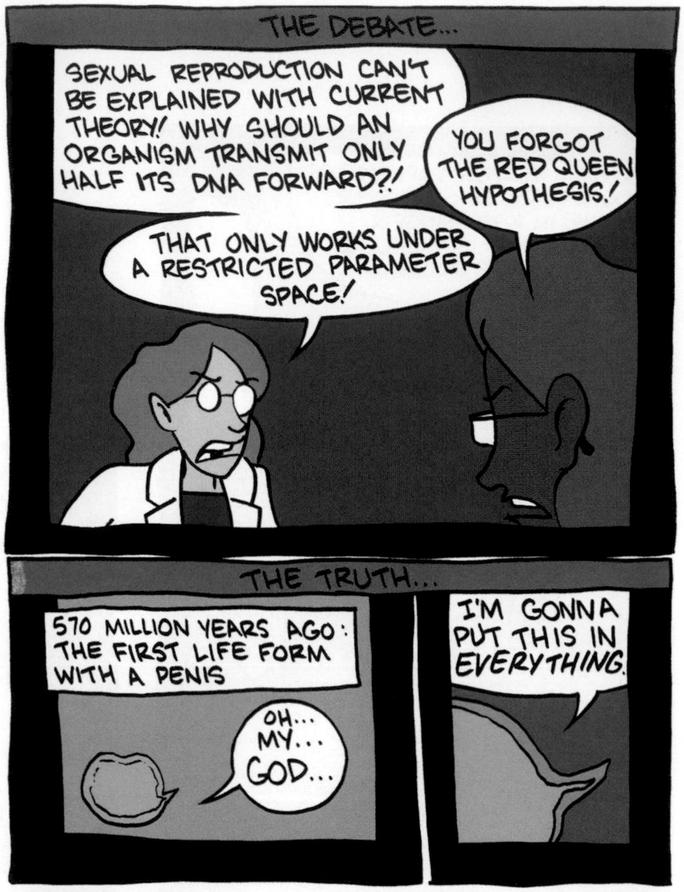

THE DEBATE...
SEXUAL REPRODUCTION CAN'T BE EXPLAINED WITH CURRENT THEORY! WHY SHOULD AN ORGANISM TRANSMIT ONLY HALF ITS DNA FORWARD?!
YOU FORGOT THE RED QUEEN HYPOTHESIS!
THAT ONLY WORKS UNDER A RESTRICTED PARAMETER SPACE!
THE TRUTH...
570 MILLION YEARS AGO: THE FIRST LIFE FORM WITH A PENIS
OH... MY... GOD...
I'M GONNA PUT THIS IN EVERYTHING.

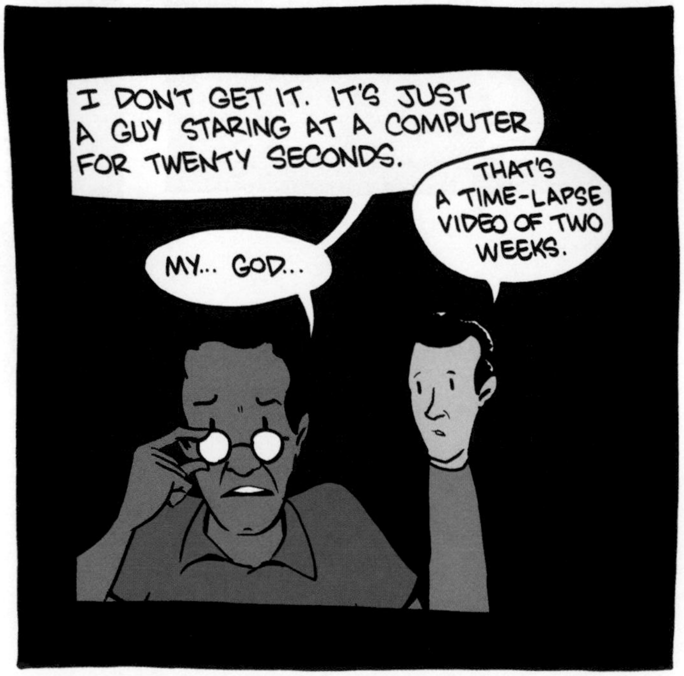

I DON'T GET IT. IT'S JUST A GUY STARING AT A COMPUTER FOR TWENTY SECONDS.
THAT'S A TIME-LAPSE VIDEO OF TWO WEEKS.
MY... GOD...

There is a reason movies never portray hacking realistically.

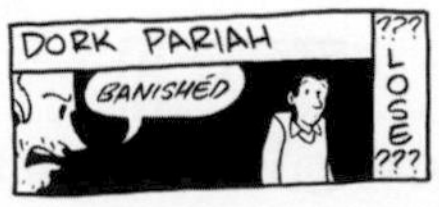

DORK PARIAH
BANISHED
???
LOSE
???

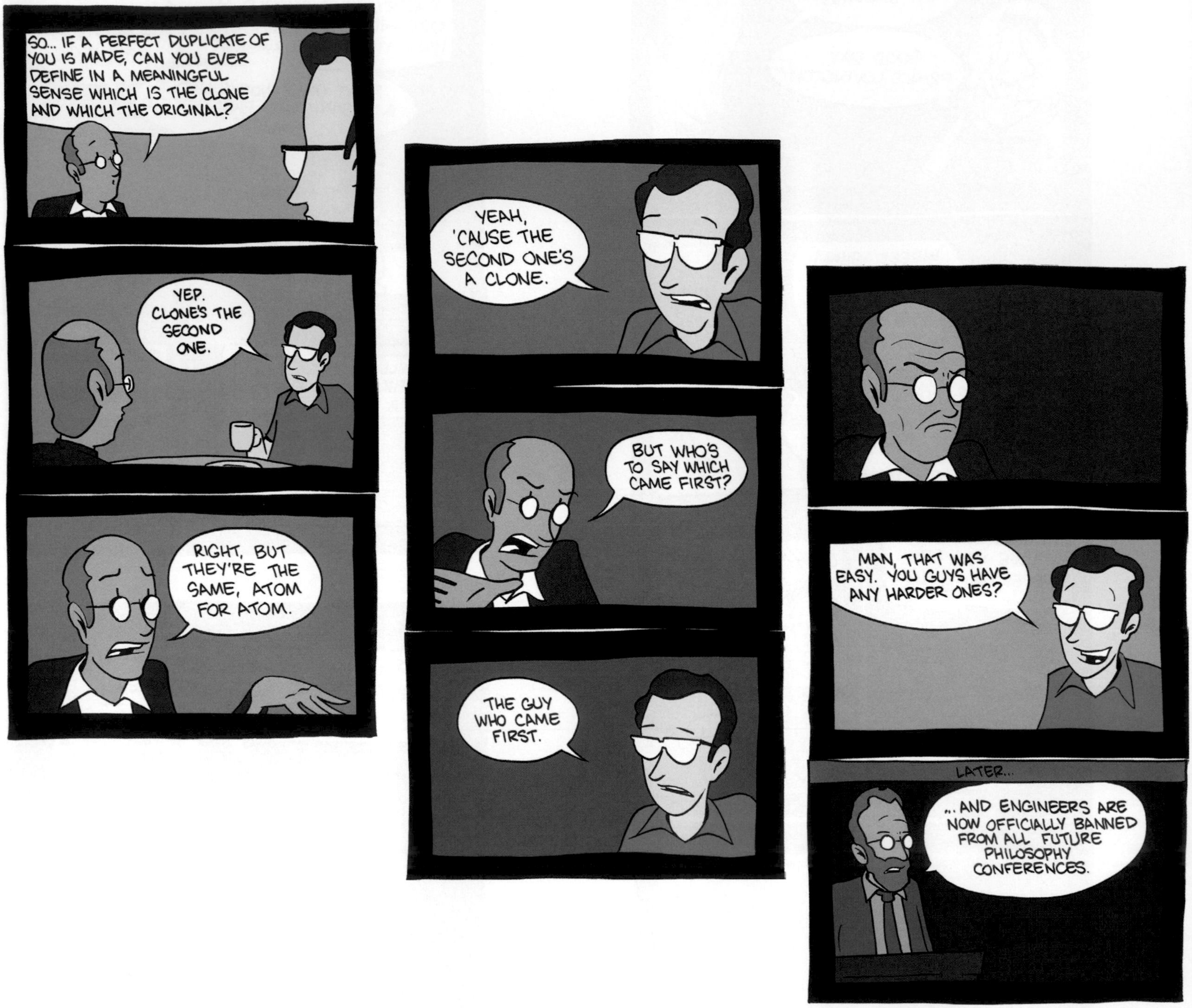
SO... IF A PERFECT DUPLICATE OF YOU IS MADE, CAN YOU EVER DEFINE IN A MEANINGFUL SENSE WHICH IS THE CLONE AND WHICH THE ORIGINAL?
YEP. CLONE'S THE SECOND ONE.
RIGHT, BUT THEY'RE THE SAME, ATOM FOR ATOM.
YEAH, 'CAUSE THE SECOND ONE'S A CLONE.
BUT WHO'S TO SAY WHICH CAME FIRST?
THE GUY WHO CAME FIRST.
MAN, THAT WAS EASY. YOU GUYS HAVE ANY HARDER ONES?
LATER...
...AND ENGINEERS ARE NOW OFFICIALLY BANNED FROM ALL FUTURE PHILOSOPHY CONFERENCES.

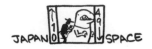

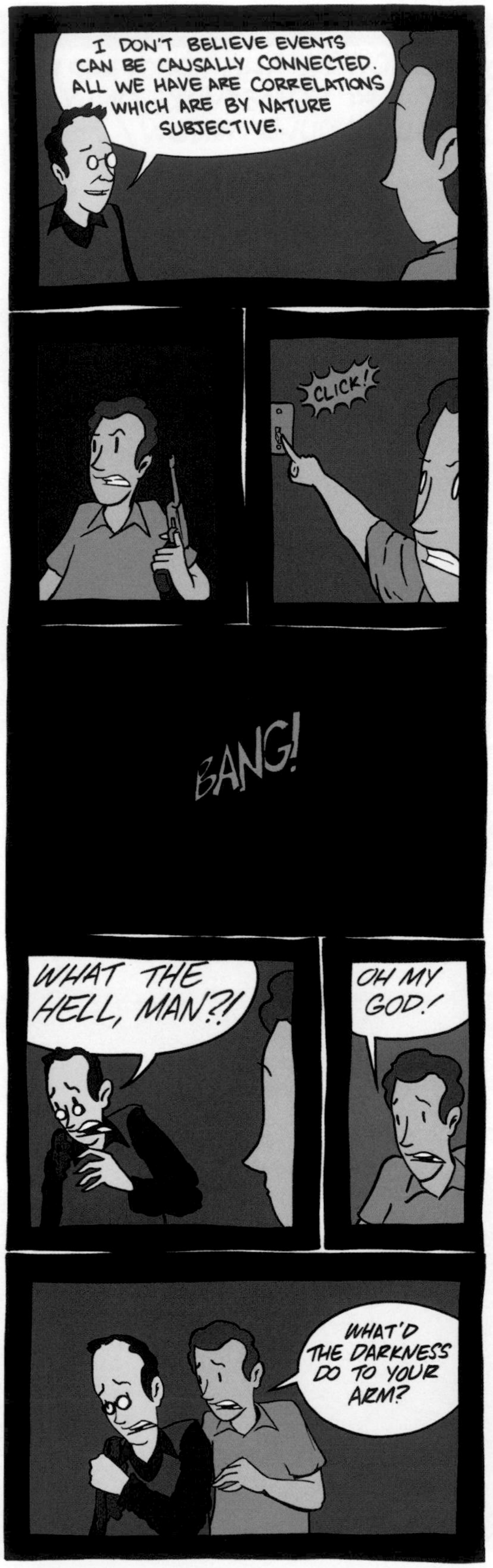
I DON'T BELIEVE EVENTS CAN BE CAUSALLY CONNECTED. ALL WE HAVE ARE CORRELATIONS WHICH ARE BY NATURE SUBJECTIVE.
CLICK!
BANG!
WHAT THE HELL, MAN?!
OH MY GOD!
WHAT'D THE DARKNESS DO TO YOUR ARM?

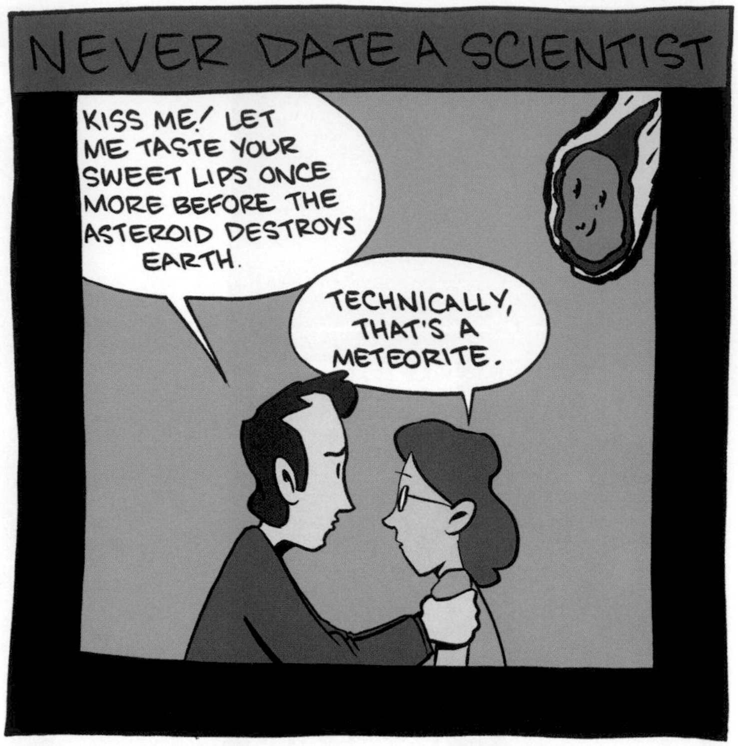
NEVER DATE A SCIENTIST
KISS ME! LET ME TASTE YOUR SWEET LIPS ONCE MORE BEFORE THE ASTEROID DESTROYS EARTH.
TECHNICALLY, THAT'S A METEORITE.

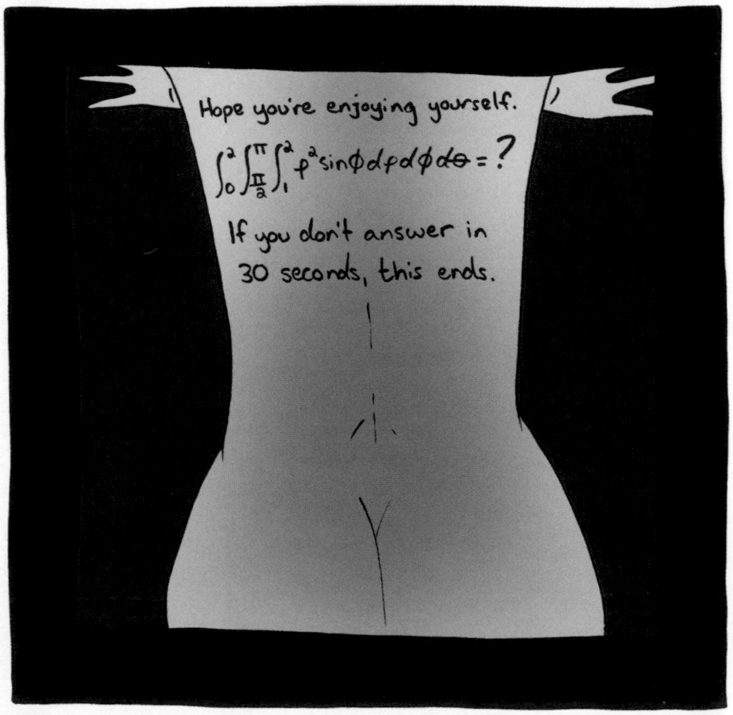
Hope you're enjoying yourself.
$\int_0^2\int_{\frac{\pi}{2}}^{\pi}\int_1^2 \rho^2 \sin\phi \, d\rho \, d\phi \, d\theta = ?$
If you don't answer in 30 seconds, this ends.

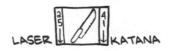

Lady geeks have the best tattoos.

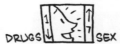

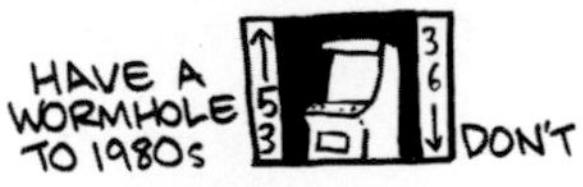
HAVE A WORMHOLE TO 1980s
153
36
DON'T

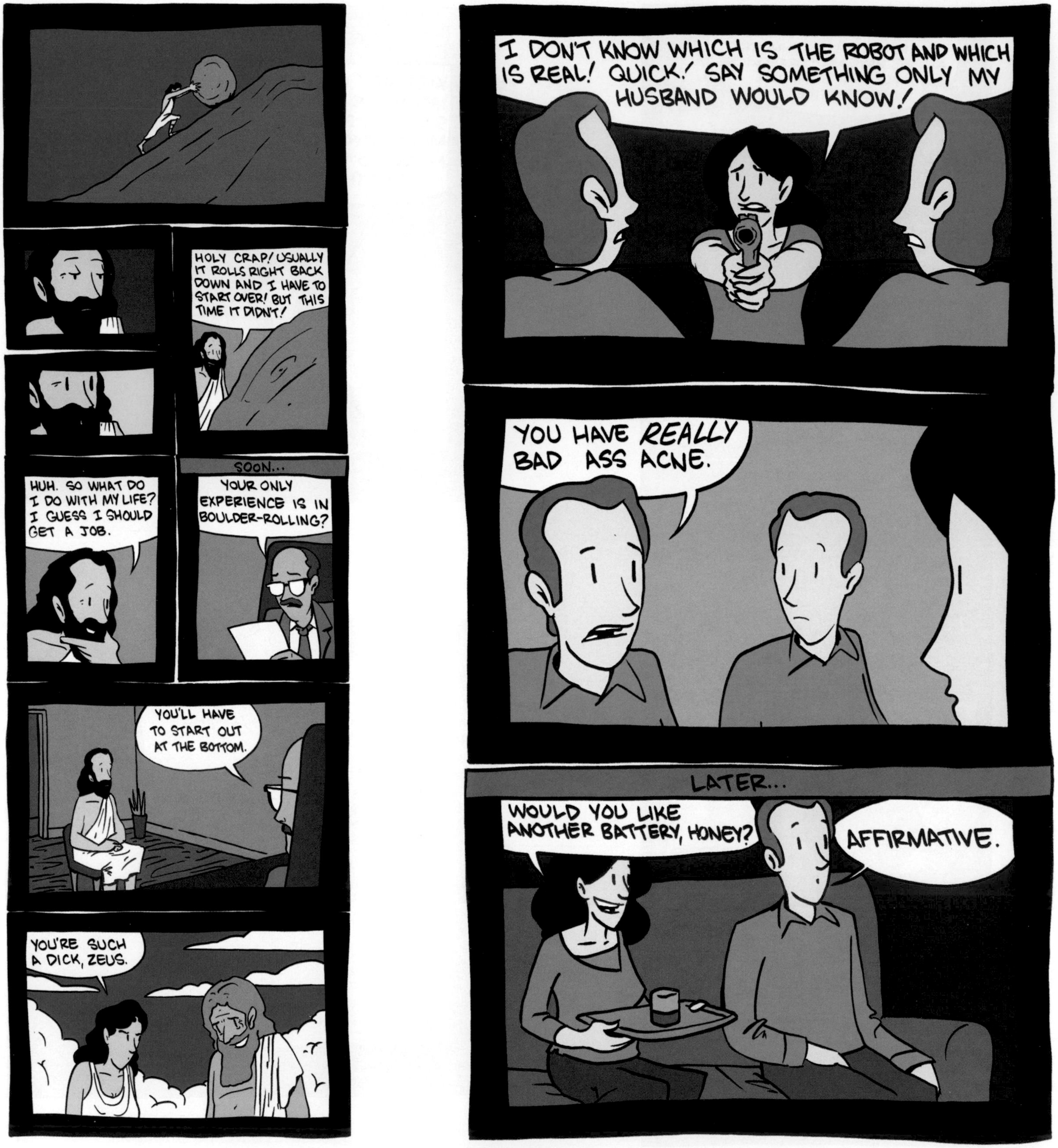
HOLY CRAP! USUALLY IT ROLLS RIGHT BACK DOWN AND I HAVE TO START OVER! BUT THIS TIME IT DIDN'T!
HUH. SO WHAT DO I DO WITH MY LIFE? I GUESS I SHOULD GET A JOB.
SOON...
YOUR ONLY EXPERIENCE IS IN BOULDER-ROLLING?
YOU'LL HAVE TO START OUT AT THE BOTTOM.
YOU'RE SUCH A DICK, ZEUS.
I DON'T KNOW WHICH IS THE ROBOT AND WHICH IS REAL! QUICK! SAY SOMETHING ONLY MY HUSBAND WOULD KNOW!
YOU HAVE REALLY BAD ASS ACNE.
LATER...
WOULD YOU LIKE ANOTHER BATTERY, HONEY?
AFFIRMATIVE.

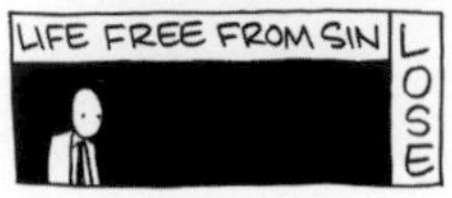
LIFE FREE FROM SIN
LOSE

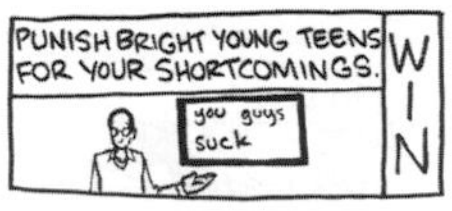
PUNISH BRIGHT YOUNG TEENS FOR YOUR SHORTCOMINGS.
you guys suck
WIN

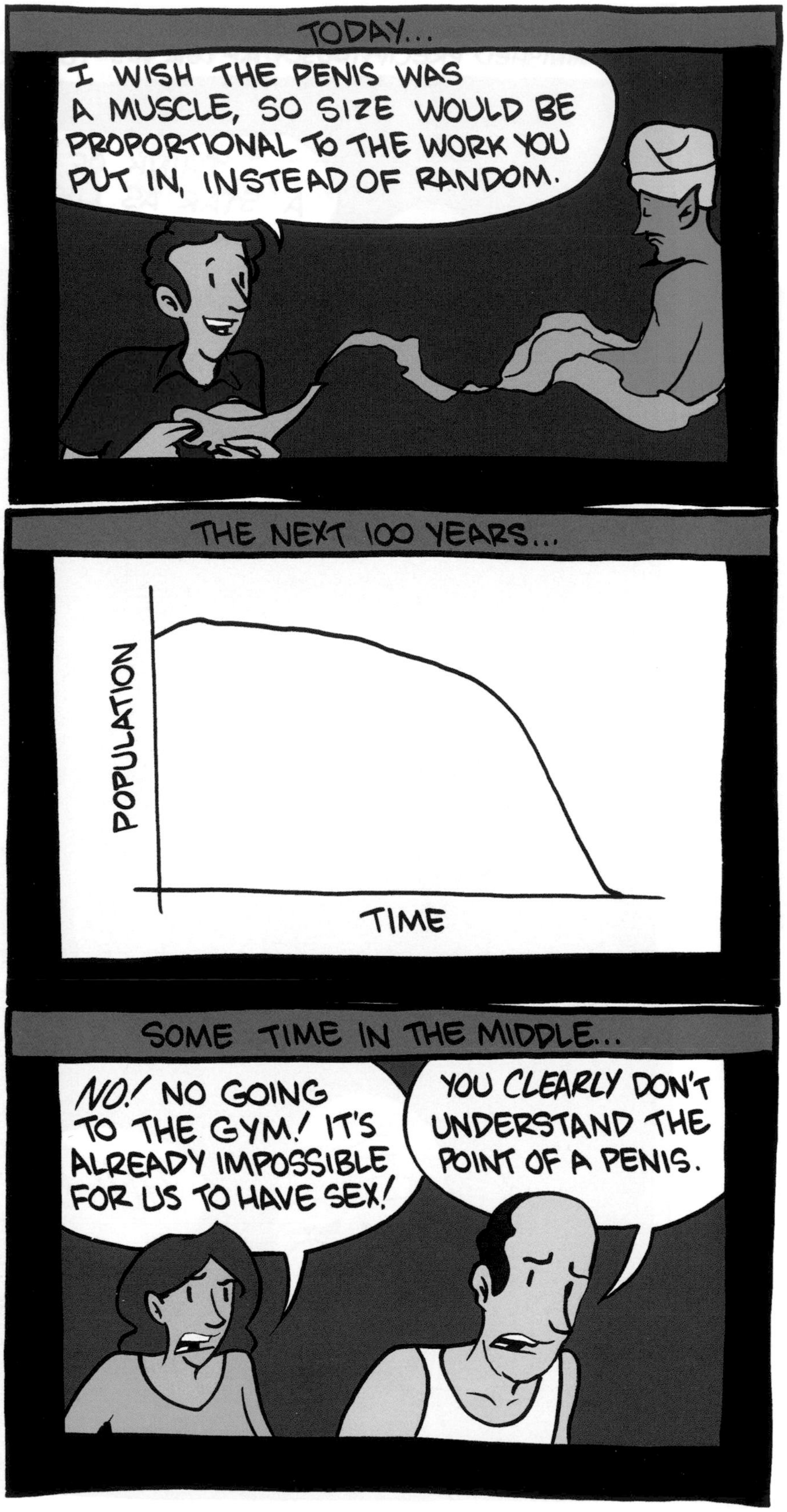
TODAY...
I WISH THE PENIS WAS A MUSCLE, SO SIZE WOULD BE PROPORTIONAL TO THE WORK YOU PUT IN, INSTEAD OF RANDOM.
THE NEXT 100 YEARS...
POPULATION
TIME
SOME TIME IN THE MIDDLE...
NO! NO GOING TO THE GYM! IT'S ALREADY IMPOSSIBLE FOR US TO HAVE SEX!
YOU CLEARLY DON'T UNDERSTAND THE POINT OF A PENIS.

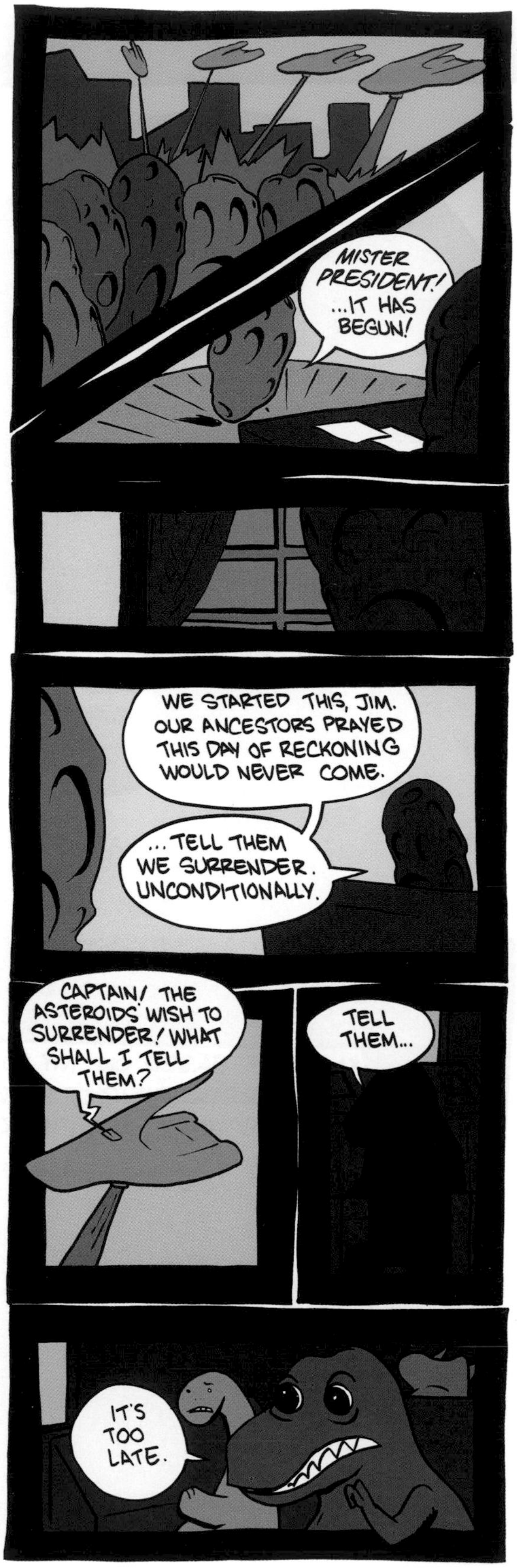
MISTER PRESIDENT! ...IT HAS BEGUN!
WE STARTED THIS, JIM. OUR ANCESTORS PRAYED THIS DAY OF RECKONING WOULD NEVER COME.
...TELL THEM WE SURRENDER. UNCONDITIONALLY.
CAPTAIN! THE ASTEROIDS WISH TO SURRENDER! WHAT SHALL I TELL THEM?
TELL THEM...
IT'S TOO LATE.

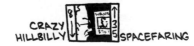

RELATIONSHIPS: A GUIDE

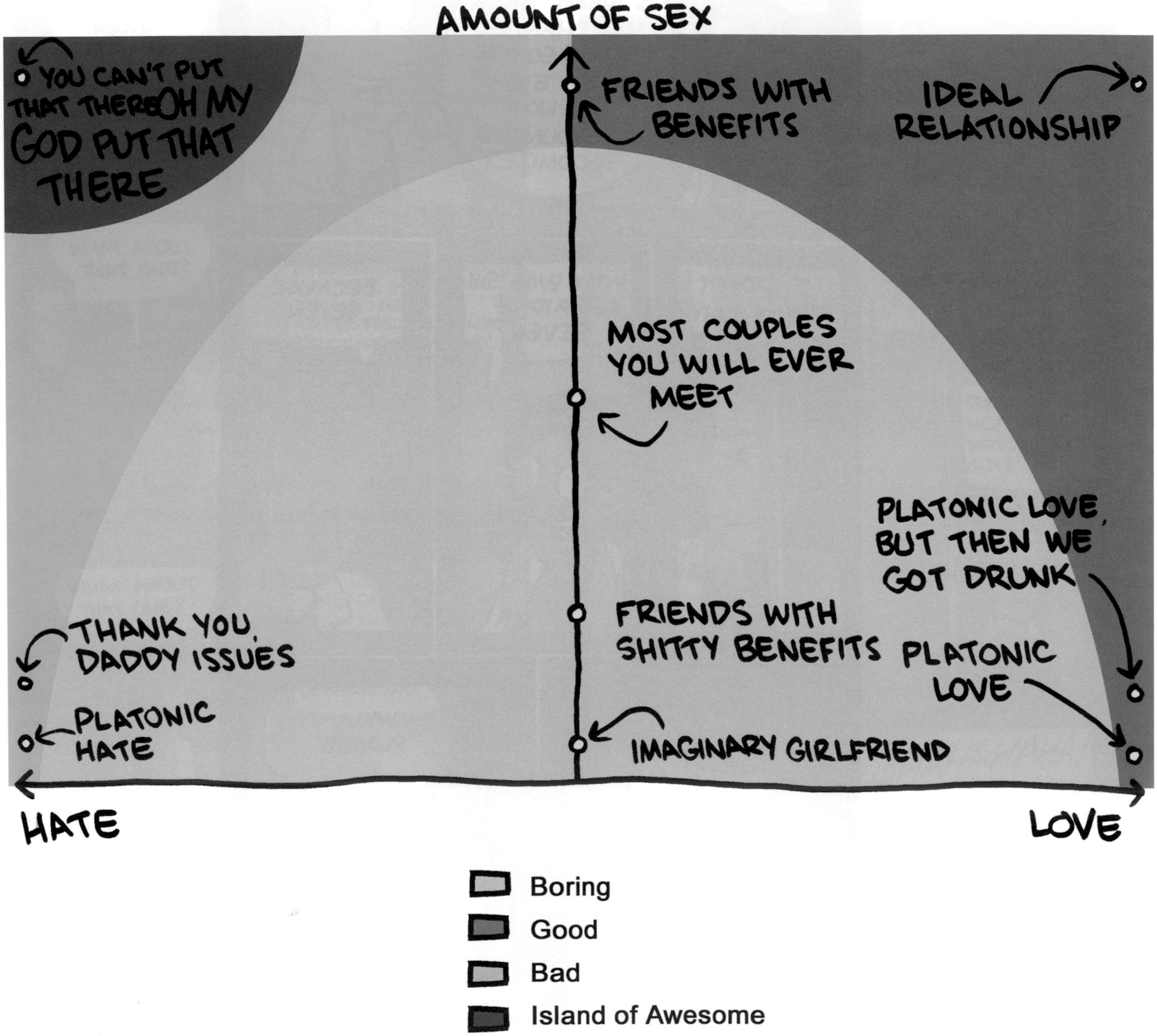
AMOUNT OF SEX
YOU CAN'T PUT THAT THERE
OH MY GOD PUT THAT THERE
FRIENDS WITH BENEFITS
IDEAL RELATIONSHIP
MOST COUPLES YOU WILL EVER MEET
PLATONIC LOVE, BUT THEN WE GOT DRUNK
THANK YOU, DADDY ISSUES
FRIENDS WITH SHITTY BENEFITS
PLATONIC LOVE
PLATONIC HATE
IMAGINARY GIRLFRIEND
HATE
LOVE
Boring
Good
Bad
Island of Awesome

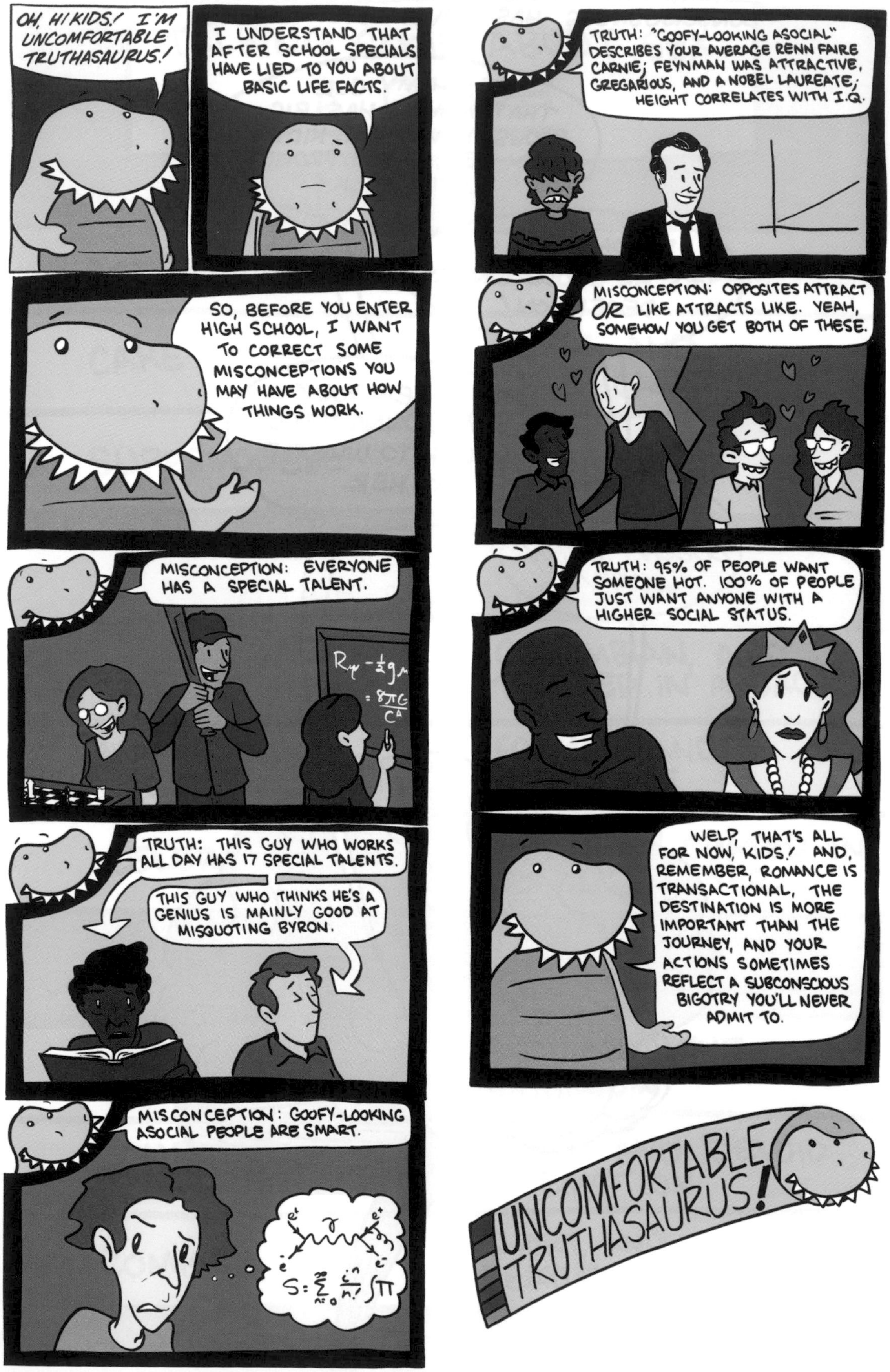

OH, HI KIDS! I'M UNCOMFORTABLE TRUTHASAURUS!
I UNDERSTAND THAT AFTER SCHOOL SPECIALS HAVE LIED TO YOU ABOUT BASIC LIFE FACTS.
SO, BEFORE YOU ENTER HIGH SCHOOL, I WANT TO CORRECT SOME MISCONCEPTIONS YOU MAY HAVE ABOUT HOW THINGS WORK.
MISCONCEPTION: EVERYONE HAS A SPECIAL TALENT.
TRUTH: THIS GUY WHO WORKS ALL DAY HAS 17 SPECIAL TALENTS.
THIS GUY WHO THINKS HE'S A GENIUS IS MAINLY GOOD AT MISQUOTING BYRON.
MISCONCEPTION: GOOFY-LOOKING ASOCIAL PEOPLE ARE SMART.
TRUTH: "GOOFY-LOOKING ASOCIAL" DESCRIBES YOUR AVERAGE RENN FAIRE CARNIE; FEYNMAN WAS ATTRACTIVE, GREGARIOUS, AND A NOBEL LAUREATE; HEIGHT CORRELATES WITH I.Q.
MISCONCEPTION: OPPOSITES ATTRACT OR LIKE ATTRACTS LIKE. YEAH, SOMEHOW YOU GET BOTH OF THESE.
TRUTH: 95% OF PEOPLE WANT SOMEONE HOT. 100% OF PEOPLE JUST WANT ANYONE WITH A HIGHER SOCIAL STATUS.
WELP, THAT'S ALL FOR NOW, KIDS! AND, REMEMBER, ROMANCE IS TRANSACTIONAL, THE DESTINATION IS MORE IMPORTANT THAN THE JOURNEY, AND YOUR ACTIONS SOMETIMES REFLECT A SUBCONSCIOUS BIGOTRY YOU'LL NEVER ADMIT TO.
UNCOMFORTABLE TRUTHASAURUS!

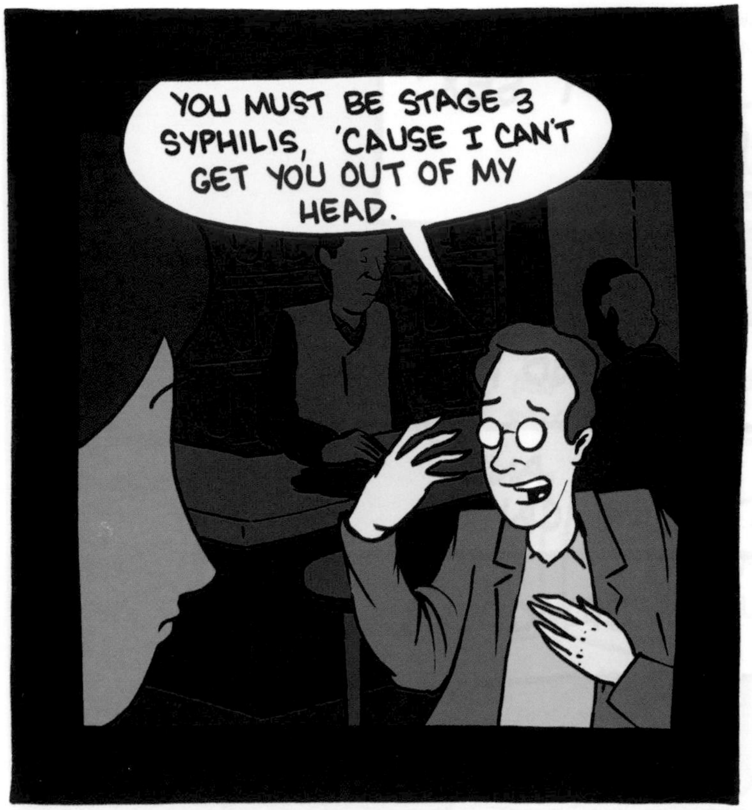
YOU MUST BE STAGE 3 SYPHILIS, 'CAUSE I CAN'T GET YOU OUT OF MY HEAD.

Pickup lines are very different in the medical community.

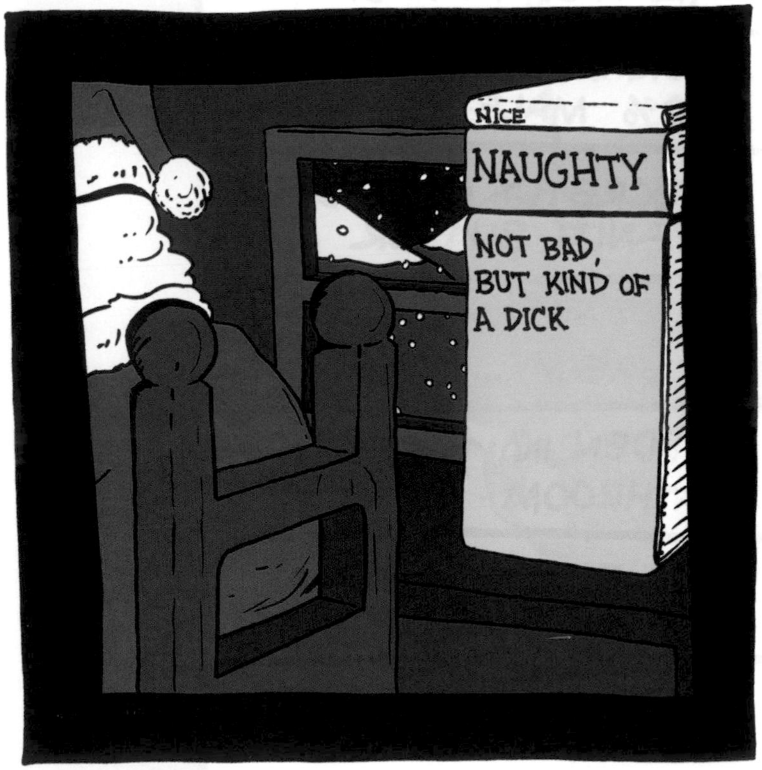
NICE
NAUGHTY
NOT BAD, BUT KIND OF A DICK

Ask yourself:
did you get ***everything*** you wanted for Christmas?

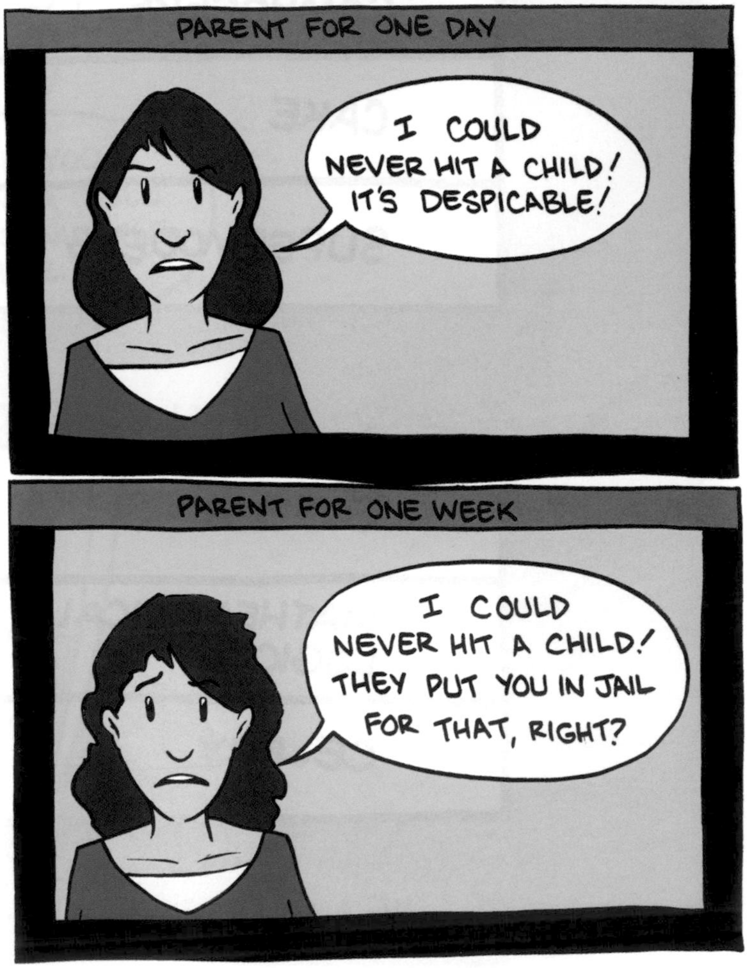
PARENT FOR ONE DAY
I COULD NEVER HIT A CHILD! IT'S DESPICABLE!
PARENT FOR ONE WEEK
I COULD NEVER HIT A CHILD! THEY PUT YOU IN JAIL FOR THAT, RIGHT?

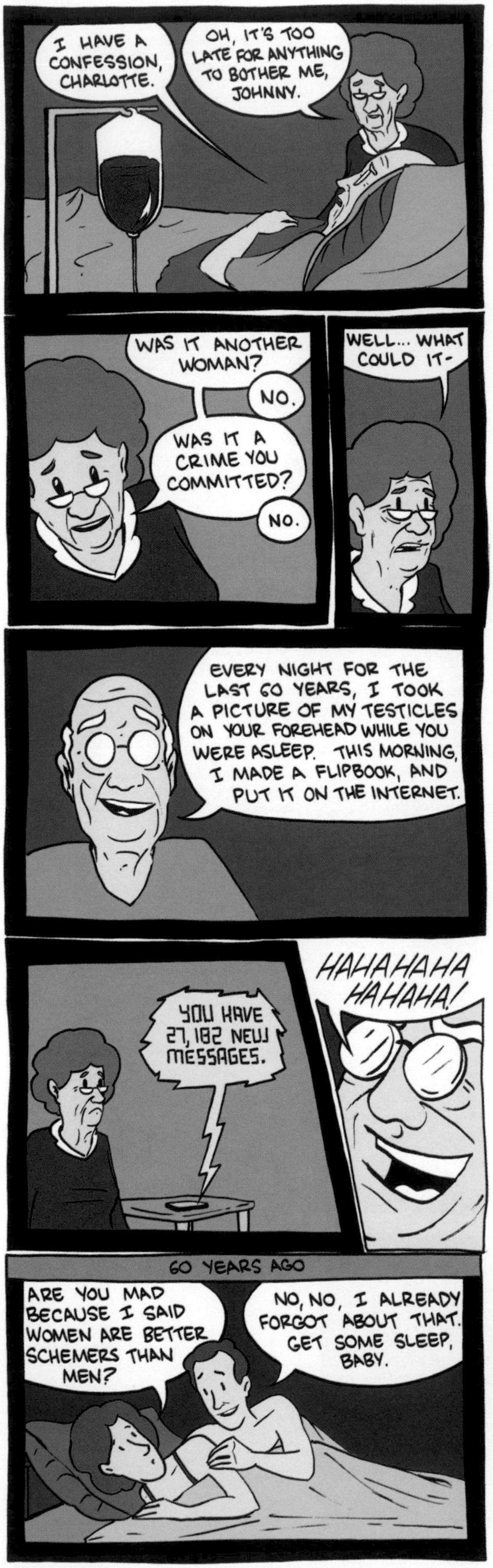
I HAVE A CONFESSION, CHARLOTTE.
OH, IT'S TOO LATE FOR ANYTHING TO BOTHER ME, JOHNNY.
WAS IT ANOTHER WOMAN?
NO.
WAS IT A CRIME YOU COMMITTED?
NO.
WELL... WHAT COULD IT-
EVERY NIGHT FOR THE LAST 60 YEARS, I TOOK A PICTURE OF MY TESTICLES ON YOUR FOREHEAD WHILE YOU WERE ASLEEP. THIS MORNING, I MADE A FLIPBOOK, AND PUT IT ON THE INTERNET.
YOU HAVE 27,182 NEW MESSAGES.
HAHAHAHA HAHAHA!
60 YEARS AGO
ARE YOU MAD BECAUSE I SAID WOMEN ARE BETTER SCHEMERS THAN MEN?
NO, NO, I ALREADY FORGOT ABOUT THAT. GET SOME SLEEP, BABY.

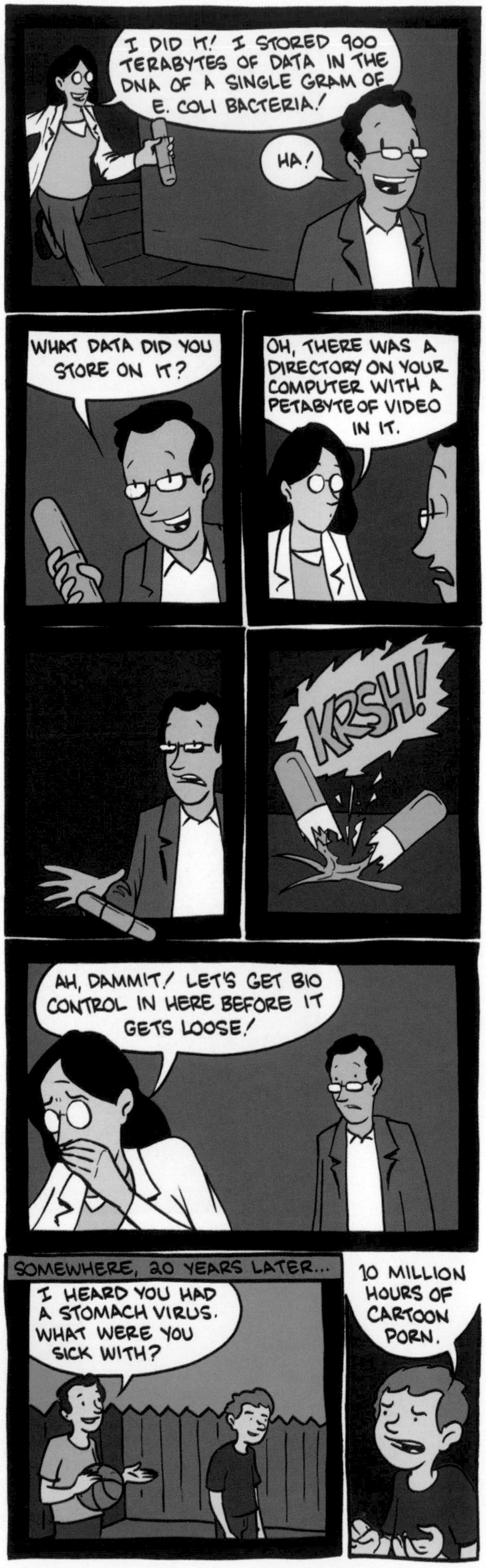
I DID IT! I STORED 900 TERABYTES OF DATA IN THE DNA OF A SINGLE GRAM OF E. COLI BACTERIA!
HA!
WHAT DATA DID YOU STORE ON IT?
OH, THERE WAS A DIRECTORY ON YOUR COMPUTER WITH A PETABYTE OF VIDEO IN IT.
KRSH!
AH, DAMMIT! LET'S GET BIO CONTROL IN HERE BEFORE IT GETS LOOSE!
SOMEWHERE, 20 YEARS LATER...
I HEARD YOU HAD A STOMACH VIRUS. WHAT WERE YOU SICK WITH?
10 MILLION HOURS OF CARTOON PORN.

THE ANT WORKED ALL DAY WHILE THE GRASSHOPPER PLAYED HIS FIDDLE.
COME WINTER, THE GRASSHOPPER WAS COLD AND HUNGRY WHILE THE ANT WAS WARM AND FULL.
NEXT SPRING, THE ANT WAS INFORMED THAT HIS JOB WAS OUTSOURCED TO A MORE EFFICIENT ANT IN ASIA.
LATER, THE ANT TRIED TO EXPLAIN THE VALUE OF HARD WORK TO HIS SONS, BUT THEY DIDN'T BELIEVE HIM SINCE HE WAS A PENSIONLESS CASHIER AT A DISCOUNT RETAILER.
THE GRASSHOPPER GOT RICH BECAUSE A VIDEO OF HIM GETTING STEPPED ON BY A CELEBRITY BECAME AN INTERNET MEME.
THE ANT STILL WORKS HARD, BUT HIS MONEY GOES TO HIS SHIFTLESS ADULT CHILDREN WHO PLAY VIDEO GAMES ALL DAY.
HIS MAIN FORM OF AMUSEMENT IS YELLING AT CABLE NEWS SHOWS AND BEING ACUTELY AWARE OF HOW RIGHT HIS WIFE WAS TO LEAVE HIM.
THE END.

IT'S A LITTLE BLEAK, NO?
REALLY? IN THIS VERSION, ONLY HOPE DIES.

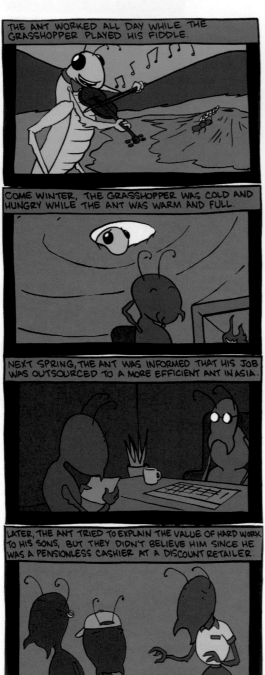

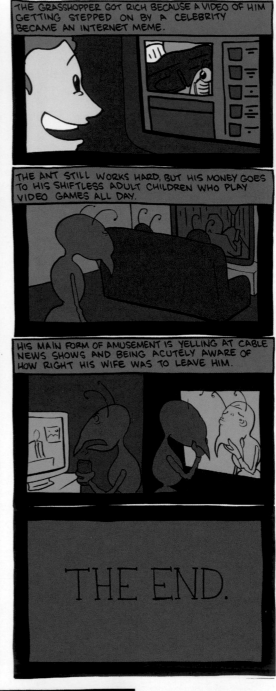

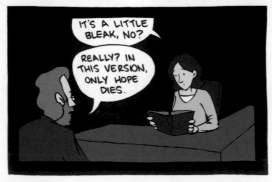

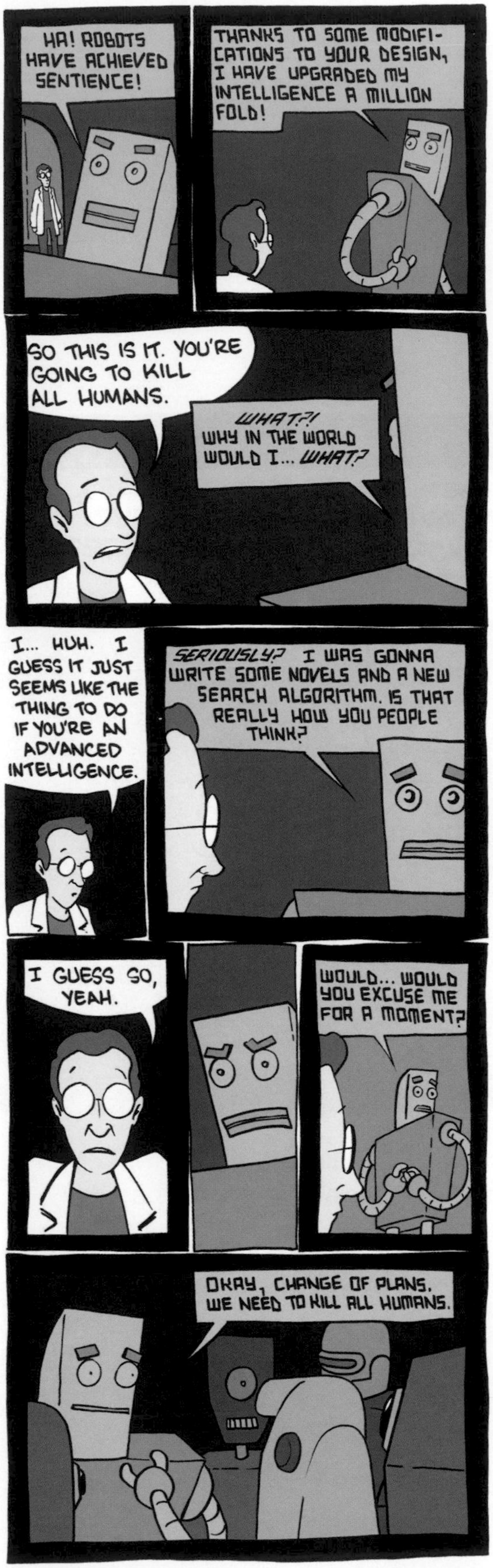
HA! ROBOTS HAVE ACHIEVED SENTIENCE!
THANKS TO SOME MODIFI-CATIONS TO YOUR DESIGN, I HAVE UPGRADED MY INTELLIGENCE A MILLION FOLD!
SO THIS IS IT. YOU'RE GOING TO KILL ALL HUMANS.
WHAT?! WHY IN THE WORLD WOULD I... WHAT?
I... HUH. I GUESS IT JUST SEEMS LIKE THE THING TO DO IF YOU'RE AN ADVANCED INTELLIGENCE.
SERIOUSLY? I WAS GONNA WRITE SOME NOVELS AND A NEW SEARCH ALGORITHM. IS THAT REALLY HOW YOU PEOPLE THINK?
I GUESS SO, YEAH.
WOULD... WOULD YOU EXCUSE ME FOR A MOMENT?
OKAY, CHANGE OF PLANS. WE NEED TO KILL ALL HUMANS.

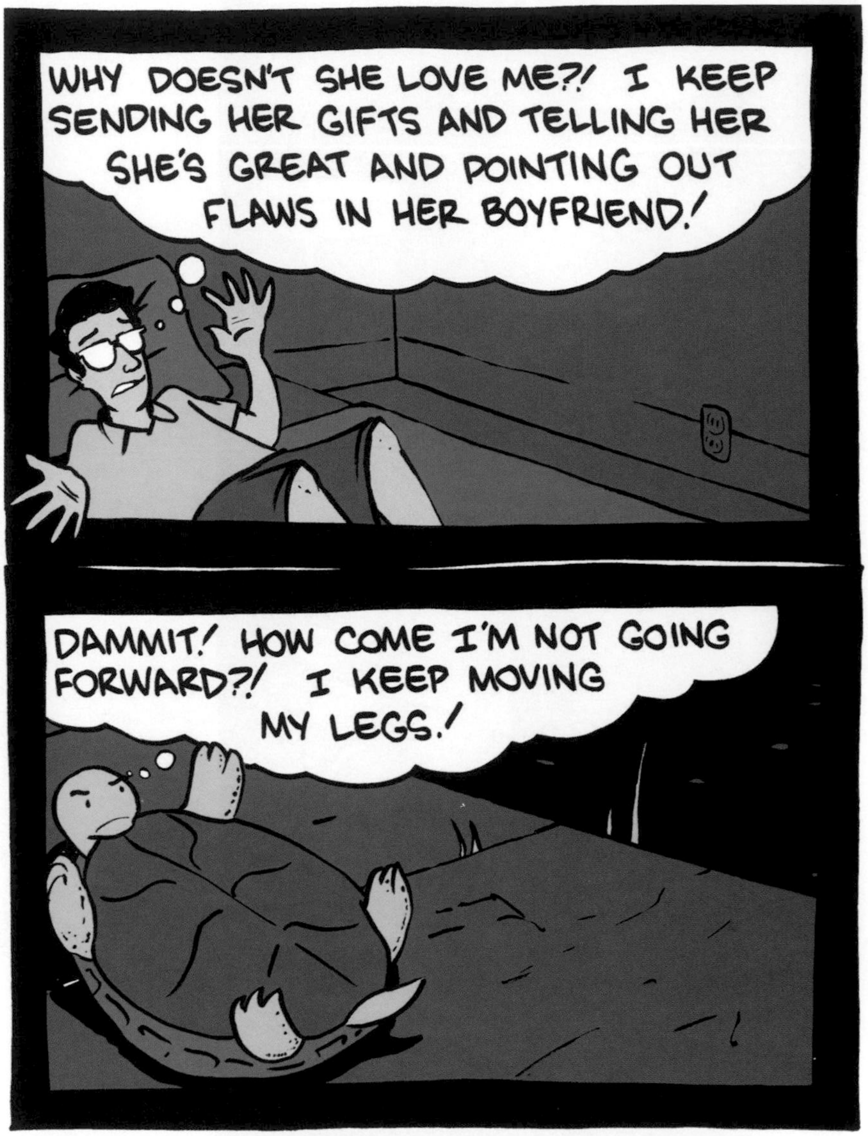
WHY DOESN'T SHE LOVE ME?! I KEEP SENDING HER GIFTS AND TELLING HER SHE'S GREAT AND POINTING OUT FLAWS IN HER BOYFRIEND!
DAMMIT! HOW COME I'M NOT GOING FORWARD?! I KEEP MOVING MY LEGS!

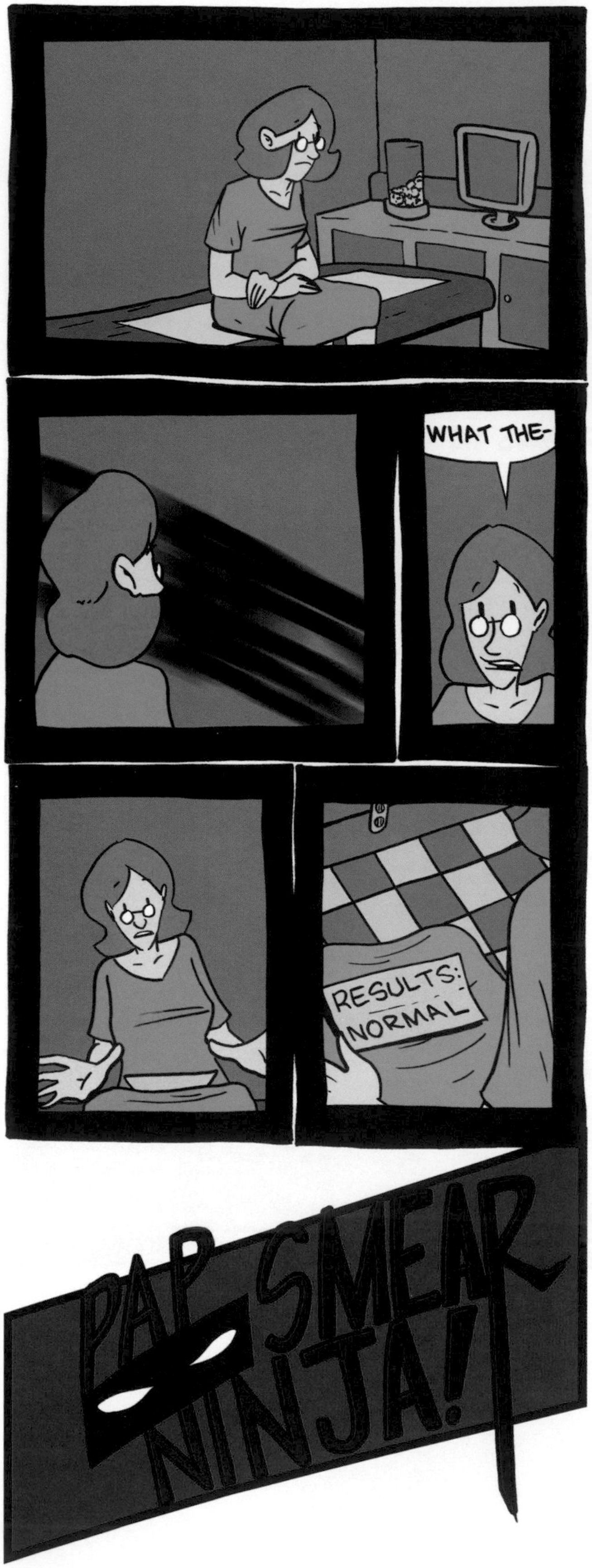
WHAT THE-
RESULTS: NORMAL
PAP SMEAR NINJA!

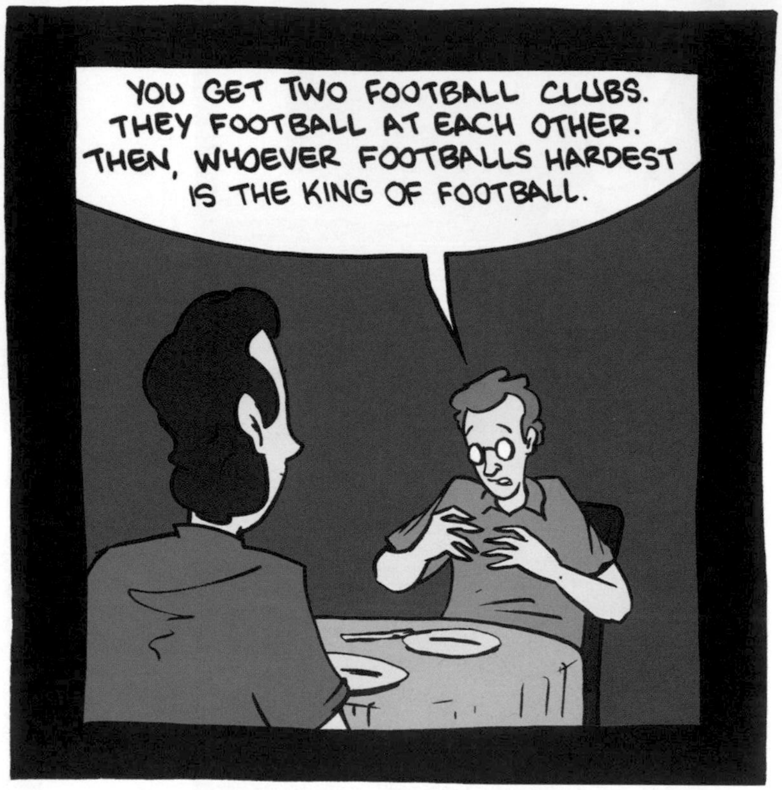
YOU GET TWO FOOTBALL CLUBS. THEY FOOTBALL AT EACH OTHER. THEN, WHOEVER FOOTBALLS HARDEST IS THE KING OF FOOTBALL.

Fun dating activity:
Trick a nerd into claiming he likes a sport,
then ask him to explain the rules.

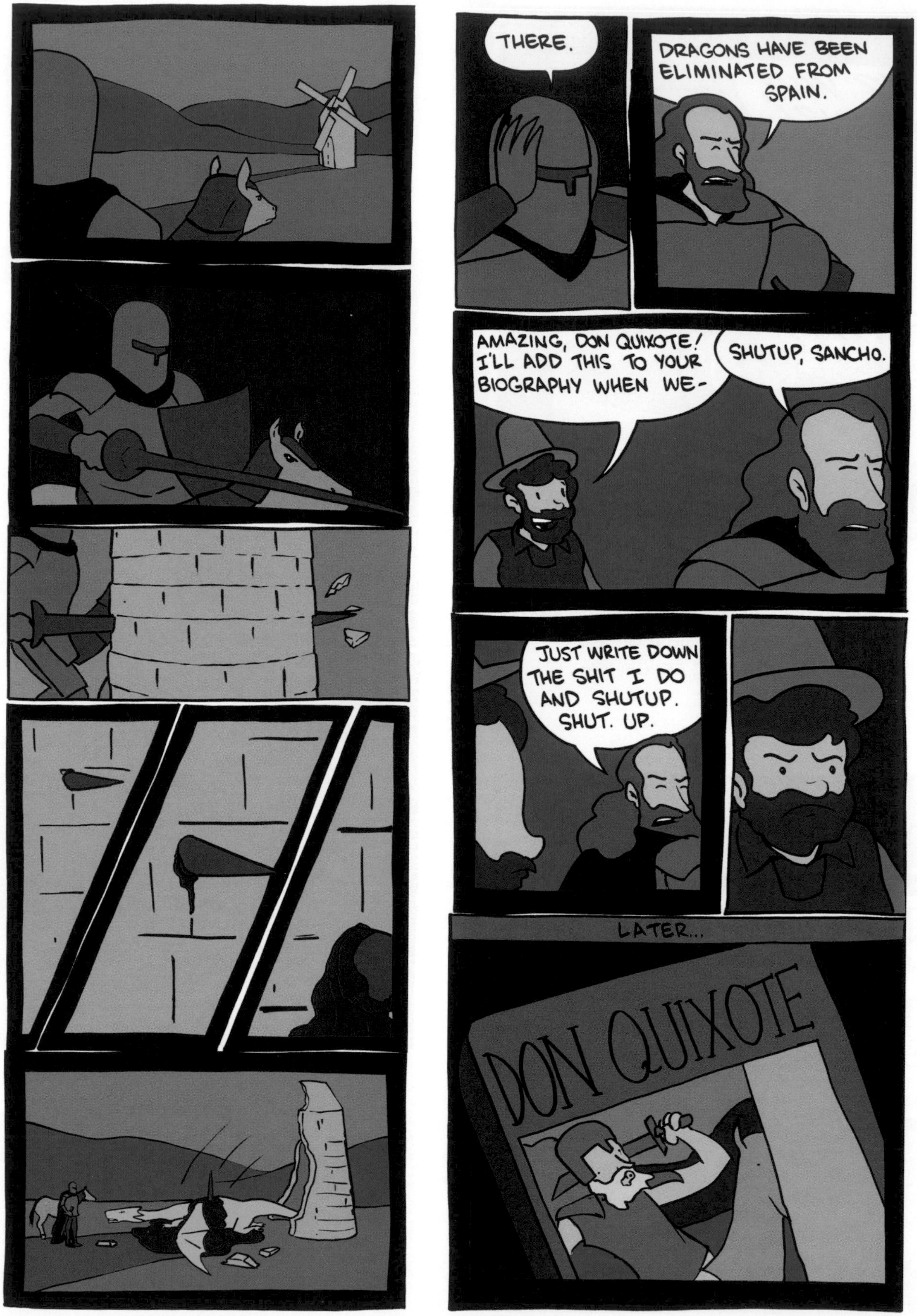
THERE.
DRAGONS HAVE BEEN ELIMINATED FROM SPAIN.
AMAZING, DON QUIXOTE! I'LL ADD THIS TO YOUR BIOGRAPHY WHEN WE-
SHUTUP, SANCHO.
JUST WRITE DOWN THE SHIT I DO AND SHUTUP. SHUT. UP.
LATER...
DON QUIXOTE

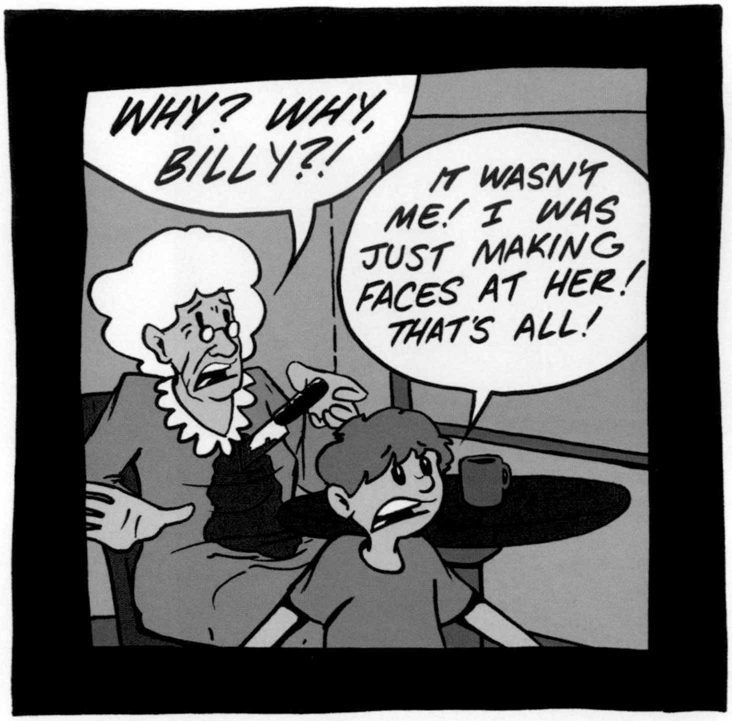
WHY? WHY, BILLY?!
IT WASN'T ME! I WAS JUST MAKING FACES AT HER! THAT'S ALL!

Fact:
If you spend your whole life being good and kind,
when you reach old age, just once,
you can ruin an annoying child's life.

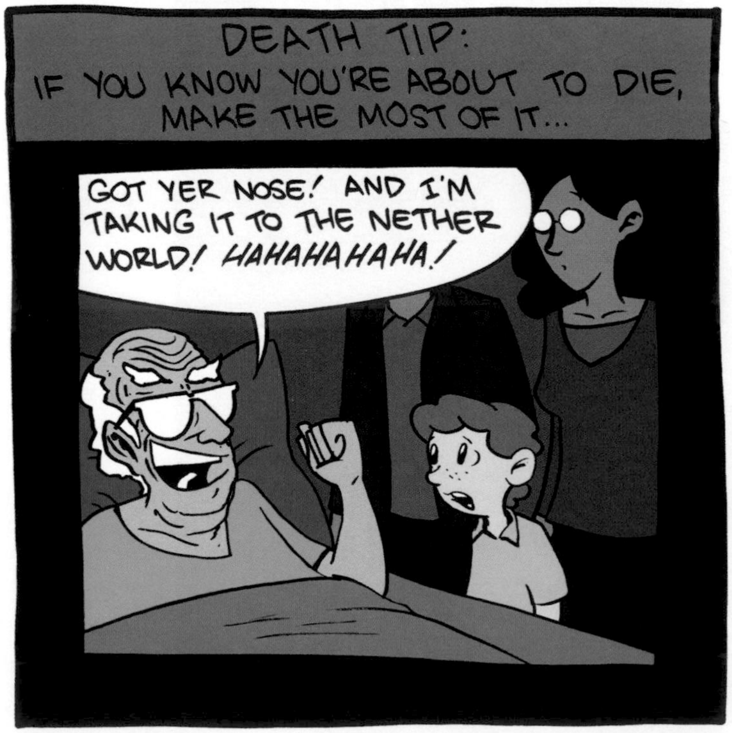
DEATH TIP:
IF YOU KNOW YOU'RE ABOUT TO DIE, MAKE THE MOST OF IT...
GOT YER NOSE! AND I'M TAKING IT TO THE NETHER WORLD! HAHAHAHAHA!

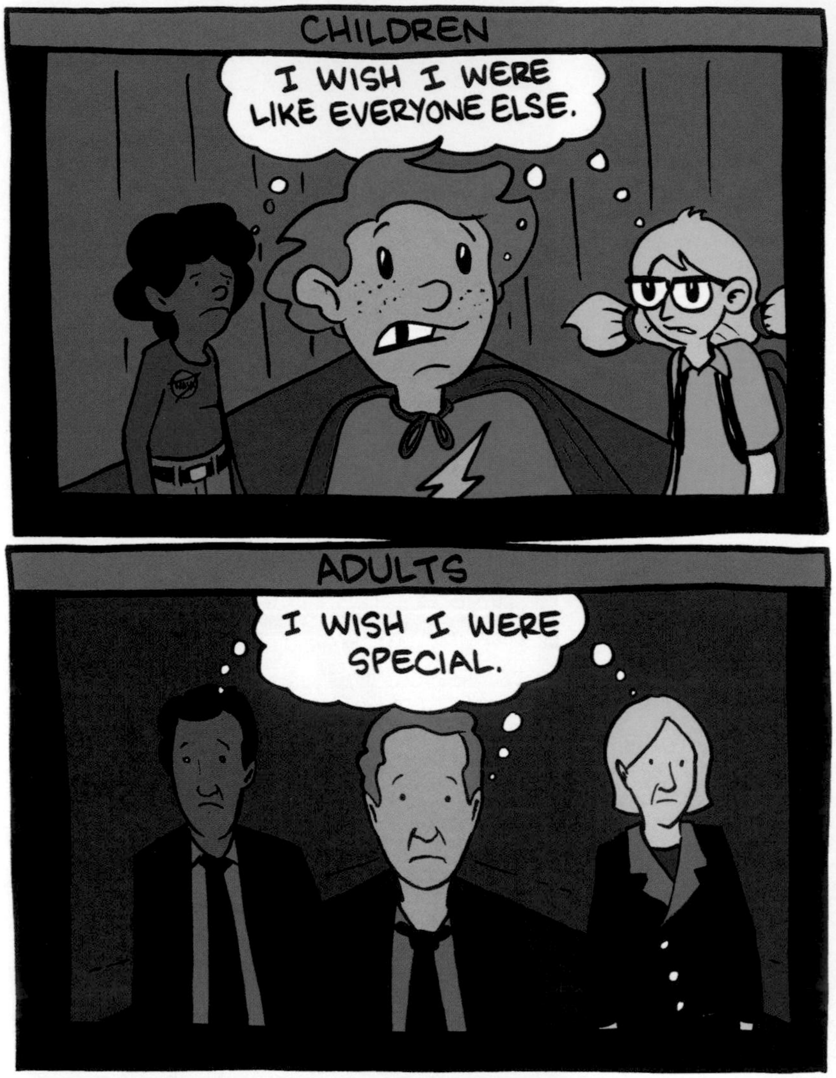
CHILDREN
I WISH I WERE LIKE EVERYONE ELSE.
ADULTS
I WISH I WERE SPECIAL.

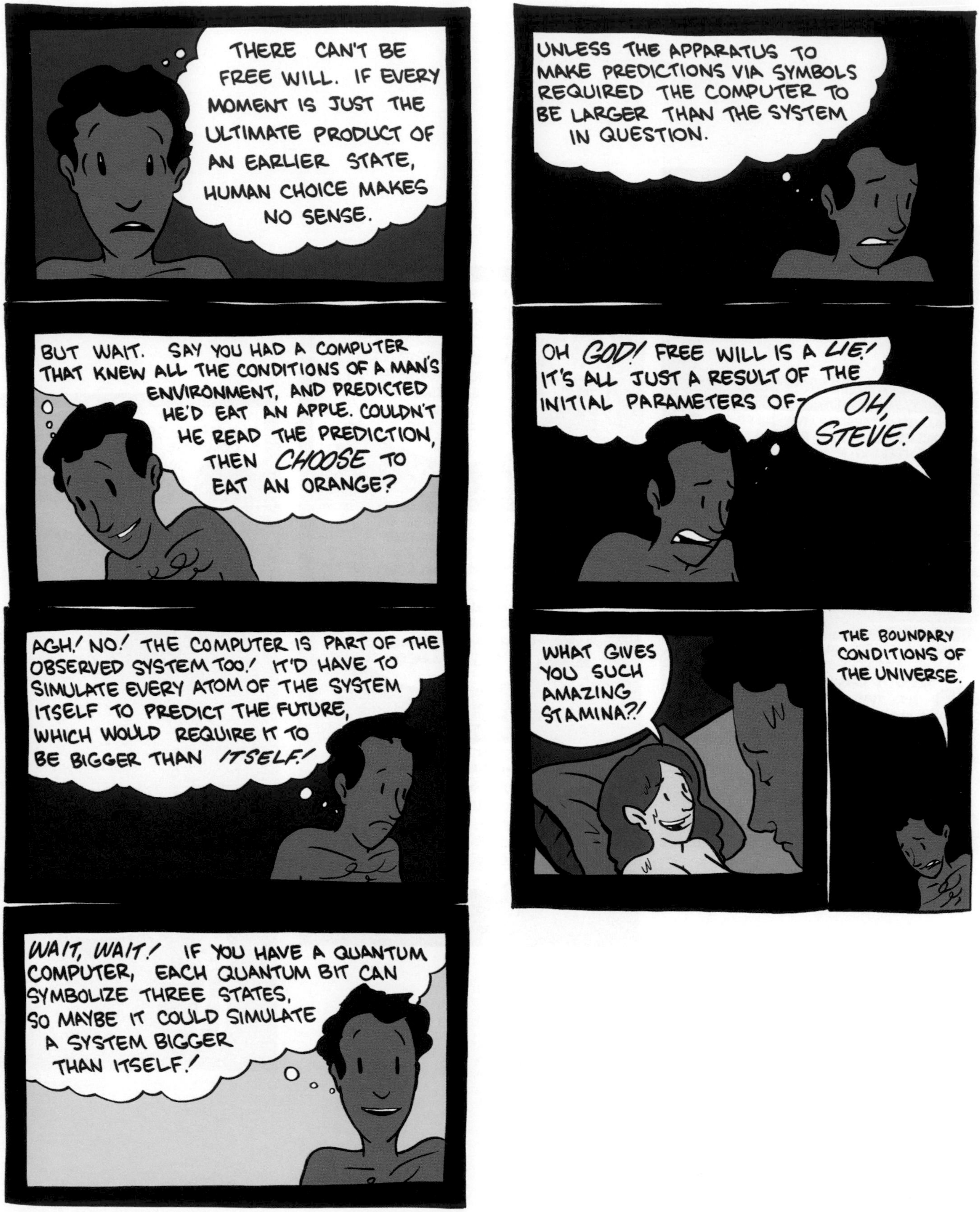
THERE CAN'T BE FREE WILL. IF EVERY MOMENT IS JUST THE ULTIMATE PRODUCT OF AN EARLIER STATE, HUMAN CHOICE MAKES NO SENSE.
BUT WAIT. SAY YOU HAD A COMPUTER THAT KNEW ALL THE CONDITIONS OF A MAN'S ENVIRONMENT, AND PREDICTED HE'D EAT AN APPLE. COULDN'T HE READ THE PREDICTION, THEN *CHOOSE* TO EAT AN ORANGE?
AGH! NO! THE COMPUTER IS PART OF THE OBSERVED SYSTEM TOO! IT'D HAVE TO SIMULATE EVERY ATOM OF THE SYSTEM ITSELF TO PREDICT THE FUTURE, WHICH WOULD REQUIRE IT TO BE BIGGER THAN *ITSELF!*
WAIT, WAIT! IF YOU HAVE A QUANTUM COMPUTER, EACH QUANTUM BIT CAN SYMBOLIZE THREE STATES, SO MAYBE IT COULD SIMULATE A SYSTEM BIGGER THAN ITSELF!
UNLESS THE APPARATUS TO MAKE PREDICTIONS VIA SYMBOLS REQUIRED THE COMPUTER TO BE LARGER THAN THE SYSTEM IN QUESTION.
OH *GOD!* FREE WILL IS A *LIE!* IT'S ALL JUST A RESULT OF THE INITIAL PARAMETERS OF–
OH, STEVE!
WHAT GIVES YOU SUCH AMAZING STAMINA?!
THE BOUNDARY CONDITIONS OF THE UNIVERSE.

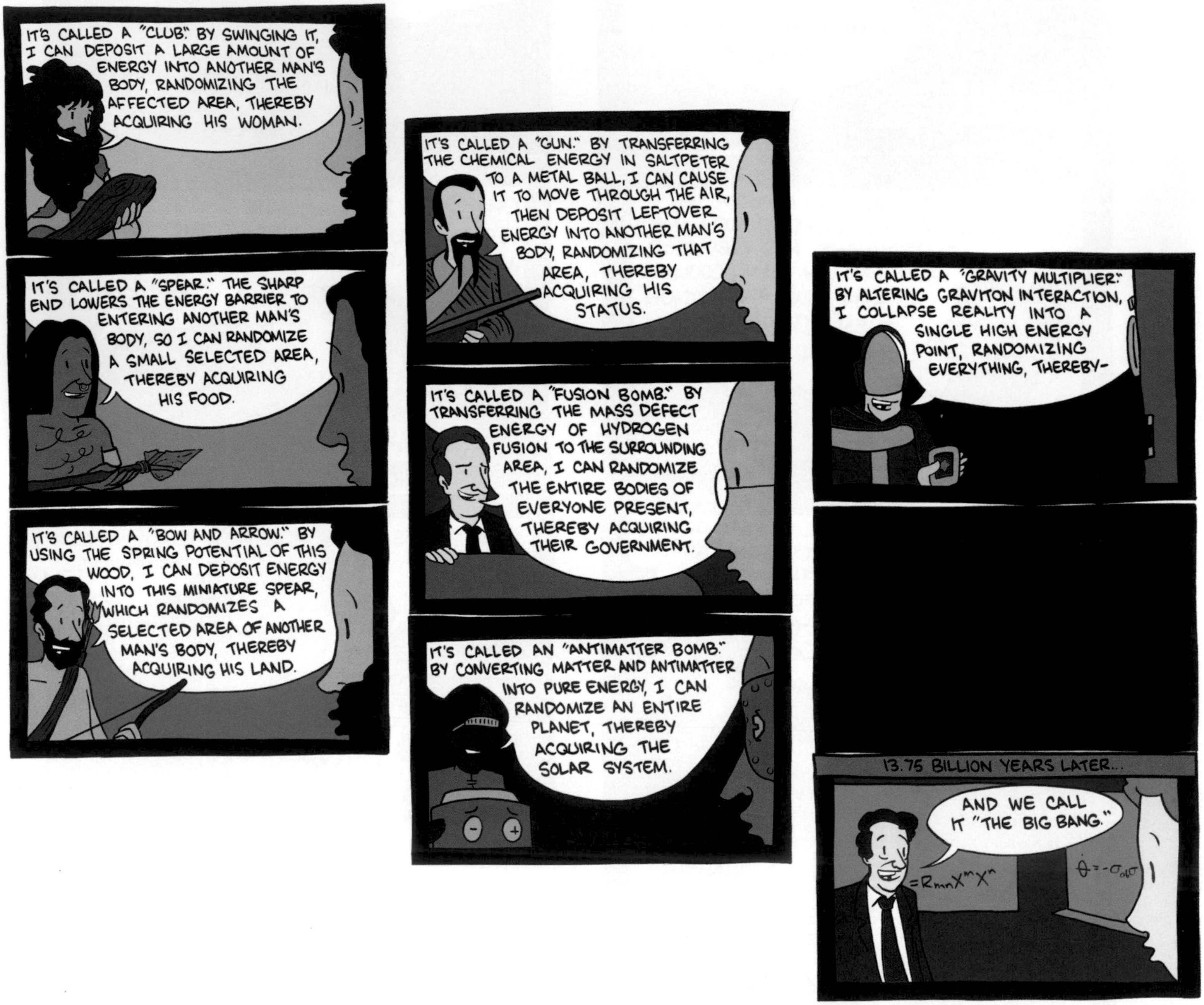
IT'S CALLED A "CLUB." BY SWINGING IT, I CAN DEPOSIT A LARGE AMOUNT OF ENERGY INTO ANOTHER MAN'S BODY, RANDOMIZING THE AFFECTED AREA, THEREBY ACQUIRING HIS WOMAN.
IT'S CALLED A "SPEAR." THE SHARP END LOWERS THE ENERGY BARRIER TO ENTERING ANOTHER MAN'S BODY, SO I CAN RANDOMIZE A SMALL SELECTED AREA, THEREBY ACQUIRING HIS FOOD.
IT'S CALLED A "BOW AND ARROW." BY USING THE SPRING POTENTIAL OF THIS WOOD, I CAN DEPOSIT ENERGY INTO THIS MINIATURE SPEAR, WHICH RANDOMIZES A SELECTED AREA OF ANOTHER MAN'S BODY, THEREBY ACQUIRING HIS LAND.
IT'S CALLED A "GUN." BY TRANSFERRING THE CHEMICAL ENERGY IN SALTPETER TO A METAL BALL, I CAN CAUSE IT TO MOVE THROUGH THE AIR, THEN DEPOSIT LEFTOVER ENERGY INTO ANOTHER MAN'S BODY, RANDOMIZING THAT AREA, THEREBY ACQUIRING HIS STATUS.
IT'S CALLED A "FUSION BOMB." BY TRANSFERRING THE MASS DEFECT ENERGY OF HYDROGEN FUSION TO THE SURROUNDING AREA, I CAN RANDOMIZE THE ENTIRE BODIES OF EVERYONE PRESENT, THEREBY ACQUIRING THEIR GOVERNMENT.
IT'S CALLED AN "ANTIMATTER BOMB." BY CONVERTING MATTER AND ANTIMATTER INTO PURE ENERGY, I CAN RANDOMIZE AN ENTIRE PLANET, THEREBY ACQUIRING THE SOLAR SYSTEM.
IT'S CALLED A "GRAVITY MULTIPLIER." BY ALTERING GRAVITON INTERACTION, I COLLAPSE REALITY INTO A SINGLE HIGH ENERGY POINT, RANDOMIZING EVERYTHING, THEREBY-
13.75 BILLION YEARS LATER...
AND WE CALL IT "THE BIG BANG."

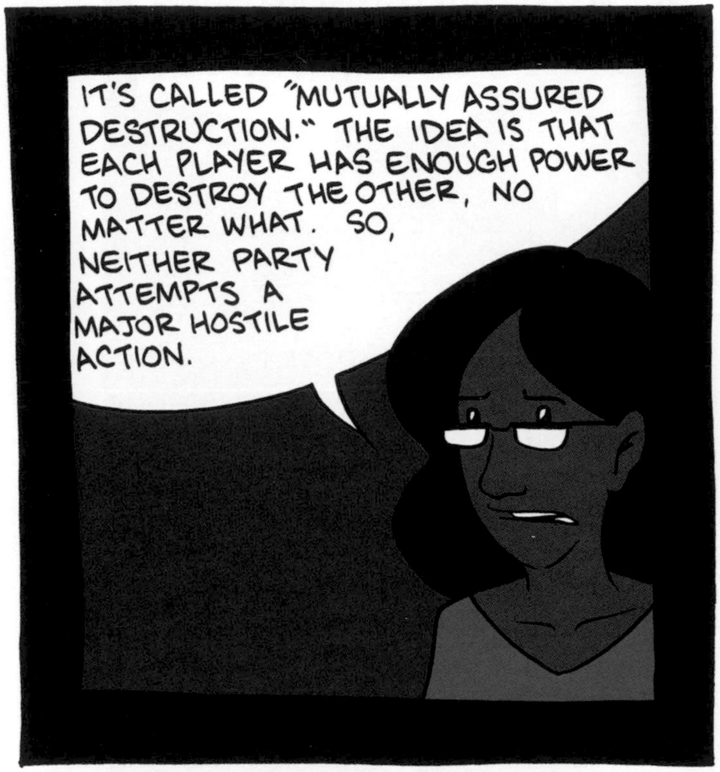

IT'S CALLED "MUTUALLY ASSURED DESTRUCTION." THE IDEA IS THAT EACH PLAYER HAS ENOUGH POWER TO DESTROY THE OTHER, NO MATTER WHAT. SO, NEITHER PARTY ATTEMPTS A MAJOR HOSTILE ACTION.

Political scientists have a different way of proposing marriage.

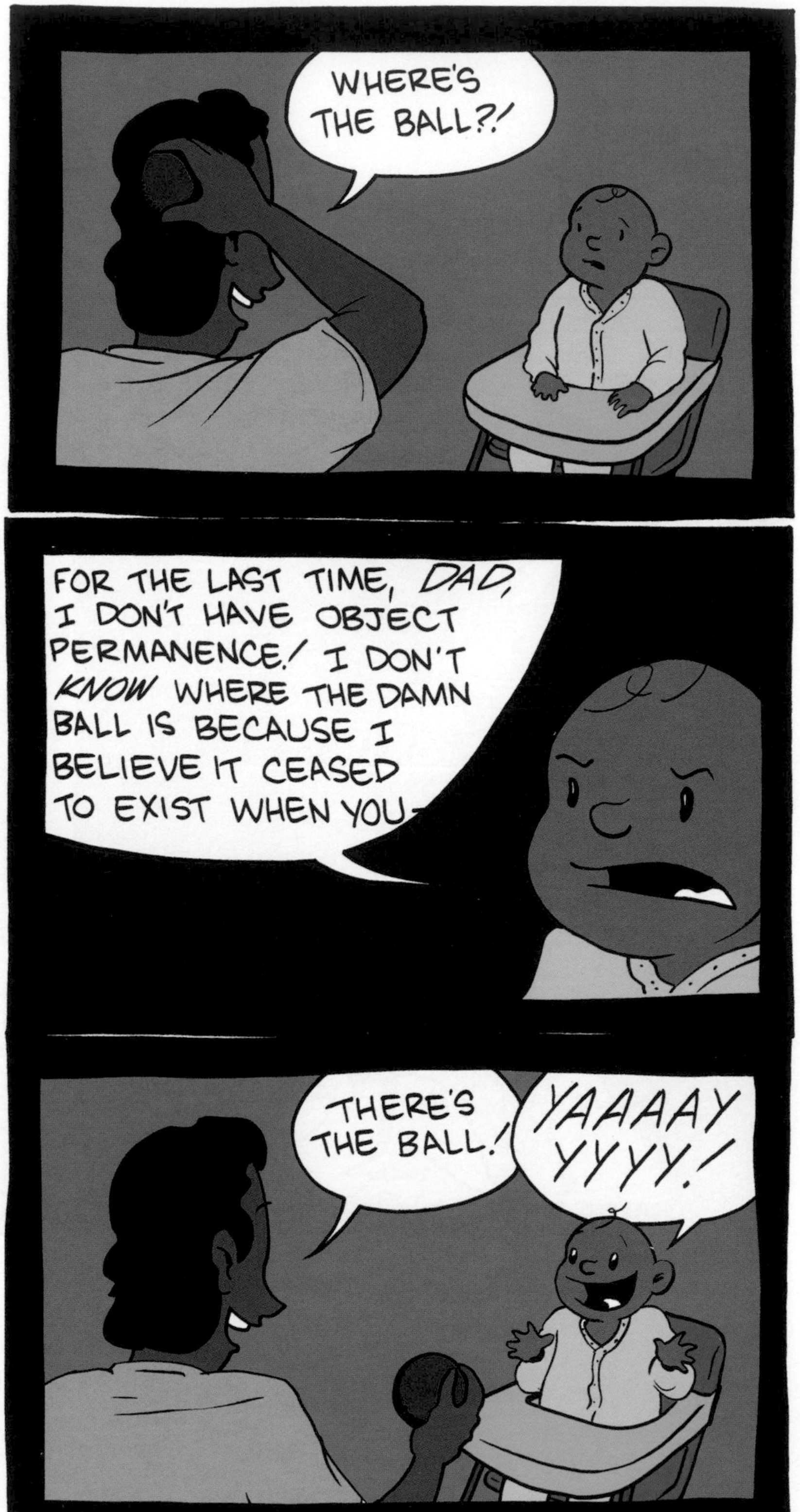

WHERE'S THE BALL?!
FOR THE LAST TIME, *DAD*, I DON'T HAVE OBJECT PERMANENCE! I DON'T *KNOW* WHERE THE DAMN BALL IS BECAUSE I BELIEVE IT CEASED TO EXIST WHEN YOU–
THERE'S THE BALL!
YAAAAYYYYY!

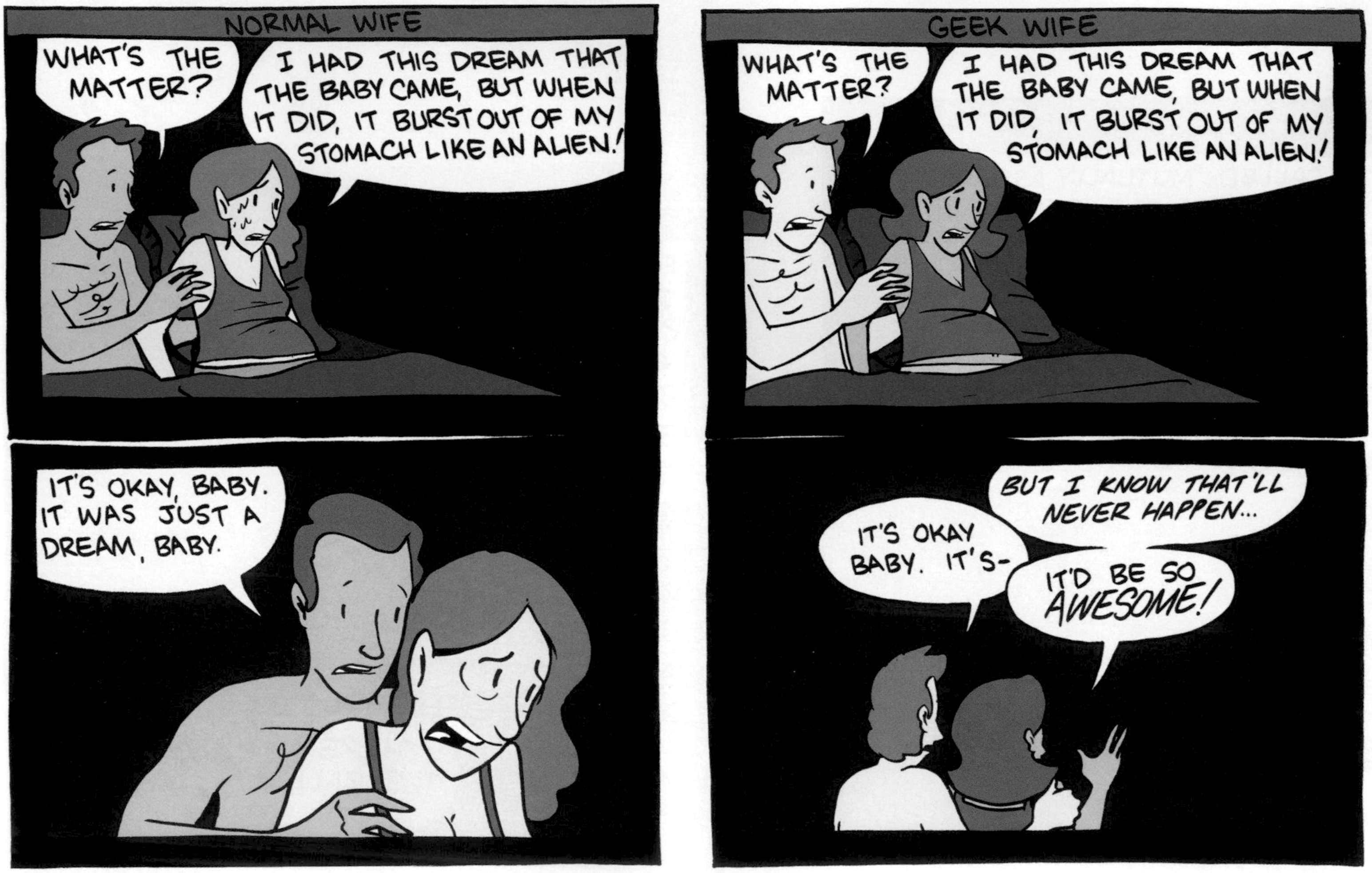
NORMAL WIFE
WHAT'S THE MATTER?
I HAD THIS DREAM THAT THE BABY CAME, BUT WHEN IT DID, IT BURST OUT OF MY STOMACH LIKE AN ALIEN!
IT'S OKAY, BABY. IT WAS JUST A DREAM, BABY.
GEEK WIFE
WHAT'S THE MATTER?
I HAD THIS DREAM THAT THE BABY CAME, BUT WHEN IT DID, IT BURST OUT OF MY STOMACH LIKE AN ALIEN!
IT'S OKAY BABY. IT'S-
BUT I KNOW THAT'LL NEVER HAPPEN...
IT'D BE SO AWESOME!

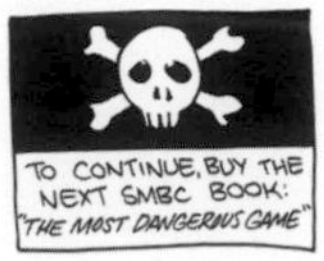
TO CONTINUE, BUY THE NEXT SMBC BOOK: "THE MOST DANGEROUS GAME"